Character Kings 2

Character Kings 2
Hollywood's Familiar Faces Discuss the Art & Business of Acting

by Scott Voisin

Foreword by John Badham

BearManor Media
2014

Character Kings 2:
Hollywood's Familiar Faces Discuss the Art & Business of Acting

© 2014 Scott Voisin

All rights reserved.

For information, address:

BearManor Media
P. O. Box 71426
Albany, GA 31708

bearmanormedia.com

Typesetting and layout by John Teehan
Cover design by Tim Ferrante

Published in the USA by BearManor Media

ISBN—1-59393-580-3
978-1-59393-580-1

*For the three most beautiful and important women in my life:
My wife, Alysia, and my daughters, Trinity and Hallie.
You thought I was just goofing off in the basement,
but look what I made…*

Love you all.

Table of Contents

Acknowledgements ix
Foreword xi
Introduction 1

Jon Polito 3
Charles Martin Smith 27
Dale Dye 45
James Hong 67
Richard Riehle 83
James Rebhorn 107
Duane Whitaker 125
Raymond J. Barry 147
Stephen Root 169
Tony Todd 187
Frank Vincent 205
William Forsythe 223
Jeffrey DeMunn 245
William Atherton 263
Mike Starr 281

Acknowledgements

There are many others who also deserve my deepest gratitude in the creation of this book:

All of the actors profiled here, whose talent and contributions to the world of entertainment inspired me to share their stories.

The agents, managers and publicists (and especially their assistants) who worked me into their clients' schedules.

Tim Ferrante, the greatest friend, mentor, cheerleader—and former boss—anyone could ask for.

Joe Kane and *The Phantom of the Movies' VideoScope* magazine, for providing a forum and the encouragement to write about these men.

And last but not least, Ron "The Godfather" Ketchum, for continuing to treat my family as his own.

Foreword

For a director, assembling the cast of a film or TV project is like a chef assembling the ingredients for a meal. You spend much of your time thinking about the main ingredients, the things that give the dish its name, but you're not doing your diners any favors if you neglect the wonderful seasonings that bring the meal to life—these are the character actors.

In my film *Bird on a Wire*, the stars were so big the studio figured just using their first names Mel and Goldie on the poster would be enough! But the meal wouldn't have been so spicy without the talents of great character actors like David Carradine, Bill Duke and Stephen Tobolowsky to keep things exciting. Another example: The *Nick of Time* poster only features Johnny Depp (who himself would be a great character actor if only he wasn't so famous!), but as great as he is, something would be missing without such "Character Kings" as Christopher Walken, Charles S. Dutton, Bill Smitrovich and G.D. Spradlin. And let's not forget there are "Character Queens" here too—Marsha Mason, Roma Maffia and Gloria Reuben. Perhaps the next volume will share some of their stories?

I am glad to be able to help bring some attention to these unsung "ingredients" of some of our favorite films. Within these pages, you'll not only get to put some names to faces that you always recognize on your screens, but hear some wonderful stories from these gentlemen. You'll also learn a bit about how they got started in this business and how they feel about their niche in this industry. It's not always an easy road but these men have got that special something that allow them to keep doing the thing we all love—bringing stories and characters to life. I hope you enjoy it as much as I did.

– John Badham

Introduction

"Don't do it."

That's the advice most of the men profiled in this book have for those chasing the unrealistic dream of making a living as an actor.

The numbers don't lie: According to the U.S. Bureau of Labor Statistics, nine out of every ten actors face long-term unemployment in an industry rife with uncertainty and rejection. SAG-AFTRA, the union that represents over 160,000 media performers, offers its own cautionary warning: "Even the most talented performers may do everything right and still not end up with acting jobs. Success in this business is an unpredictable combination of talent, training, residence, 'look,' energy, attitude and the completely uncontrollable factor—luck!"

Those that manage to beat the odds and find a job will often discover the financial compensation to be greatly diminished from years past. Thanks to the Great Recession, billions of dollars in financing has disappeared, meaning that producers who somehow manage to scrape together a little money for their production can't afford to splurge on actors' salaries. Once that job is completed, it's time to start looking for the next one, competing against hundreds of other underemployed thespians hoping to book a few weeks of work.

Yet, as dire as the prospects are for turning a passion for acting into a full-time career, these men have proven it *is* possible. Their insight and advice won't help you become a movie star or lead you on a path to fame and fortune, but their shared experiences provide a solid foundation for aspiring actors to build on. From surviving the audition process to the behavior on a set that has earned them future employment opportunities, the stories dispensed here are from those who have used their talent and skills to create a lifetime's worth of memorable characters, becoming instantly recognizable even if their names don't quickly come to mind.

Ladies and gentlemen, these are the Character Kings.

Jon Polito

Whereas most thespians dream of being stars, Jon Polito's main goal was to be a successful character actor. Mission accomplished! After building his resumé with appearances in *Remo Williams: The Adventure Begins, Highlander* and *Miami Vice*, Polito finally landed his breakout role as a mobster hell-bent for revenge in the 1990 Coen brothers film, *Miller's Crossing*. Since then, Polito has parlayed that exposure into a career that has seen him portray a wide array of oddballs, lowlifes, and miscreants, but instead of trying to escape the typecasting, he embraced it—a strategy that has kept him in demand for nearly three decades.

How did you get your start in acting?

I was in West Catholic Boys High School in Philadelphia, and at that time in the '60s, there was a lot of interesting theater going on in the universities around that area. One of the Christian Brothers, Dominic Garvey, had just moved to our high school and was teaching at West Catholic while he was studying for his second Ph.D. in Theatre History at Villanova University. He came in and shook up our theater department. We were just doing regular musicals and these little plays, and he came in and began to do very serious theater. The advantage was that he went to the directing students and writers at Villanova and told them they could come down to our little theater at West Catholic and do their projects. There were some amazing people at Villanova at the time… David Rabe—the playwright who wrote [*The Basic Training of*] *Pavlo Hummel* and *Sticks and Bones*—was just back from Vietnam, and he was studying at Villanova. There was a wonderful

Benno Blimpie

black playwright named Leslie Lee, and there were very interesting theater people that were coming down to West Catholic to look at the students and use the students for their projects. When Villanova offered for the first time in history an undergraduate scholarship, Dominic Garvey pushed them to consider me for it, which I got. I could never have afforded Villanova. I was a city kid from Philadelphia, and I wasn't very good in my classes, but I basically got a fully paid scholarship to Villanova. That led to a very good education as well as the fact that we had a theater company that was being produced in New York. We were going up to New York to present plays, David Rabe was becoming pretty famous at the Public Theater, and our theater was actually being reviewed by *The Philadelphia Inquirer* and even some New York papers. After graduation, I went to New York and was very fortunate to get a play within the first two months that was reviewed in *The New York Times*. That began my career as a character actor in theater, and I didn't start doing film and television until I was thirty. I always wanted to be an actor, and I wanted to be an actor like Peter Lorre and Sydney Greenstreet and Charles Laughton. That was my thing… I remember seeing *The Phantom of the Opera* with Lon Chaney when I was a kid, and I wanted to be *that* kind of an actor—somebody in disguise.

One of your early film roles was in Remo Williams: The Adventure Begins. *How did you get involved with that?*

I was doing *Death of a Salesman* on Broadway with Dustin Hoffman, and I couldn't really do a long film because of our commitment to the theater. At some point—I think it was in June—Dustin decided he was going to take the summer off, which was kind of unheard of, but because the production was making so much money, they gave him the summer off and I was offered a one-day part on *Remo Williams*. There weren't really any lines or anything; it was just some kind of a goon that was chasing Remo Williams around the Statue of Liberty. My reason for doing it was because I was a fan of the old [Alfred] Hitchcock film *Saboteur*, and I loved the idea that I was going to be working on the Statue of Liberty and that I would be working with Joel Grey. We were actually shooting on the statue during the remodel, so we really got up close and walked all over it. It was terrific.

Your next film was Highlander. *What was it like making that movie?*

That was a wonderful and important experience. After the *Death of a Salesman* play ended, I went into another play called *Digby* that was produced at the Manhattan Theatre Club. One of the casting people for *Highlander* saw the production and thought I would be right for this one part. She contacted my agents and said, "We are going to fly Jon Polito to London to meet the director, Russell Mulcahy." Now, this was kind of unheard of—I was shocked—but they flew me to London and I had lunch with Russell Mulcahy, who offered me this smallish part in the film. It was a very exciting time because this was London in the '80s, so you can well imagine the excitement of all the discos and the funky clothes, and needless to say, lots of drugs and drinks were being partaken, so it was a very exciting time for a guy in my thirties. I very much enjoyed doing that film, although I always regretted that a lot of my favorite scenes ended up on the cutting room floor. They called me about five years later about having my character return in the sequel, and I said to them, "I'll do it if you can find my lost footage!" They didn't have it because in those days they didn't keep that stuff. There weren't DVDs with additional scenes, so I never got to see these scenes that I thought I was brilliant in, which they obviously thought were pieces of crap and couldn't be used in the film! But it was an exciting time and an exciting film… I was very happy to work with Clancy Brown. I am such a fan of that man's work; I think he's just wonderful. I did not work with Sean Connery because all of his scenes were set in the past and I was involved in the contemporary stuff, but it was a lot of fun to work on the film. I do remember one of the most exciting things was all technical because it was the first time I'd seen the Skycam used, and the Steadicam was being used all of the time. Those cameras were new, and that was an exciting thing to watch. My brother was a special effects man who did dinosaur movies and stop-motion things in our little row home in Philadelphia. He was making these movies, and one of the things I did through my high school and college education was to make my own movies for the different academic projects that were needed. For me, that technical stuff was exciting to watch.

One of the films you're best known for is Miller's Crossing.

That's kind of the *real* beginning of my film career, and that didn't happen until I was thirty-nine. I had seen *Raising Arizona* and *Blood Simple*, and I got the word that the Coens had written a new film and were considering me for a part. I read the script and I immediately flipped out. I thought it was one of the greatest scripts I've ever read; the dialogue was so wonderful it was like reading music. So I immediately said to my agent, "I very much want to read for Johnny Caspar," and she said, "You're not being considered for Johnny Caspar, they want to see you for the Dane." I did not want to go in for the Dane, so I said, "No, I will not go in for that. Just tell them I only want to be seen for Johnny Caspar." They said no, so I thought that was the end of it and I went off to Miami to do this very weird *Miami Vice* arc with Don Johnson, and then I was cast in the play *Other*

People's Money in Hartford, Connecticut. I then got word that they had not yet finalized the casting of Johnny Caspar, and they'd consider reading me for it. I went in and read the opening scene for Joel and Ethan, and I was told to go outside in the waiting room while somebody else came in. They asked me to come back in and they had me read cold—without preparation—the entire role from beginning to end, every scene. I read the whole script cold with the way I was going to do that character, and I was very, very fortunate to be cast. To be honest with you, my career was a basic "Character Actor 101" career. There were a lot of actors like me, and I'd not yet really found the best way to act in film. I was a better theater actor than I was a film actor, and my career would have gone nowhere—and still would be nowhere—if it wasn't for the Coens and *Miller's Crossing*. The film was not a success then but now it's considered a cult classic, and it was the big break for me in terms of people seeing the kind of work I could do. I did not know I could do that kind of work… I hadn't played gangsters very much and really didn't know how to do them very well, but I was in a Michael Mann show called *Crime Story*, and that character was sort of like the big mob boss who wasn't very astute and really kind of weak. I used that to develop the character of Johnny Caspar—almost in a comedic way—because he was a threat and dangerous but also kind of a buffoon, and that's the kind of thing you can only do in a Coen brothers script. I would truly say, without a doubt, people who know my name and young directors who want to work with me know me from my connection to the Coen brothers and *Miller's Crossing*.

Miller's Crossing *was the first of five films you've done with the Coens. Did you have any idea when you were making it that you would become a regular member of their acting troupe?*

Not really, they just seem to think of me in very interesting roles. After *Miller's Crossing*, I went back into the play *Other People's Money*, which had come to New York. Joel and Ethan sent me a script for their next film, *Barton Fink*, and they were offering me the part of Lou Breeze, this very nerdy ex-studio head. I, of course, wanted to play the head of the studio, the role that Michael Lerner played. That was the part I felt would be right but they said no, it was too much like *Miller's Crossing* and they'd written this other part with me in mind. Lou Breeze was a very pear-shaped, frightened, nervous, nerdy guy. Where they got the idea for me to play that guy after playing the bombastic Johnny Caspar, I don't know.

Gabriel Byrne and Polito in *Miller's Crossing*

They're geniuses, and you never know how a genius's mind works. They told me then they had ideas for different roles ahead, all of which pretty much came true. I was doing *The Crow* in North Carolina while they were shooting *The Hudsucker Proxy*, and they asked me to do a cameo in that. While I was shooting that, they said, "We have an idea… Would you like to make a pass at Brad Pitt?" I said, "Absolutely! Who *wouldn't* want to make a pass at Brad Pitt?" They said, "Well, we have this other movie that we're going to be doing, and we're going to cast you in it." That turned out to be *The Man Who Wasn't There*, and Billy Bob Thornton ended up playing the role instead of Brad Pitt. They somehow get these ideas, and they wrote that part for me as well. That was a wonderful gift. They wrote for me these beautiful roles and it's been quite a joy, quite a ride. As I said, they are responsible for anything that separates me from every other average, working character guy.

The Crow

Speaking of The Crow, *what was it like working on that film?*

I'll be honest with you about *The Crow*, that movie was haunted from day one. It was all night shoots, and the first night of the shoot, a young guy was moving a cherry picker light system onto the studio lot. As he was driving it, the front wheels went through a covering in the ground and the whole cherry picker was lifted straight up—with him on it—and he slammed into an electrical pole and was electrocuted. He did survive, but I think he's blind, and it was a horrible situation. That was the first night… On the third night when we were shooting a scene with an explosion, a prop truck caught on fire. We had a tornado during the shoot that destroyed a lot of our street sets. The Coens were on the same lot doing *Hudsucker Proxy*, but their sets were in studios and our stuff was outside and got destroyed. We also had flooding at our hotel. It was an all-the-way-around haunted experience, the worst part being what happened to Brandon Lee. He was a wonderful young actor and a very sweet man. I remember in the scene after he bursts through the glass door of the pawn shop, I noticed he was bleeding in several spots. They stopped the shoot and they patched him up, and he was ready to go back in. Before he went back in, I pulled him aside and I said, "You've got to be careful with this stuff." He said, "I do all of my own stunts. There won't be a problem." I said, "Whatever you do, don't pull a Vic Morrow," because Vic Morrow had been killed on the *Twilight Zone* movie. That was kind of my first conversation with him, which is very disturbing in retrospect. When I would sit with him, we talked about his father, and we did talk about the old curse on Bruce Lee. There was a darkness over the film that you could feel… Toward the end of my shoot, I had to do my death scene, which involved being covered in exploding blood squibs because I was going to be shot with an Uzi and I had a sword in my throat. I was very nervous for some reason about the guns, and we were in a location that really bothered me. They always test the guns and the rounds in front of the actor, and I felt there was a problem. We had been working about a fourteen-hour day, and they were about to go into my death scene. I went to the producer and I said, "Look, I think we're very tired and I'm a little

nervous about this Uzi and these gunshots. Perhaps we can wait and do this tomorrow." He said, "Absolutely not. We're gonna shoot it tonight. You cost too much money to keep you another day." I said, "I'll do it for free. I just don't want to shoot tonight because I have a bad feeling about the gun." He insisted we were going to shoot the scene, so I then went to the gun wranglers who were friends of mine I had worked with before. I told them, "Let's figure out how we can do this because I'm very nervous about the rounds." They went down to one-quarter blanks, and then they actually went down to one-eighth blanks. I went to the producer and said, "I don't like any of them and I don't feel safe, so I'm going to ask you not to use any rounds." They didn't use any rounds in the gun sequence with me, and they actually added the gunfire and all of that in post.

I think one of the really interesting films on your resumé is With Friends Like These…, *which is about a group of friends who are character actors competing for the same role.*

There's a story about that… Bobby Costanzo played the lead guy, and character actors like Bobby have ten years on me. I was very fortunate as an actor to come in in my thirties and be able to play forties, and when I did *Miller's Crossing*, I was able to advance into the area of fifties. As a character guy, I could always play older. I went in to read for a show called *Ohara* with Pat Morita, and the other actor up for the part that I was reading for was Bobby Costanzo. This was back in 1987, and it was the first time I met him. I ended up getting the part, and Bobby and I have been—and still are—up for the same roles quite often. Bobby called me one day and said, "I'm doing this movie and there's one part that you *have* to play because you've taken parts from me. You're gonna play this damn part because you've got to finally acknowledge that you've always been in competition with me, and we're going to have a confrontation scene on the golf course." That was the reason for me to do it because I was sort of making up for any roles I got from Bobby, and Bobby was challenging me on any roles that he got from me. It was quite a serious, *real* competition between Bobby Costanzo and me. I thought the movie had an interesting premise too, and it had a terrific cast.

The characters in the film have all been typecast and they're trying to break out of it. Would you say that you've been typecast?

Absolutely, but I never wanted to break out of it. The best roles ever for men have either been as a cop or a crook. Look at the performances of [Robert] De Niro and [Al] Pacino, guys like that. It's not like you're going to see a great role as the father who has two kids. The reason for doing these things is that you want to play an exceptional character either on the right side of the law or the wrong side of the law. That seems to be what most films are about. I never minded typecasting, and what I always loved about people like Walter Brennan and Sydney Greenstreet is that these actors were the kind of people that when they walked on screen, you knew who they were so you didn't have to have background history. Initially when I went into films, I wanted to be a character guy but I played a lot of different things, and that wasn't working for me. With the Coens, I was able to be a character type that was recognizable as soon as I walked on the screen. You know what you're getting when you see me and hopefully you'll enjoy the ride. So I like being typecast—I've always liked it—and it's a way for a character man to get his bread and butter because you are then cast based on the fact that people know you're reliable in a type of character that's recognizable to the audience. No work has to be done; you walk on the screen and they already recognize you and say, "Oh, there's that guy." I've found that very valuable. It's not the same in theater and that's actually why I eventually gave up theater because there were so many different things to prove. I had twenty years in theater and I won awards and then it was time to move on to film, but for film it's very important to be typecast because you go into a reliable area where people call and say, "Is Jon Polito available?" That means they know what they're getting. From *Miller's Crossing*, I have had a good twenty-five years of being called and offered gangster-type roles or these kind of crazy comedy roles based on what I did in *Seinfeld*. I've been very fortunate to be able to go back and forth between film and television—and between comedy and drama—and it seems like I'm accepted by audiences in each one of those areas, which is very fortunate for me. I don't think there's any problem with being typecast. As a matter of fact, I think it's one of the greatest gifts you could have. My feeling is to say that being typecast is the gift of a film actor, not a curse.

You were part of the groundbreaking TV show, Homicide: Life on the Street. *How did you get involved with that?*

That was interesting... I had just officially moved from my New York apartment. I still had it, but I was now moving to Los Angeles. My agent

Clark Johnson and Polito in *Homicide: Life on the Street*

called and said there's a script for this Barry Levinson show that's shooting in Baltimore. I'm from Philadelphia and I said, "I don't want to read this script. I've already got two places in two different areas, and I don't want to be moving to Baltimore." There was very little money involved because it was a new, experimental technique they were using, and they weren't going to pay much money for this ensemble group. Anyway, the agent sent me three scripts to read, and the third script was actually the opening scene from *Homicide*. I read it and fell in love with it, and I said, "Okay, I want to read for it." But there was a bit of a problem... The part that I wanted was not the part they were reading me for. They wanted to read me for the part that ended up going to Clark Johnson, and I didn't like that part, so I said no to the reading. I went back to New York to work on something else and I got a call from my agent saying, "You've got to read for *Homicide*." I decided to read for it, but when I went in for the audition, I said, "Mr. Levinson, I am reading for this part but I don't want this part. I want to play the character that I'm reading opposite of, so if you do like me and want to bring me back, I only will come back for the other part." And I'll be damned if they weren't kind enough to bring me back for the other part to see what I would do with it. That was the part I ended up getting, which was Crosetti, although he wasn't named Crosetti in the original script. So then we all trekked down to Baltimore, and they were making up all of the camera stuff as we were doing it. It was a very, very exciting show to be involved with. I did have problems with it toward the end of the first season because NBC was making so many demands about guest stars and they started to write things about Crosetti's home life, and I was only interested in doing it as a workplace drama. NBC was not fond of me, I gather, and thought they needed another woman in the cast. They said they wanted a more attractive woman than Melissa Leo—who I think was brilliant on that show—because she was not going to do makeup or try to pretty herself up; she was going to play it like a real detective, so they decided to add another woman. They actually told me I was not going to be in the next season right away, and I stupidly took that as a rejection. Even though [writer/executive producer] Tom Fontana told me they would bring me back, I didn't believe him, so I kind of bad-mouthed them and got myself in a lot of trouble and was not invited back at all. That was a big drama... There was actually a fight in the papers back-and-forth. I said something, then Tom Fontana said something, but in the end, I did end up going back for the movie. I was invited back for that, and I worked for Tom Fontana again. Out here, nothing lasts too long. None of these battles do and none of the friendships do. It's Hollywood.

You've done a lot of guest-starring roles on TV, but one that really stood out was on the show Millennium.

Keegan Tracy, Michelle Beauchamp and Polito in *Millennium*

I loved that show. First of all, I love Lance Henriksen... I've always loved him, and I liked the show a lot. That was really a lovely episode for me because I learned a lot from him. My acting style was over the top—I'm not known as a subtle actor—and I remember getting on that set and thinking that I've *got* to tone down my work because I'm working with Lance Henriksen, who barely opens his mouth! Lance is a wonderful and subtle performer who works from the inside; he's just all there. Me, I'm all over the place: I'm outside, inside, oozing at the seams, sweat pouring out from me... So I really had to learn how to be a better actor from watching Lance and working with him, and I think that performance was a good one. The episode itself was interesting; the Christmas episode that was really more Easter-like because it was about resurrection. I played a gangster, but I got to do a lot of colors in it, and it was a different kind of a gangster. It was totally the opposite of any gangster I ever played before, so if you're worried about being typecast and not being able to play certain things, there are lots of variations within the same kind of role.

Have there been other instances where you've altered your acting style based on who you're working with?

Yes, you learn from everyone. Going back to *Homicide*, I learned a lot working with Clark Johnson. He was a joy to work with—and a *bad* boy—so he was always a challenge every minute. I felt my work was the most natural it's ever been. I learned how to be natural as opposed to theatrical in *Homicide*, and that was mostly due to Clark Johnson. In my life, there have been some wonderful people that I've learned from. Lance is one, Clark Johnson is another and certainly Dustin Hoffman in *Death of a Salesman*. You have to realize that in acting, you're playing tennis with these people in scenes, and what you have to do is adjust your game to the people you're playing with. For the most part, you'll realize that if you are open to it, you'll be a better player for absorbing how to play opposite certain actors. If you're smart, you will not fight for *your* ways, you will learn from *their* ways. There's an actor named Derek Cecil, and he worked on a show called *Push, Nevada*. I really learned a lot about how to listen by working with him. He's such a fine actor, and we also got to work together years later on an episode of *Masters of Horror*, and I had a ball with him. When you're doing these television shows, you're in different styles all of the time, and they know the rules and you don't. You're cast, you walk in, you have no prep and you're starting to rehearse and film within the first half hour. You have to quickly learn what their style is and what the director's style is, and you have to basically adjust your performance to what the rules of the game are. You know you're playing a baseball game but you're in a different park and you have different players on the team. When I was younger, I was very stubborn and I thought I knew what I was doing and I really didn't; I wasn't very good on the screen. I know the basics… I know how to speak and I know where to stand and I know how to look good—or look bad, based on what I need—but what I don't know is how the style of that particular show works until I actually open myself up to my fellow performers.

Aside from the Coen brothers, you've worked with some very renowned filmmakers like Ridley Scott, Clint Eastwood, and John Boorman. What are some of the traits a good director has that gets the best out of you as an actor?

They're all very different, but there is a common ground. Ridley Scott is like a lion. He stands there like a bull, and you feel the power around him. Same thing with John Boorman… There is a strength and a power in

The Man Who Wasn't There

these directors. You feel immediately that you want to impress them and please them. It's very father-like. You don't want to be told what to do, but you want to work well under them. You want to feel that you have fulfilled what they need. Most of the time, these men are people of few words. They will encourage you, but for the most part, you know whether you're doing well or not. You just feel the need to please in a parental way, but at the same time—as the son would be with the father—you want to make your own statement. You know that you feel confident with them at the helm, and that you're on that ship with them. You want to impress them and you want to hold your own.

Do you have a specific process when preparing for an audition?

There are two things… First of all, I'm an external actor, so I always sort of physicalize how I want to make him look, and I always dress as the character for an audition. But more than that, there is usually always one friggin' line in the audition that I can't get my mouth around. There's one line or one speech or one part that I always think, Oh, God, I would *never* say it like that, or I don't know quite what it means. There's always one point in an audition that you know you've got to learn how to say that line and make that work, and then you'll be able to figure out how to play the character. I call that the "click"... In the play *Cat on a Hot Tin Roof*, there's a character named Brick and he talks about how he drinks until he feels the click, the moment when he's at peace with himself. I always use that term for what I need as an actor. I need something that makes me click into how to play the part, and that something is usually that goddamn line that I can't get my mouth around! When that happens, I've got a way of playing the performance. If I get my mouth around that and I figure out a way to play that, then I usually have a hook for the character. The clicks make no sense…Not everyone would have the same reaction to that line, and in my early days, I used to change those lines, and that's why my acting was no good on film. What I learned is that by finding out how to say those lines and understand what you're saying, you will find a way into the character.

Once you get a role, how do you prepare for it?

Since I'm external, I want to know what they're going to dress him like because I need to know how I'm going to feel in the clothes. Then I look at my face and try to figure out what I want to do with that so I know what to ask the makeup people to accent. When I did *Miller's Crossing*, I want-

Big Nothing

ed to look like a bowling ball with a pencil-thin mustache, and I think I did. The wonderful hair and makeup woman had the side of my hairline shaved back so I was just all face with a slash of a mustache. When I did *Barton Fink*, I wanted him to look like a bowling pin: Small head, wider and wider and wider, with small feet. I go by physical images like that, and when I've got that, usually the voice comes in and I know how to place the voice. I'm known for this gravelly voice in some ways but there are other things you have to find, like the accent I did in *Seinfeld*. I did a film called *Big Nothing* with Simon Pegg and David Schwimmer, and with that character, I had to use a very nasal voice. You use those things as building blocks for the character and then hopefully you find out when you get on set that it works with what the other actors are doing.

Are you in a position to be able to pick and choose your projects or do you still have to worry about paying the bills?

I've never made much money in my life on any film at all. People always say, "Oh my God, actors make so much money," but actors *don't* make a lot of money. We make bursts of money, and then we don't work for months. So I basically take everything that's offered to me, and thank God there are still offers. For the most part, I still have to audition and really fight to get roles. The downside to being typecast is that many times I have to fight to get in for roles because casting people don't see me outside of the way I've been typecast. For the most part, I have to fight to pay the bills, and as I get older, I have to fight more. What's happening these days is that you have shows on television with such high-quality actors doing cameos. I watched *The Good Wife* last night, and *every* part was played by a star. The parts that would have been given to me—or that I could have read for—are no longer going to actors like me. They're going to stars because stars are drawn to the brilliant television scripts. It's harder now to make enough money to get insurance through the year, so it's a struggle. I'm fortunate to be in a situation where I have *some* kind of a name so there are some offers, but for the most part, I have to go out there and pound the streets, as they say. The funny thing is, when I was younger, I always had great admiration for people who had normal jobs. I would say to them, "You don't quite know how much I envy the fact that you have a steady job." Now of course, in this economy, everybody's in the same boat as an actor. Everybody's out there fighting and struggling day by day just to get their next gig, so to speak. Everybody's living the life of the artist…

Stiffs

My battle is to make enough every year to be able to just get insurance and pay the bills.

Are there any projects or roles you've done that you're really proud of and wished had gotten more of an audience?

Yes, there are many. I'm very proud of my work in the film *Big Nothing*, and it never even played in the States—it just got a video release. With *Miller's Crossing*, had the Coens been then what they are now, I think my work as Johnny Caspar would have been nominated, but they weren't famous then. I played a woman on *The Chris Isaak Show*, and that was one of my best performances ever, but no one saw it. I thought my work on *Homicide* should have been acknowledged more, but Andre Braugher got all the attention on that show. I think there's many of us out there that have done great performances that are not recognized, but they're respected. For instance, I recently met Mark Wahlberg for a film that I did not get, and I learned that Mark had been a fan of mine for years from the show *Crime Story*. It's really great to know that some people admire that work, but you'd like it to be more well-known. I thought my work in *The Man Who Wasn't There* with Billy Bob Thornton was very good, and it was being talked about by many critics that it was worthy of being nominated, except the movie didn't do anything. There are people who have won Oscars for five minutes on the screen because the film was popular, and I have not really been in popular films. For the most part, the movies I've done were not successful and did not make money. They have become cult films but they were not financially successful when they opened, therefore I think the performances were overlooked then and now are respected. People talk about me in *Miller's Crossing*, and that movie opened and closed in two weeks. It was not a hit at the time. I did two films back-to-back, *Big Nothing* with David Schwimmer and *Stiffs* with Danny Aiello. Neither film was a success but I was proud of both performances. Had they been successful, it would have been a great year where people would have said these are two *entirely* different perfor-

mances from the same actor. What I find encouraging is what happens to someone like Melissa Leo. I love Melissa… I loved her on *Homicide*, and who would've thought that a tiny film like *Frozen River* would've made a name for her? It just so happened that they sent it out at the right time, her performance was solid, and it led to her rise to being famous now. I'm very close with an actor named Mark Margolis, who was just nominated for an Emmy for his performance on *Breaking Bad*. This is the same Mark Margolis who I've known since I first got to New York in the '70s who is now being acknowledged for his work. All you can really hope for is that you get one role on one hit and somebody says now's the time for that old bugger to get acknowledgement. I'm very sad that many things were not popular in their day, but I'm happy that I'm still here and I feel very privileged to still be working.

What advice would you give to aspiring actors?

That's tough… I don't know what to say to young actors now because it's hard to live and be an actor. I guess there's always the same old thing like, "If you believe, and if you keep it up," that kind of stuff, but it's hard for people, and I've seen many people fall by the wayside. I've seen certain performers that come in with a bang and they're gone with a bang as well. I've seen Oscar-winning actors who have come and gone too. I would tell them to enjoy their journey. It *will* be a roller coaster ride, and hopefully you'll end up making it to the end of that ride. There are no rules, don't be discouraged, don't have your self-worth be based on whether you're cast or not, and just keep on pluggin'.

Remo Williams: The Adventure Begins (1985)
Director: Guy Hamilton
Starring: Fred Ward, Joel Grey, Wilford Brimley, J.A. Preston
An ordinary cop (Ward) is forcibly recruited by a secret crime-fighting organization and placed under the tutelage of a wise old martial arts master (Grey). This fun hunk of '80s cheese has some good action set-pieces but is at its best—thanks to great chemistry between Ward and Grey—when it focuses on the cantankerous relationship between student and teacher. Nominated for an Academy Award for Best Makeup.

Highlander (1986)
    Director: Russell Mulcahy
    Starring: Christopher Lambert, Roxanne Hart, Clancy Brown, Sean Connery
    Throughout time, a war has been waged between immortal beings. One of them, Connor MacLeod (Lambert), fights for good. Another, Victor Kruger (Brown), embraces evil. It all comes down to one final battle where the winner will decide the fate of the world. Ultra-stylish fantasy flick has the always-great Connery and a kick-ass soundtrack by Queen, so sit back and enjoy the carnage.

Miller's Crossing (1990)
    Director: Joel Coen
    Starring: Gabriel Byrne, Marcia Gay Hardin, John Turturro, Albert Finney
    A gangster movie that could only come from the minds of the Coen brothers, *Crossing* stars Byrne as Tom, the right-hand man to boss Leo (Finney). As Tom deals with the consequences of his secret relationship with Verna (Hardin)—Leo's girlfriend—he is approached by a rival crime kingpin who wants Tom to kill Bernie (Turturro), a sleazy gambler who happens to be Verna's brother. In a genre that has become overpopulated with *Godfather* clones and *Goodfellas* wannabes, this visually striking, densely plotted and lyrically unique film earns a spot at the top.

Barton Fink (1991)
    Director: Joel Coen
    Starring: John Turturro, John Goodman, Judy Davis, Michael Lerner
    Barton (Turturro) is an acclaimed New York playwright who is lured to Hollywood with the promise of being able to pen important films. His first assignment turns out to be a Wallace Beery wrestling movie, and as Barton struggles with writer's block, he eventually loses his grip on reality. The Coen brothers have concocted an utterly surreal and bizarre comedy so layered in details that it becomes deeper and funnier every time you watch it. Nominated for three Academy Awards, including Best Supporting Actor (Lerner).

The Crow (1994)
    Director: Alex Proyas
    Starring: Brandon Lee, Rochelle Davis, Ernie Hudson, Michael Wincott
    Dark comic book fantasy tells the story of Eric Draven (Lee), a mu-

sician who, along with his fiancée, is murdered by gang members led by a psychotic crime lord (Wincott). Eric is resurrected one year later, and with the help of a mysterious crow, exacts revenge on his killers. Although it's a well-made and entertaining movie, watching the final performance of the charismatic Lee makes *The Crow* a bittersweet experience.

The Hudsucker Proxy (1994)
Director: Joel Coen
Starring: Tim Robbins, Jennifer Jason Leigh, Paul Newman, Charles Durning
Norville Barnes (Robbins) is a naïve mailroom clerk at Hudsucker Industries who becomes president of the company thanks to Sidney J. Mussburger (Newman), a scheming executive who believes Norville will fail spectacularly, giving Sidney a chance to seize power and become rich in the process. At first glance, the movie comes across as a vehicle valuing style over substance, but like most Coen brothers' films, this paean to screwball comedies of the '30s and '40s appreciates greatly with multiple viewings.

With Friends Like These... (1998)
Director: Philip Frank Messina
Starring: Robert Costanzo, Adam Arkin, David Strathairn, Jon Tenney
Small-time character actor Johnny (Costanzo) is ecstatic when he gets the inside track on an audition for a star-making role in a Martin Scorsese movie. Although it's supposed to be a secret, Johnny's buddies—bit players hoping for their own big break—find out and start maneuvering for a shot at the part, setting up a competition amongst friends that could destroy their relationships. If you're interested in a witty and engaging behind-the-scenes look at the lives of working actors, this is the movie to watch.

The Man Who Wasn't There (2001)
Director: Joel Coen
Starring: Billy Bob Thornton, Frances McDormand, Michael Badalucco, James Gandolfini
A beautifully lensed homage to '40s film noir, Thornton plays Ed Crane, a barber living a thoroughly ho-hum and uneventful life. When a cagey businessman offers Ed the opportunity to invest in a dry clean-

ing enterprise, it starts a devastating chain of events that includes blackmail, infidelity and murder. Thornton delivers a quietly devastating performance in one of the most underrated efforts from the Coen brothers. Oscar-nominated for Best Cinematography.

Big Nothing (2006)
Director: Jean-Baptiste Andrea
Starring: David Schwimmer, Simon Pegg, Alice Eve, Natascha McElhone

Charlie (Schwimmer) is a failed writer forced to take a demeaning job at a call center. His co-worker, Gus (Pegg), is in dire need of cash, and he enlists Charlie in a scheme to blackmail a local reverend who's been looking at naughty things on the internet. Of course, things go horribly wrong, but that's when the fun begins. This darkly comic thriller keeps the plot twists coming at a furious pace, and the acting is terrific across-the-board. Director Andrea also helmed the criminally underseen flick *Dead End*, which begs the question: Why isn't this guy getting a chance to make movies that people actually know about?

Stiffs (2010)
Director: Frank Ciota
Starring: Danny Aiello, Jon Polito, Louis Vanaria, Lesley Ann Warren

Frank (Aiello), John (Polito) and Nino (Vanaria) work at a struggling funeral home on the verge of going under. John, who's made some enemies over the years with the local mob, comes up with an idea that will settle a few personal vendettas *and* drum up much-needed business. *Stiffs* is an entertaining black comedy that works thanks to a veteran cast led by Aiello and Polito.

Charles Martin Smith

Before the age of twenty, Charles Martin Smith began making his mark in Hollywood with appearances in *The Brady Bunch* and Sam Peckinpah's *Pat Garrett and Billy the Kid*, but it was his role as Terry "The Toad" in *American Graffiti* that put his career into the fast lane. Following performances in the Oscar-nominated films *The Buddy Holly Story*, *Starman*, and *The Untouchables*, Smith turned his attention to working behind the scenes, directing such diverse projects as the cult horror flick *Trick or Treat*, the lighthearted caper *Stone of Destiny*, and family favorite *Dolphin Tale*. As an actor, writer and director, Smith is a triple threat who continues to engage audiences from both sides of the camera.

How did you get your start in acting?

I'd been interested in it since I was young, and I acted in high school stuff, which is pretty organized in L.A. It sounds somewhat amateur but actually in L.A. it isn't. It's sort of like playing high school basketball in Indiana—it's taken very, very seriously. I got an agent after graduating from high school, I went to university to study theater, and I worked very hard at it. Then I went on auditions and began getting roles.

Kris Kristofferson and Smith in *Pat Garrett and Billy the Kid*

One of your earliest film appearances was in Pat Garrett and Billy the Kid. *What was it like working with director Sam Peckinpah?*

He was quite a character. He was a volatile guy, he had a terrible temper and was a heavy drinker, but he was also very, very smart and very knowledgeable about film. People often think about the hard-drinking, sort of "crazy man" aspect of him, but he was actually very knowledgeable and he worked very hard. Particularly, I remember his attention to detail on the set. The way the room looked, the way the shots were framed… He was very meticulous. I know a lot of actors had problems with him because he was difficult to get along with, but I got along with him fine and had a good experience. He was nice to me but I was a kid too, so he probably treated me a little gentler than he did some of the other guys.

How did you get the role of Terry "The Toad" in American Graffiti?

Well, I had taken a semester off of university and gone traveling in Europe on my own for a while. When I got back, I had heard from my agent that they had been auditioning kids for this film and that there were a lot of roles in it for young actors, but I had missed the audition by being away. He took me there anyway and they had actually not quite finished casting yet. They were going to make the final decisions in three days, so I went in and did a reading for the casting assistant, Gino Havens, and he introduced me to Mike Fenton and Fred Roos, the casting directors. They called me later and brought me in for a screen test—which I did—and to my surprise, they offered me the part.

Did you have any expectations about whether or not the film would be successful?

Well, it was a very, very good script written by George [Lucas] and Gloria Katz and Willard Huyck. It was a cast of very dedicated young actors and we were all just kind of getting started, but I think we all really believed

Candy Clark, Smith and Ron Howard in *American Graffiti*

in the film and we really believed in George. We were so anxious to do a good job for him, and we all worked really, really hard on it. We rehearsed hard, we knew our lines, and we were ready and prepared. We all thought it could be a really, really good film but we didn't think anybody would notice. It was a small-budget film, only $750,000 or something, but then again it also had Francis Coppola as the producer and Haskell Wexler was shooting it, so it had sort of a great pedigree. We all believed in it and just hoped people would notice.

More American Graffiti

Was it a no-brainer for you to do More American Graffiti *or did you have some concerns about doing a sequel?*

I think all of the cast had concerns about doing a sequel, but our only stipulation was that it would be for George. If George was doing a sequel, we were absolutely in. If Universal was going to make a sequel without him, then we were not interested. That just speaks to the loyalty and respect and affection we all felt—and still have—for George. As soon as we found out that it *was* George's project, we were happy to be a part of it, and we were pleased with the way it came out. I, particularly, was pleased with what he wrote for my character to do. Terry "The Toad" going off to Vietnam was very, very cool and I really enjoyed it.

How did you get involved with Never Cry Wolf?

That was interesting… [Director] Carroll Ballard knew George, and *More American Graffiti* was shot by Caleb Deschanel, who had also been the cinematographer on Ballard's film, *The Black Stallion*. I was at the Universal Studios commissary for a meeting about another project and I bumped into Caleb, who happened to be having lunch with Carroll Ballard. Carroll was getting ready to do *Never Cry Wolf*, and we had a bit of a chat. I later got a call from Caleb saying that Carroll wanted to know if I'd be interested in playing the lead in this movie, and I said, "Absolutely." I loved *The Black Stallion*, and we were all kind of family—part of the Lucasfilm bunch—and that meant a lot to us. So Carroll sent me the script, we talked it over and he ended up offering me the part.

Was it intimidating for you as an actor to carry most of the movie on your own?

No, it was fascinating. I had discussions with Carroll about how that was going to work and about how the film was going to be shot. One of the things that really surprised me was that although there was an existing screenplay, he was going to veer pretty much away from it. His background is in documentary filmmaking, so he was going to go off and make it more or less like a documentary, which would mean a lot of improvisation for me, which I was totally cool with. It was an unorthodox way of making the movie but I really liked the idea.

Smith and Farley Mowat on the set of *Never Cry Wolf*

How did you come to end up writing some of the narration?

We worked without a script a lot of the time, and there were different writers who would come up and work on it for a while. Sam Hamm came up and worked for a while, a very good writer named Richard Kletter wrote a lot of the winter stuff, and Ken Kesey was actually part of it for a while, which was interesting. The filming went on for nine months, and there were a lot of times that we didn't have a scene written at all, and I would just sit and write with Carroll. I think he knew that I was a writer, and because I think he had confidence in my ability to write, by the time he was in post-production, he thought that I would have a good ear for the voice of the character, so he invited me to come and help write the narration.

Starman is a film that has a very devoted following after all of these years. What attracted you to the project?

Starman

I always thought it would be fun to do a science fiction movie. What boy doesn't want to be the first one to actually go into an alien spacecraft, you know? It's every kid's fantasy, but it's also just a really good film. I think it's a really smart, interesting love story with a twist, and I think it has a lot of interesting things to say about human behavior as seen through the eyes of an alien. The script was from a writing team named [Raynold] Gideon and [Bruce] Evans, and it was the first script that I'd ever read that I thought you could just shoot verbatim and was basically ready to go. I haven't seen it in a long time but I certainly am proud of the film.

The Untouchables *is another movie that you're well-known for. What was it like making the film?*

That was another kid's fantasy. It was a gangster period piece with these beautiful suits designed by [Giorgio] Armani, and I enjoyed working with Brian De Palma, who had made some great films. I didn't really know Kevin [Costner] or Andy [Garcia] because they hadn't really done much at that point, but I was very happy to work with Sean Connery because I admired his work over the years. We had talked about one of my favorite films, *Robin and Marian*, which is one of his favorites that he had done, so that was really great. It was just a very fun experience.

Andy Garcia, Sean Connery, Kevin Costner and Smith in *The Untouchables*

Trick or Treat was your first film as a director. What led you to making a heavy metal horror movie as your debut?

I was introduced to [writers/producers] Joel Soisson and Michael Murphy, and they had seen a little short film I did in Canada. They had this rock 'n' roll monster movie and they sent me the script. I gave them my notes and my thoughts on it, we talked about it, we saw eye-to-eye that it needed another draft, and they offered it to me. It's nothing I would have thought of… It was their film and they hired me on to direct it, and when you're looking to direct a film, you're pretty much happy to get involved with anything. How many chances do first-time directors get to do a feature film? It's not like Hollywood is giving you a hundred movies to choose from. With that being said, we ended up making a movie that I think we were all really happy with, and I very much enjoyed it.

At what point in your career did you decide you wanted to direct?

I was a directing student at university, and what I wanted to do as a career was to direct theater. I was an acting student too, but by my third or fourth year at university, I was pretty much just a directing student. I was directing plays there and some theater in Los Angeles, and it was always an interest of mine. I wasn't sure that I would ever understand the technical side of filmmaking enough to direct a film, and I ended up learning that mostly from George Lucas and Carroll Ballard. Ballard was always my hero as a filmmaker and I learned so much from him.

What lessons did you learn making Trick or Treat *that you carried over to your other films?*

There's a few things... Certainly you have to make a movie or two to be able to figure it out, and you have to understand editing and post-production before you can effectively direct a movie. I learned a huge amount about the basic craft of making a movie, but I think the main thing I took away from that was the necessity for a director to focus properly on the right things. When you're shooting a film, you tend to get pulled in a hundred different directions at once and it's very, very difficult to stay focused on what you need to focus on. Whenever I talk to young directors or mentor people or speak on panels, I always point out that it's your job to have the story in your head and to be the one telling it. You should not allow yourself to get distracted too much or caught up in things like visual effects meetings and all of the other details. There's a lot of things that will take a director's attention away from what he should be concentrating on, and I really learned that on *Trick or Treat*. With all of the visual effects, all

Marc Price and Smith on the set of *Trick or Treat*

of the stunts and all of the stuff that was going on in there, I sometimes felt very overwhelmed by all of that. If I were to give advice to a young director, it would be this: Don't allow what everybody else is doing distract you from what you should be doing.

The Snow Walker was the first film that you wrote and directed. How did the project come to life?

I got to know Farley Mowat when I was doing *Never Cry Wolf* and we became friends over the years. One time at his house, he told me that he was willing to let me adapt any of his books into a film, which was a very generous offer from a world-famous author. I had already read a bunch of Farley's stuff and I was reading more just looking for something, and I found this little short story that I thought would make a very good film. I asked Farley if I could have it for a dollar option, and then I started working on the script. I worked on it for a few years and then I put it down because I had trouble solving some story problems. I did *Air Bud* with Will Vince—who was the producer—and Will was going to set up his own company. He asked me what other movies I was interested in making, I told him about *Snow Walker* and he encouraged me to finish it. Will and Rob Merilees helped get the money together and we ended up making the film.

Did you draw on your experiences with Never Cry Wolf *when you were making it?*

On the set of *The Snow Walker*

I certainly did. I already knew what the problems were going to be shooting in the Arctic. I understood what the issues were going to be working with the Inuit people, and I knew what their strengths and weaknesses were. I also understood what life is like in the Arctic, and that certainly helped me in writing the movie too, because I'd been up there and I lived that experience of being a guy from the South stranded up there. I knew what that situation was like and that experience was hugely helpful.

You've said that you dreamed of making your film, Stone of Destiny, *for many years. What was it about the story that you found so appealing?*

Well, it's about a bunch of university students pulling off a wonderful heist, and I guess I remember when I was in university and having that feeling that you could change the world and that kids are going to make all of the difference. I remember the Vietnam War protests and the civil rights movement when I was a little kid, and I loved the idea that with that sort of passion, you can, in fact, change the world. These kids did something non-violent that was so inspirational to the entire county of Scotland, and I loved the fact that they did a prank that sort of changed society there forever.

After living with the project for so long, were you able to fully realize your vision of how the film should be?

I don't know that you ever really have a vision that you can fully realize… I'm skeptical of the word "vision." You know what movie you're trying to make and then you have to make it within the parameters of whatever situation you're in. It never looks like the movie you imagined in your head when you're writing it—where the sets are, what the people you end up casting actually look like—but you have to try and stay true to the story and make the best version of the movie that you have in your head that you can. There are a lot of times when you end up having to simplify things much more than you thought you would, or you have to make certain compromises for the shooting schedule or for the availability of locations. It's always a process… The movie you end up with is never exactly the movie you set out to make, but what you hope to do is to keep the heart and soul of it.

On the set of *Air Bud*

Is there a big difference between directing material that you've written as opposed to being hired to direct someone else's script?

Yeah, you certainly have a better understanding of the stuff you wrote. You understand why every single word is there and you know why every scene is there because you put it there. On the other hand, I think when you're directing someone else's screenplay it's like you have a bit of a collaborator. You have the writer's ideas *and* you have your ideas. When you're directing a script that you wrote yourself, you don't have that other person to help with the ideas. There's definitely pros and cons to both situations.

Do you think your experience as an actor has helped your directing, or are those two separate skills?

No, no, they're totally connected. I learned an awful lot as an actor from an acting teacher I had named Nina Foch, and she was a terrific teacher. She talked about the fact that we're all in it telling the same story, and she discussed what the actor's role is and what the director's role is. Those are very similar skills because actors and directors have to know how to break the script down and how to understand what each scene is. Having been an actor for so many years, I think that I'm—I hope that I am—of some help to the actors when I direct. I certainly understand what they're going through, and I've worked in enough different styles as an actor that I think I'm able to figure out how each actor approaches the work and then kind of help them to do what they do.

These days when you're hired to act, is it hard to just be an actor when you're on the set?

Actually, it's easier than it used to be. For one thing, I understand that the director is the only one that really sees the movie in his head, so I think I'm probably easier to direct than I ever was. I'm not aware of everything the director is doing when I'm acting, nor do I want to be because I have

Smith and Morgan Freeman on the set of *Dolphin Tale*

to concentrate on what *I'm* doing. It's like being the editor of a newspaper as opposed to being a columnist… You're either supervising other people that are doing the job or you're doing the job itself. It's just a different way of thinking.

How would you describe your process when preparing for an acting role?

I just get extremely familiar with the script and do as much research as I can on the character and the situation. I think it's different for everybody but I do a lot of that kind of work. You just have to really understand the script inside and out, and I do a breakdown of the character on where he is in each scene, what he's trying to accomplish, and then I learn the lines. I think it might have been [John] Gielgud who said the best advice he could give any young actor is to learn your lines. It actually sounds stupid but it's kind of true. A lot of actors don't really quite have their lines down and that makes it much more difficult on the day. There are some actors who have actually memorized the entire script before they show up, and then there's some who don't know what they're supposed to say.

When you're asked to act in a movie, what do you look for that decides whether or not you'll do it?

Good writing… Good writing is the main thing. I also look at the director and see who that person is, what they've done and if I liked their films. I just look for a good script—a story that means something to me, a character I can understand that would be interesting to play, and dialogue that's actable. Unfortunately, you see a lot of badly written scripts in Hollywood, and sometimes you look at these things and think, 'How can anybody say these lines?' It's very, very hard to turn in a good performance when you've got bad dialogue.

In the future, do you see yourself concentrating on writing and directing or do you like mixing it up with acting too?

I like to mix it up and do all of those things. I haven't done very much acting at all in the last ten years because I've been busy with the directing and so forth, which is great. Writing and directing is something that I love doing, but I'd be happy to do some more acting when I'm available and have the time. I like doing all of those things.

What advice would you give to aspiring actors?

The advice that I always give to people is don't do it, it's just too hard a way to make a living. It's really, really difficult, it's really frustrating, and I think it's very unfair a lot of times. Anybody that I could encourage to *not* be an actor I would certainly do so. I think the only people that have any possible chance of succeeding are the ones that can't be talked out of it. If I can talk them out of it, they shouldn't do it. I had people that tried to talk me out of it too, and I wouldn't listen, so I think that's the only way you have a chance.

American Graffiti (1973)
    Director: George Lucas
    Starring: Richard Dreyfuss, Ronny Howard, Paul Le Mat, Charlie Martin Smith
    Taking place on the last night of summer in 1962, *Graffiti* focuses on a group of small-town teenagers facing the crossroads in their lives. Curt (Dreyfuss) is supposed to leave for college but is having second thoughts; Steve (Howard) struggles with whether or not to continue dating his longtime girlfriend; and Terry "The Toad" (Smith) finally gets a chance to impress a blonde bombshell. Featuring an infectious soundtrack of classic songs and engaging performances from everyone involved, *Graffiti* raised the bar for teen-oriented films and has rarely been surpassed. Nominated for five Academy Awards, including Best Picture, Best Director and Best Screenplay.

Pat Garrett and Billy the Kid (1973)
    Director: Sam Peckinpah
    Starring: James Coburn, Kris Kristofferson, Richard Jaeckel, Katy Jurado
    If anyone could've made the definitive movie about Garrett (Coburn)

and Billy (Kristofferson)—former friends who found themselves on opposite sides of the law in the old West—it should've been Sam Peckinpah. However, the director's personal demons and fights with the studio led to a compromised product that merely scratches the surface of its potential. Coburn and Kristofferson are very good and they make the film worthwhile, but this is a case where the behind-the-scenes stories are a lot more interesting than what ended up on screen.

More American Graffiti (1979)
Director: B.W.L. Norton
Starring: Ron Howard, Paul Le Mat, Charles Martin Smith, Candy Clark

Conceptually ambitious but unnecessary sequel takes the characters from *Graffiti* and splits them into four separate stories taking place during four different years in the 1960s. The segments vary in quality, from good—1965 Vietnam, where Terry "The Toad" (Smith) desperately tries to escape from the Army—to downright bad—1966 San Francisco, featuring Debbie (Clark) as a pot-smoking hippie. While it's nice to see the gang back together (so to speak), the original film said pretty much everything that needed to be said.

Never Cry Wolf (1983)
Director: Carroll Ballard
Starring: Charles Martin Smith, Brian Dennehy, Zachary Ittimangnaq, Samson Jorah

Beautifully filmed story of a scientist named Tyler (Smith) who is sent to the Arctic for six months to study wolves and their effect on the caribou population. Although woefully unprepared for the grueling conditions, Tyler eventually comes to adapt to his surroundings and the creatures themselves. *Wolf* is essentially a one-man show, and Smith does an incredible job carrying the movie. Oscar-nominated for Best Sound.

Starman (1984)
Director: John Carpenter
Starring: Jeff Bridges, Karen Allen, Charles Martin Smith, Richard Jaeckel

An alien (Bridges) lands on Earth and takes on the physical form of a grieving widow's (Allen) deceased husband. The two hit the road to rendezvous with the Starman's rescue ship as a government scientist (Smith) doggedly pursues them. Director Carpenter is best known for his horror films, but he shows a sure and steady hand with this winning sci-fi love story. Bridges earned an Oscar nomination as Best Actor.

Trick or Treat (1986)
    Director: Charles Martin Smith
    Starring: Marc Price, Tony Fields, Lisa Orgolini, Doug Savant
    A fun and nostalgic flick for heavy metal horror fans, *Treat* tells the story of Eddie (Price), a bullied high school headbanger whose music idol, Sammi Curr (Fields), dies in a hotel fire. Eddie obtains a copy of Sammi's unreleased last album and plays it backwards, resurrecting the dead rocker who's ready to exact some revenge from beyond the grave. Price gives an endearing performance, and real-life rock stars Gene Simmons and Ozzy Osbourne make amusing contributions in small roles.

The Untouchables (1987)
    Director: Brian De Palma
    Starring: Kevin Costner, Sean Connery, Charles Martin Smith, Andy Garcia
    Federal agent Eliot Ness (Costner) is sent to Chicago during Prohibition to dismantle the bootlegging empire created by mobster Al Capone (Robert De Niro). When his efforts are thwarted by crooked officials, Ness forms an unlikely team of incorruptible men—a sage flatfoot (Connery); an academy rookie (Garcia); and an accountant (Smith)—to bring down Capone. This supremely entertaining film is, quite simply, one of the best gangster movies of all time. Nominated for four Academy Awards and winner for Best Supporting Actor (Connery).

Air Bud (1997)
    Director: Charles Martin Smith
    Starring: Michael Jeter, Kevin Zegers, Wendy Makkena, Bill Cobbs
    Predictable but ultimately winning family fare has Zegers as Josh, a kid adjusting to the death of his father and life in a new town. He finds a dog he names Buddy, a sweet pooch with a talent for playing basketball that has escaped the clutches of a hateful owner (Jeter). Aside from the novelty of seeing a Golden Retriever shooting hoops, the formulaic script sticks to the familiar Disney clichés, but thanks to director Smith's deft handling of the material, most viewers will be satisfied with the ride *Air Bud* delivers.

The Snow Walker (2003)
    Director: Charles Martin Smith
    Starring: Barry Pepper, Annabella Piugattuk, James Cromwell, Kiersten Warren
    A cocky pilot (Pepper) transporting a sick Inuit woman (Piugattuk) crash lands deep in the Arctic. With no one to rely on but each other, the duo struggles against the harsh elements to survive. Returning to the themes and environment he explored as an actor in *Never Cry Wolf*, writer/director Smith creates a compelling drama with terrific performances from Pepper and Piugattuk.

Stone of Destiny (2008)
    Director: Charles Martin Smith
    Starring: Charlie Cox, Kate Mara, Stephen McCole, Billy Boyd
    Based on a real-life incident, *Destiny* tells the story of Ian Hamilton (Cox), a Scottish university student who concocted a plan in 1950 to break into London's Westminster Abbey and steal the fabled Stone of Scone, a treasured artifact England took from Scotland centuries ago. More than a history lesson, the movie is an infectiously fun heist flick with gorgeous locations and a winning cast.

Dale Dye

After two decades of service to his country, Capt. Dale Dye retired from the United States Marine Corps and began waging a different kind of battle in the trenches of Hollywood. His mission: Bring an accurate and authentic depiction of military life to the silver screen. While working as the technical advisor on Academy Award winners *Platoon*, *Born on the Fourth of July*, and *Saving Private Ryan*, Dye embarked on a second career as an actor, appearing in such popular movies as *Under Siege*, *Mission: Impossible*, and *Starship Troopers*. Not content with his success both in front of and behind the camera, Dye is also a bestselling author of several novels and will be making his writing/directing debut with the film *No Better Place to Die*. Follow Capt. Dye's continuing adventures at www.daledye.com.

According to your bio, during the twenty years you served in the Marine Corps, you did everything from being a drill instructor and working as a combat correspondent in Vietnam to serving on the Secretary of Defense's staff at the Pentagon. How did you end up in Hollywood?

It was actually a surprise to everyone, including me. I really had planned on spending the rest of my life in the Marine Corps as long as they would let me stay. Then I had a very strange, final combat assignment in Beirut, Lebanon, in '82 and '83. The Marine unit I was attached to was serving as what were euphemistically called "peacekeepers." That mission rapidly began to creep, and we found ourselves becoming targets over there with no real way to respond because of the political nature of the mission. I left in May of 1983, and in October of 1983 after I had come home, we had the bombing of the Marine barracks that killed 241 men. I think that broke my warrior's heart… It made me really look around at what I was doing. I was a captain at that time and a leader of Marines, but it's hard to be a good, effective, honest leader if your warrior's heart is broken. So, I decided there were two reactions I could have: One was to just suck it up and continue the march, but that seemed dishonest to me; the other reaction was to rage at the machine, so to speak, but that wasn't my nature—that wasn't my way of going about things. I thought maybe it was time for me to retire, and I had enough time in to retire with a pension and that sort of thing. What I *didn't* have was any idea of what I was going to do. So, I did what good Marines do: I went out and bought a case of beer, I got one of those long yellow legal pads, and I sat down and drew a line down the middle of the pad. On one side of it I wrote "Assets" and on the other side I wrote "Liabilities," and then I started drinking beer. By dawn, the beer was gone and I had about sixteen pages of liabilities and about three lines of assets. One of those assets was that I had always been a movie fan. I'd seen every military movie there was because that was my life, and the common denominator was that all of those movies had pissed me off. They didn't reflect the professional military as I knew it. They didn't reflect the life I had led. They didn't reflect the people that I knew or the relationships between people that I knew, and I wondered why… Why does Hollywood get it so absolutely, gut-wrenchingly *wrong*? I would see credits that listed military advisors, and the movies would be nonsense. When you're ignorant, you can do a lot of things that people tell you you can't do—and I was certainly ignorant—so I decided to hell with it, I was just going to come out to Hollywood and sniff around and see if I could find out what this was all about. The glimmering idea in the back of my mind was that I wanted to fix this… I wanted to get involved in motion pictures and television and see if I couldn't convince them that who we really were and how we really act and how we really operate is much more interesting and dramatic than what was being presented. That was the germ of the idea when I came out here.

Was it difficult getting executives to listen to you?

I spent about a year talking to anybody I could. I'd go onto studio lots and attack the first guy I saw carrying a briefcase and wearing a tie. I'd say, "Do you make movies? Let me tell you…." Of course, I'd usually get arrested and thrown off the lots. I quickly became convinced the problem was simply that no one out here understood what I was going for. They didn't understand it because no one out here had experience in it. There was a generation of filmmakers in the '50s who had actually been to war in World War II, but those guys were gone, they were out of the business. They were replaced by people who were of the Vietnam era where everything was anti-military, anti-war, and full of stereotypes about who the military really was. I knew that what was needed was someone who could show them the truth—someone who could teach the actors, teach the writers, teach the directors what the reality is, and let them get a look at how interesting it really is. It was very difficult to sell anybody on my ideas for a lot of reasons, the biggest being that I had no experience in it. I'd never made a movie or even been on a movie set, but I had this idea and I wouldn't give it up.

The first movie you worked on was Invaders from Mars. *How did that come about?*

A friend of mine who had been in Vietnam with me was a storyboard artist, and he was working on *Invaders from Mars*. He called me one day and he said, "Are you still looking to work on movies?" I said, "Yeah," and he said, "Well, in our movie, it's the Marines that fight the Martians, and the director doesn't know anything about the military and he's looking for somebody who can stage combat between the Marines and the Martians." I had no compunction against killing Martians, so I quickly volunteered for the job. I was able to sort of "borrow" a Marine reserve unit from Southern California, and they became the Marines who fought the Martians. It was a great experience… It was another leadership challenge, and the Marines responded to me and did exactly what I told them to do. We staged it like a regular battle, and I was figuring it out as I flew. The great thing about it was that when I wasn't actually running the Marines or helping the director—Tobe Hooper—choreograph the action, I was working for every department head I could find. I found out about costumes, camera, props, weapons… In other words, I went to school the whole time we were making that movie, and because I was interested and was willing to do anything, the department heads taught me a lot about how movies were made. *Invaders from Mars* was like a community college of filmmaking for me.

You also made your debut as an actor in the film. Did you audition for the part or were you just asked to do it?

Well, I had watched Tobe run the actors and I thought, I can do this… It's simply performance, and it's stuff I've done in the Marine Corps. At this point, Tobe was really relying on me; I was his go-to guy. I saved him time and effort and frustration and everything else just by running the Marines around like crazy, so I finally went up to him one day and I said, "Listen, there's this little role of a rocket gunner who blows away a Martian and

says a few lines." He looked at me and said, "Do you want to do it?" I said, "You know, I'd really love to," and he said, "All right, let's try it." Without any audition, he just put me in there. Everybody loved it, and I qualified to become a Screen Actors Guild guy, which was the start of yet another career.

Did you harbor any ambitions about becoming an actor or was it something you just felt like trying?

I only thought about trying it after seeing actors doing what they do. I did that all the time in the Marine Corps when I was teaching, when I was instructing, when I was training people… I was acting, and I was good at it. My success and my promotions and everything else kind of demonstrate that, so I thought it was something I could do. Of course, I had a very superficial and shallow understanding of what acting is. There's a lot more to it than simply manipulating a weapon properly and screaming, but I thought I could do it. I got kind of interested in it, and I got more and more interested in it the more I did it.

How did you get involved with your next movie, Platoon?

By that time, I had learned to read the trade papers, and I saw a notice in *Daily Variety* that a relatively unknown writer/director by the name of Oliver Stone was going to do a Vietnam movie based on his own experi-

Platoon

ence as a combat infantryman. I knew that if I could just get to this guy, he would get it because he had been a soldier. Through a series of machinations, I managed to get his home phone number. I called him one Sunday morning and I went into my best two-minute drill. I said, "Look, you don't know me and there's no reason you should know me, but if you're really going to do what the papers say you're going to do, you *need* me," and I told him why. He said, "You know, you may have a point. Let's meet." We had a meeting, and I convinced him that what I was telling him was right, and he knew it was because he had experienced it personally. So I got hired for this little movie called *Platoon*, and he gave me the thirty-five actors who would comprise the primary unit. He let me take them for three weeks into the mountains of the Philippine jungle and train them, living twenty-four hours a day/seven days a week in the environment with no civilian contact whatsoever. They lived as soldiers, and by the time I brought them down out of the hills, they *were* real Vietnam-era G.I.s. We then proceeded to make the film, and when we brought it home, it won four Academy Awards, including Best Picture. Oliver was kind enough to credit me with much of its unique nature, and from that point on, I was the hot ticket as a military advisor in Hollywood.

What was the boot camp like that you put the actors through?

It was intense. I isolated them about fifteen kilometers up on a jungle hillside. There were absolutely no civilians anywhere around them, there was no contact with anybody, no phones, nothing. They worked about fourteen hours a day and I let them sleep about two hours a night if they didn't piss me off. They only ate about twice a day, and they humped through those hills up and down and up and down, cutting their way through the jungle carrying about sixty-five pounds of gear on their backs. They cleaned their own weapons, they dug their own holes and they slept in them at night. I had brought some guys with me and we would ambush and attack them every night. And as I got them going through this routine, I trained them… I trained them in how to react to these things and how to go into immediate action drills. More importantly, every evening I would talk to them about the psychology of a soldier, about the relationships that one soldier has with another. As I told them these things, they would then see it as they went through a training day. They really, *really* got into the mind and into the heart and into the philosophy of combat soldiers. That's what made the performances in the film so special.

You also wrote the novelization of the film. How did that come about?

I had written one book prior to this time, and it was released during my last year of active duty. It was a novel called *Run Between the Raindrops*, sort of a semi-autobiographical tale of my fighting in Hue, Tet, 1968. Oliver and I were very close after *Platoon* was released because we were running around the country doing publicity tours and Oprah Winfrey's show and that sort of thing. So, Oliver came to me one day and said, "Oh, God, I don't know what I'm going to do. They want a novel to sell because the movie is so popular." I told him, "I'll write it," and he said, "You? What do you know?" I handed him my book and I said, "Well, I've already written one, and if anybody knows these characters and knows the story, I do because I was at your shoulder the whole way through." He kind of paged through my book and he said, "Yeah, maybe you can." He made a pitch to his agents and told them he wanted me to write the book, and they were fine with it. We arranged a contract, I got a little bit of money and I sat down and wrote the book in about three weeks.

You've worked with Stone on several other films over the years, including Born on the Fourth of July, JFK, *and* Natural Born Killers. *What is it about him that keeps you coming back for more?*

Well, I guess I'm one of the only guys who consistently survives a movie with him. Oliver is really a visionary filmmaker, and he's very, very good at what he does. I don't always *agree* with what he does, but he's an excellent storyteller. Because we were so close during his first real big film, we became not only colleagues and workmates, we also became friends. I admired his vision, and I really wanted to learn more and more and more from him. When I work with him on a set, he lets me go behind his eyes and into his mind, more than he does with anybody else who he

Tom Hanks, Dye and Steven Spielberg on the set of *The Pacific*

works with. I guess that's because we're fellow travelers and he trusts me. I have a real curiosity about things, and I really, really learn a lot from him. That's not to say that we're politically kindred spirits… We're not; we're at opposite ends of the poles. In fact, on sets the guys used to call me "John Wayne" and Oliver was "Ho Chi Min." That was their code words for which one of us they were talking about. But I admire his vision and skill as a storyteller, and it's nice to be involved and watch him work.

A few years after Platoon, *you were hired as an actor for Steven Spielberg's movie,* Always. *How did that happen?*

Steven was a huge fan of *Platoon*. He loved that film, and he had seen my performance as Capt. Harris, the company commander. I had never met him, but when he got ready to do *Always*, he had this role of a fire boss who he envisioned as kind of a company commander in the Forest Service. He told me later that he wanted the guy Oliver used as his company commander, so he looked at the credits, called my agents and he said, "Look, I want to hire your guy." Of course, everybody just fainted, especially me! When I met him, he said, "I want you to be Capt. Harris like you were in *Platoon*, but I want you to be running these guys in the Forest Service." I said, "Can do," so I went up to Montana where we were shooting on location. He and I got to talking, and he's a very curious guy. He was very curious about the military and my military experiences, and we were sort of simpatico. I think we both realized it, and that was the beginning of a long and productive relationship.

At that point in your acting career, I assume that gave you some major validation when Spielberg calls and asks for you.

It certainly did. I had managed to sign on as an actor for representation with this little boutique agency in L.A., and I had been out on a few auditions and not gotten any work. When the Spielberg call came, the nature of the beast changed. Suddenly, my agents were like, "Whoa… Whoever this guy is that we're representing, some people have some respect for him, so maybe we'd better pay a little more attention." And they did start doing that.

When the time came for Spielberg to make Saving Private Ryan, *were you one of the first people to get the call?*

Dye (center) and the cast of *Saving Private Ryan*

I *was* the first. Steven called me one day on my cell phone and said, "What are you doing?" I said, "Right now? I'm actually grocery shopping." He asked me what I was doing on a certain date and I said, "I'm doing whatever you want me to do." He said, "Well, here's what I want you to do... I'm going to send you a script. I want you to read it, I want you to comment on it and I want you to talk to the writers. Then I'm gonna need you to train the actors and help me stage all of this combat." And I said, "Can do." So he sent me the script for *Saving Private Ryan*, and at that point, I didn't know who was going to be in it. The next thing I know, I'm over in England getting ready to do this and working with all the department heads and helping everybody out with props and wardrobe and weapons and everything else. Then I met Tom Hanks and Tom Sizemore and Eddie Burns and Vin Diesel and the rest of the cast and took them to the field and trained them for about ten days.

When you're hired as an advisor, do you always come in that early during pre-production?

It used to be kind of late in the game because in the early stages I was only known as the trainer of actors and the stager of combat scenes. I was known as the best at doing that, but that's *all* I was known for. As I began to do more and more films with bigger and bigger directors, it became obvious that the earlier they brought me in, the better off they were because I could work with the writers and get the script right so that we

Dye, Sean Young, Tommy Lee Jones and director David Green on the set of *Fire Birds*

wouldn't have to be tearing it apart and re-doing it on the fly. These days, I'm involved very early so that I can provide script notes and possible changes and help the writers with incongruities and anachronisms. I also can help the department heads get the right stuff because I know where all the right stuff is.

The landing at Omaha Beach in Ryan *has some of the most harrowing combat footage I've ever seen in a film. What was it like creating and staging that sequence?*

It was really interesting. Steven pulled me aside one day and said, "Look, I'm not really sure how to do this, but you are. You stage the war and I'll film it." That was carte blanche, and I got my Eisenhower fix on that deal. By this time, I had formed my company, Warriors Incorporated, and I had a few people who worked for me. I took them over there to help me run 1,000 men who were all Irish Territorial Army, fourteen armored vehicles, and seven ships at sea. I was able to kind of get a feel for what the invasion was going to be like, and I positioned my guys in the middle of it. They were wearing earbuds and talking to me on the radio, and I was talking to guys on the ships and in the vehicles. In fact, I had a bunch of production assistants who walked around and slapped radios in my hand for whatever I needed to get done. We knew that for the wide shots, once it started, it was not going to stop. You can't stop something like that for take two, it's just a monster. So after about three days of milling around with it and training the guys, I went to the boss and said, "Okay, I think we're ready." We went out and shot a little bit in the boats and the landing craft just to get everybody warmed up and ready to go. When the tide was right and the troops were ready and we'd done all of the preparation we could conceivably do, Steven nodded at me and I keyed the radios and said, "Go." The cameras were rolling and we just ripped it off.

Another director you've worked with a couple of times is Brian De Palma, and I think Casualties of War *is one of his more underrated efforts. What was it like making the movie?*

It was odd… They originally wanted us as the technical advisors, and while I was cementing that deal, I asked Brian if he had hired anybody to do the company commander role. He said that he hadn't, and I said, "Well, I'd like to audition for you." He brought me in with the casting director, and I did the audition. And I guess I did a good job because before I even got home from the audition, he called and said, "You're hired." I was working on a TV series as an actor at the time, so I couldn't immediately go over there and do the technical advising thing. I had to get my

Dye and Michael J. Fox in *Casualties of War*

Executive Officer, Mike Stokey—my number one guy who's been with me for forty years now—and send him to represent us as the advisors. Mike was a sergeant with me in Vietnam, and he knows exactly how we do things. He went over and trained the troops and when I finished my TV gig, I jumped on a plane and went over and did the company commander role. It's interesting working with Brian… He's very much a film technician. Unlike Oliver Stone, Brian is not as focused on the story sometimes as he is on the visual presentation, and I think that's to his detriment in some of his films. In order to do a really good job with him, you've got to know camera and you've got to know staging. After that is when you worry about your acting.

You've also worked with acclaimed director Terrence Malick on The Thin Red Line. *What was that experience like?*

Terrence is another visionary, he really is, but he has a mind that's very difficult to fathom sometimes. I remember that when it was announced Terrence was going to do the picture, we were working on another film in Texas, and Terrence lived down there. He wanted us to work on the film, so we left the set we were on and went to meet him and talk it over with him. I couldn't really get a handle on Terrence… During the meeting, I was looking at things as a practical filmmaker and Terrence was talking as an ethereal thinker. He handed us a script that was huge and would've been about a four or five-hour movie, and I was thinking I had no idea what we're going to do here… As it turned out, I got a call from Hanks and Spielberg to begin work on *Band of Brothers* about the same time, so I sent Mike Stokey to do *The Thin Red Line*. He told me some *very* interesting stories about working with Terrence, and he'd often call me and say, "I'm not sure what's gonna happen with this film." I only shot with Terrence once on set when they came back to the States after filming in Australia. They had to do some pick-up shots here in California in San Pedro aboard the Lane Victory, so I worked with him there. I found it very hard—as Mike did—to ever second-guess Terrence. He knows what he wants and what he wants to do, but sometimes he doesn't communicate it well.

Speaking of Band of Brothers, *you got some rave reviews for your portrayal of Col. Robert Sink in the show. Did you do any kind of research for the role?*

Band of Brothers

Tons of it. I was very lucky to be able to talk to Col. Sink's family, particularly his daughter, and I was able to acquire some recordings of speeches he'd made so I could get his voice and his cadence and his accent. I guess all of us who spend our lives in the military are amateur military historians, so I knew a lot about him, but the family really gave me some insight—some personal stuff—that I was able to bring to the character. That's what made it so rewarding… The greatest acting experience, in my judgment, is accurately and effectively portraying a real person. I was able to get my teeth into the Col. Sink character because I felt like I knew him.

What directors have helped you the most when it comes to acting?

I guess the directors who influenced me most as an actor would be Oliver Stone and Steven Spielberg. Oliver because he understands people and how contrary and unpredictable they can be. He's rarely averse to genuine emotion and lets his actors do what's necessary to convey those emotions while serving the storytelling. He gave me the courage to expose emotions as an actor with no formal training. Steven is probably the best in the world at hitting all the right buttons in a given scene: Background, props, camera angle, the interplay between characters, emotional tone, and everything else you can think of. He taught me to use it all if it serves the story. He respects actors and really wants them to contribute beyond hitting the mark and saying the lines. You can't ask for much more than that.

Are there any actors you've trained in your boot camps that you think would make good soldiers in real life?

Ron Livingston who played Nixon in *Band of Brothers* would've made a good soldier. Tom Hanks, Tommy Lee Jones, Eddie Burns, and Tom Berenger would've made excellent soldiers. Believe it or not, Tom Cruise would've made a good soldier... They all had heart. Not only did they understand emotions, they "got it" about being part of a team. They understood that the sun doesn't always rise and set on their asses, and they were willing to give and to support the people around them. It would have been very easy to take that kind of mentality—that kind of heart—and mold it and teach them the technical skills and let them run with it. I think they would've done fine as soldiers.

You received credit as second unit director on Oliver Stone's film Alexander. *How did that come about?*

On the set of *Alexander*

At the point we were getting ready to do *Alexander*, I knew that I was becoming a complete filmmaker… Not just a technical advisor, not just an actor, but I was also a writer and had helped produce a few things. I had trained so many actors that I really understood staging and performance and emotional beats and all of those buzzwords that are tossed around in showbiz. I just thought, I want to tell my stories my way, and in order to do that I need to become a director. But in order to become a director, I needed a shot at it. So once again, I hit my default position, which was to go to Oliver. I went to him and said, "This is what I want to do. Can you give me a shot? You know I can do it. You've seen me work with actors, you've seen me stage stuff, I know camera because you taught me! Will you let me direct the second unit on *Alexander*?" He thought about it for a week and then came back to me and said, "All right, you're on. I'm paying your dues for the Director's Guild of America, so you're going to do it." Interestingly, I think I'm the only second unit director that ever completely survived an Oliver Stone film. It was really a great experience… I don't want to use the cliché "learning experience" but that's essentially what it was. It confirmed in my mind that I could do this, that I could be good at this. I'm now pursuing it, and I'm soon going to be directing my first feature film called *No Better Place to Die*, which is based on a story I wrote.

What advice do you have for anybody looking to break into the business?

You need to have focus… Find out how movies are made and then find out what it is specifically in that process that you want to do. I get this question from thousands of people all the time. "I want to make movies, I want to be in the movies…" And do what? Do you want to be a cinematographer? Do you want to be a writer? Do you want to be a director? Do you want to be an accountant? What do you want to do? Sometimes you don't know unless you've worked on film sets, so I usually say find yourself some sort of intern job where you can hang around and see what people do. Don't expect it to pay your bills, but get on a set or two and be a runner or be a craft service grunt and watch what people do and see what trips your trigger. Then you can get some focus and you can go specifically for a job in that area. What's really tough is talking to people who want to be actors. So many young people have driven themselves to destruction trying to make it big because they're focused on becoming "stars" instead of "actors." It can be *very* difficult for people to get a start

in this industry, but those that make it are the ones who have the tenacity and determination to survive.

Invaders from Mars (1986)
　　Director: Tobe Hooper
　　Starring: Karen Black, Hunter Carson, Timothy Bottoms, Laraine Newman
　　By-the-numbers remake of the classic 1953 sci-fi flick about a boy (Carson) who sees a UFO crash behind his house. Soon after, the adults in town begin acting very strangely, and the boy turns to the military for help in defeating the Martians. While this new *Invaders* brings improved technology to the table, it loses the sense of paranoia and dread that made the original so effective. Not a terrible movie, but not that great either.

Platoon (1986)
　　Director: Oliver Stone
　　Starring: Tom Berenger, Willem Dafoe, Charlie Sheen, Forest Whitaker
　　Engrossing Vietnam drama about a young man named Chris (Sheen) who drops out of college and enlists in the Army. As he struggles to sur-

vive amidst the chaos of war, Chris becomes a pawn in a power struggle between Barnes (Berenger)—a hardcore killer who wants to win at any cost—and Elias (Dafoe)—a sympathetic leader who just wants to do his duty and go home. Following the macho escapades in films like *Rambo* and *Missing in Action*, *Platoon* is a sobering and terrifying look at war and how it changes the people fighting in it. Nominated for eight Oscars and winner of four, including Best Picture and Best Director.

Always (1989)
　Director: Steven Spielberg
　Starring: Richard Dreyfuss, Holly Hunter, Brad Johnson, John Goodman
　Pete (Dreyfuss) is a daredevil pilot fighting fires from the sky who's in love with Dorinda (Hunter), a Forest Service air traffic controller. After Pete dies in a heroic accident, he is sent back to Earth to invisibly inspire another pilot named Ted (Johnson), a task that becomes difficult when Ted falls in love with Dorinda. A remake of the 1943 film *A Guy Named Joe*, Spielberg's deliberately old-fashioned fantasy/romantic drama isn't one of his best efforts, but even a sub-par Spielberg is better than most directors working at the top of their game.

Born on the Fourth of July (1989)
　Director: Oliver Stone
　Starring: Tom Cruise, Raymond J. Barry, Caroline Kava, Josh Evans
　Stone's gut-wrenching companion piece to *Platoon* tells the true story of Ron Kovic (Cruise), a gung-ho, all-American teen who enlists to fight in Vietnam. After being wounded and paralyzed during battle, Kovic returns home to find a nation filled with indifference, leading him to rethink his allegiance to God and country. Cruise is exceptional and really gets to show his range, but Willem Dafoe steals his scenes in a small role as another disabled vet. Nominated for eight Oscars and winner for Best Director and Best Editing.

Casualties of War (1989)
　Director: Brian De Palma
　Starring: Michael J. Fox, Sean Penn, Don Harvey, John C. Reilly
　Fox stars as Eriksson, a young family man trying to adjust to life as a soldier in Vietnam. One night on a mission, battle-hardened Sgt. Meserve (Penn) kidnaps a young girl and brings her along for a little "portable

R&R." As the men in the squad take turns raping her, Eriksson refuses to participate, incurring the wrath of Meserve and the distrust of Eriksson's fellow comrades. Based on a true story, *Casualties* is a haunting film exploring the moral battles that take place during war, with great performances by Fox and Penn.

JFK (1991)
   Director: Oliver Stone
   Starring: Kevin Costner, Tommy Lee Jones, Kevin Bacon, Gary Oldman
   Oliver Stone's epic, controversial take on the assassination of President Kennedy stars Costner as Jim Garrison, the New Orleans district attorney who felt the government was covering up the murder and launched his own investigation. Garrison believed the accused gunman, Lee Harvey Oswald (Oldman), was only a pawn in a much larger conspiracy to take down JFK, and Stone goes to great lengths to prove Garrison was right. The film is filled with facts, fiction, and hypotheticals, and whether you subscribe to his theory or not, there's no denying Stone has created an emotionally-charged, thought-provoking and visually hypnotic work of art. Nominated for seven Academy Awards and winner of two (Best Editing and Best Cinematography).

Natural Born Killers (1994)
   Director: Oliver Stone
   Starring: Woody Harrelson, Juliette Lewis, Tommy Lee Jones, Robert Downey Jr.
   Young married couple Mickey (Harrelson) and Mallory Knox (Lewis) embark on a deranged killing spree and become America's favorite outlaws thanks to overzealous media coverage and people in authority looking to profit from the duo's murderous exploits. As a satire of our nation's obsession with lunatics like these, Stone delivers his message with all the subtlety of a sledgehammer to the groin, but on a purely technical level he displays a gift for creating beautifully chaotic images and a mastery of using multiple mediums that few directors can match. *Killers* is a movie that's much easier to "respect" than it is to "like."

Saving Private Ryan (1998)
   Director: Steven Spielberg
   Starring: Tom Hanks, Tom Sizemore, Edward Burns, Matt Damon

Three Ryan brothers are killed during World War II, leaving one (Damon) to carry on the family name. As a PR move to boost morale on the home front, government officials order Capt. Miller (Hanks) and his squad to find the last remaining sibling so he can be sent back to care for his grieving mother. Raw, visceral, and emotionally devastating, *Saving Private Ryan* is arguably Spielberg's masterpiece. The first twenty minutes depicting the chaotic horror and carnage of the landing at Omaha Beach is the most harrowing war footage ever recreated on film. Nominated for eleven Academy Awards and winner of five, including Best Director, Best Editing, and Best Cinematography.

The Thin Red Line (1998)
Director: Terrence Malick
Starring: Nick Nolte, Jim Caviezel, Sean Penn, Elias Koteas
If *Saving Private Ryan* has a transcendental flipside, it's *The Thin Red Line*, directed by the brilliant Terrence Malick. Both WWII-set films were released five months apart, and where Spielberg's movie displayed the carnage of war on the physical body, Malick's film focuses on the tolls taken on the mind and spirit. Characters come and go at will and little attention is paid to presenting a story in the traditional sense, but Malick's meditative approach is powerfully hypnotic, even when you're not quite sure what the hell is going on. Nominated for seven Oscars, including Best Picture, Best Director, and Best Screenplay.

Alexander (2004)
Director: Oliver Stone
Starring: Colin Farrell, Angelina Jolie, Val Kilmer, Anthony Hopkins
Stone's sweeping swords-and-sandals extravaganza tells the story of Alexander the Great (Farrell), the King of Macedon whose military prowess led him to establish one of the largest ancient empires. It's a story worth telling, but Stone and his co-writers present the tale in such a confusing manner that it becomes downright frustrating trying to figure out who's doing what and why. And with a running time of two-and-a-half hours, it doesn't take long for that frustration to turn into apathy.

James Hong

With nearly 500 film and television credits on his resumé, James Hong is arguably the most prolific actor of all time. He has appeared in prestige pictures (*Chinatown*, *Bound for Glory*), comedy classics (*The In-Laws*, *Airplane!*), family favorites (the *Kung Fu Panda* series), and popular TV shows (*The Big Bang Theory*, *Seinfeld*). However, he is perhaps best known by cinephiles for his roles in two of the biggest cult films of the '80s: *Blade Runner* and *Big Trouble in Little China*. After six decades in Hollywood, Hong shows no signs of slowing down any time soon. Fans can find out where he'll pop up next at www.jameshongfilms.com.

You got your start in show business not as an actor but as a stand-up comedian. How did that come about?

Doing stand-up comedy was the only thing I could do in Minnesota because there were no dramatic parts or comedy parts on stage for me. Even in high school, it was tough to find a role for me—a Chinese-American— because I just didn't fit their image of the roles in the plays the school was doing. College was the same way, so I figured if I wanted to entertain— which I did—I would do something in the performing arts in front of an

Lucille Ball, Desi Arnaz Jr. and Hong in *Here's Lucy*

audience like stand-up comedy and impersonations. By doing stand-up comedy, you learn how to play the house; you learn how to play around you to the different people in the audience, and you learn how to relate to the audience to get the reaction. It wasn't very difficult to transition from that to TV comedies like *Here's Lucy* and *Gomer Pyle* and *Seinfeld*. You learn how to be conscious of the cameras and the actors and the live audience, and you know all the elements on the set. Doing stand-up comedy gives you the advantage of knowing your surroundings.

Did you ever have any professional training before you started acting?

Yes, I started with Jeff Corey when I first came to Hollywood in 1953. At that time he was blacklisted and couldn't do any movie roles because [Joseph] McCarthy had branded him as one of the so-called "pink" people, so he taught acting and was a great, great teacher. He taught a lot of well-known people, and I thought his method was great. I also took lessons from director David Alexander and Joe Sargent. Joe became my primary teacher and taught me most of everything I know. After that, I just picked up advice and listened to people like Ridley Scott and [Roman] Polanski and all of these great directors. I kept my ears open, I was open-minded, and I tried out everything they told me to do. I gained a lot from that.

I read that you worked as a civil engineer in order to please your parents. How did they react when you quit in order to pursue acting?

Well, by that time, my mother had passed away but my father was still alive. He was getting older and was semi-retired but he was running a restaurant when I started doing a lot of television. I don't think he knew what I was doing because I was kind of doing it on the side while I was doing the engineering. Even later on when I was doing acting full-time, he didn't pay too much attention because he was too busy with his restaurant and other things. Later on in 1957, when I got the role in *The New Adventures of Charlie Chan* with J. Carrol Naish, we had a big party at my dad's restaurant. The press came out and people came to say their goodbyes to me, and that's when he became aware that I was an actor. My dad would be asking people what I was doing, and they said, "Your son is going to London to be in the Charlie Chan TV series, and he's going to make a lot of money." He said, "My son is making money from TV? That's pretty good." He was happy that I was making money as an actor instead of being a starving actor.

What gave you the confidence that you could make a living as an actor?

I don't think I ever questioned that, in a sense. All my life I had been interested in acting. When I was a child, my father had a grocery store in Minneapolis, and there was a small gambling room in the back. He would put me up on a soapbox in that room and say, "Okay, Jim. Go ahead and speak and see if you can raise some money for the cause of China." I would give this speech, loud and clear, about how we should fight the Japanese and not let them attack China. So as a young boy doing those speeches, I started to perform, and from that moment on, it was just in my nature to be a performer. I always did voices and impersonations, which led to jobs as a voiceover actor.

Speaking of voiceovers, one of your earliest jobs was doing voices for the original Godzilla. *How did you get involved with that?*

A friend of mine named Sammee Tong—he played the houseboy on the TV show *Bachelor Father*—he and I formed a little team called Hong & Tong. We never really got any big gigs or anything, we mainly just did it for our own pleasure. So one day we saw this ad to go down to Japanese Town and audition for voiceovers for this black-and-white movie called *Godzilla*. When we got there, this guy says, "Okay, what can you do? Let me hear it." I said, "Okay, give us a script." He didn't have a script but he had *The Hollywood Reporter*. So he gave us *The Hollywood Reporter* and said, "This is a movie about a monster called Godzilla. Just read this *Hollywood Reporter* with the best Japanese accent. I need something very authentic." We were not Japanese but we gave it our best shot. We both did comedy, so it was sort of like a take-off on a Japanese accent. Sammee did his version, I did mine, and we walked out laughing to ourselves because it seemed like a waste of time. A couple of days later, the guy called us and we dubbed the movie without ever seeing the movie, not a foot of it. Sammee did all of the older voices—probably eight of them—and I did about eight or ten of the younger voices. When you watch the movie and the two young leads are fighting, that's me talking to myself. There's only a few voices in the movie that aren't my voice or Sammee Tong's voice. The guy who hired us got this black-and-white monster movie for something like $3,000, and the rest is history.

One of the most acclaimed movies on your resumé is Chinatown. *What was it like working on the film?*

Jack Nicholson and Hong in *Chinatown*

I had just come off of a TV production of *The New Perry Mason*, and there we did one or two takes, that was it. I ran from that set to the set of *Chinatown*, and we were doing the scene where [Jack] Nicholson pulls up in the driveway, gets out, and knocks on the door of the house where Faye Dunaway was hiding out. They did about twenty-five takes of the driveway scene until it was perfect because Polanski was very detailed and precise. I did my part of answering the door in about fifteen takes, but that's the way it was on *Chinatown* and working with Polanski. It was a very painstaking art with him, and I learned a lot. One of the things I learned was that good features take a long time versus television. On *Chinatown*, you could feel the artistry of the scenes taking place. That scene where Nicholson comes into the house and pushes past me at the door and has that confrontation with Faye Dunaway where he slaps her, it just smelled of Academy Awards. That was *Chinatown*… Everything that was done had that look of a gem.

Fifteen years later you did the sequel, The Two Jakes.

Yes. I remember they offered me fairly decent money, and the whole cast went to the producer's house to read the script. After that, for whatever reasons, it came to a standstill for about five years. Later on when the movie started up again, I got paid again for doing the same role and most of the same lines, but being directed by Jack Nicholson was a great reward for waiting all those years. He respects the actor, and it was great working with him because he trusted you. To this day, it was one of the best scenes in my whole career that I did with him. People have told me that they thought I would reappear in that movie after that particular scene, which I didn't. Anytime people say they thought I would come back later in a

Hong and Jack Nicholson in *The Two Jakes*

movie, that's a great compliment to me because that means I did something that stayed in their minds and they wanted to see more. All I can do is the best I can with the scenes I'm given, and I hope that I can pull it off and people will remember it.

You had a very memorable role in The In-Laws. *Were your scenes scripted or did you do a lot of improvising?*

For my audition, I did the scene in the airplane where I'm giving safety instructions in Chinese and doing all those hand motions. That was my stand-up comedy technique coming back into play. I went in and they said, "There's no dialogue written. Just do these safety instructions, and do it in Chinese." I did the whole thing as an improv, and they fell off their chairs laughing. Later on after I got the part, I asked for the script and [director] Arthur Hiller said, "No script! Just do what you did at the audition," so that's what I did. Playing that scene with Alan [Arkin] was great because the friendlier I was to him, the more disgusted he became. *The In-Laws*, to me, was one of the funniest movies I've ever done. There's something about that chemistry between Alan and [Peter] Falk that just clicked, and it was a pleasure to work with those two guys. To this day, Alan and I still see other once in a while, and he's still the same regular guy that you love to work with. It was a lot of fun.

James Hong | 73

Blade Runner

A lot of fans know you from your work in Blade Runner. *Does it surprise you that the movie still has a very big following today?*

When you do a movie, you don't really know how it will grab the people or what kind of following it might have. It doesn't surprise me, because the sets were so awesome and Ridley Scott was so precise in his work. Again, that was a case where after that scene in the freezer where Chew tells some secrets, people thought the movie might come back to me and the replicants would want to know more—which didn't happen—but people expected that to happen. To me, that was a great accomplishment. *Blade Runner* may have been a disappointment when it originally came out but then the audience begins to wake up to the fact that it's a great movie, and something about it haunts them. I think that's what happened with the movie because people kept coming back to it. *Big Trouble in Little China* didn't catch on in the beginning either, and people are still discovering it today.

That's true. When you were filming Big Trouble, *was the character of Lo Pan pretty defined in the script or did John Carpenter give you a lot of freedom to do your own thing?*

He gave me a lot of freedom to do whatever I could create. Looking back, I would have to say that I appreciated that trust he had in my talent. He just kind of let me go, and I flew with that part. Lo Pan kind of reminded

Big Trouble in Little China

me a little bit of my father. He was strong, dominating, and sometimes wouldn't listen to reason. Most of the Chinese men I knew as a child seemed to have those qualities, so I used those memories of them to help create that character.

Was it difficult working underneath all of that makeup?

When I looked at myself in that makeup, I had trouble moving my face because the rubber was very stiff, and you can't get expressions like you can on your ordinary face. Not only did I have to move my own face, but I also had to move the layers of the rubber makeup. I had to practice "over-expressing" so that when I looked in the mirror, I could see that the eyes were starting to fold a little more and my mouth would move a little more when I laughed. I had to practice moving the makeup.

You co-wrote and co-directed The Vineyard. *How did that project come to life?*

Harry Mok was my partner at the time, and he asked me to come to the San Jose area to shoot a film. We wrote a script to fit that area, and we sort of structured the story around the vineyard. I didn't have enough trust in my own talent to let the story and the acting go… Harry and I put a little bit too much sex into the movie, and that kind of took away from the art of the movie. We should've just gone with pure horror and some sex instead of making it over-sexy. It was very low-budget; I think we completed the whole shooting for something like $125,000. The editing took quite a bit of time and the special effects were tough, so we spent too much money on the post-production. At the time of the rough-cut, we actually had a huge offer from New World Pictures for $1 million in advance, but that got trimmed down to approximately $600,000. I loved directing, especially in those days when I was younger, and I would have liked to continue doing it, but I just had too many acting jobs offered to me. Acting is easy compared to producing and directing, at least for me.

Was co-director William Rice there to do the scenes that you were acting in?

No. He was my first assistant director. I forget the exact reason why—maybe because he wanted some more money or something—so we said we'd give him credit as co-director. I did all of the directing, but it is difficult to act and direct at the same time. It's hard to tell the other actors what to do when you're in the same scene. Sometimes it doesn't come across too well, and they might think that you're just trying to play yourself up

The Vineyard

Jack Palance and Hong in *Tango & Cash*

in the scene. On the whole, though, the actors and actresses we had were very accommodating, were very cooperative, and really put forth their best effort to do a good job. We didn't get a lot of professionals because it was done in San Jose, and we couldn't afford to send actors up to San Jose from Hollywood. But I don't think there was one bad actor or actress in it.

I read an interview where you said one of the first celebrities you saw when you came to Hollywood was Jack Palance, and nearly forty years later, you worked with him on Tango & Cash. *What was that like?*

By the time I got to work with him, Jack had become much, much older and didn't have that edge he had when he was in *Shane* and all of those other movies. However, it was great to work with him. He was the first actor I saw in Hollywood, so the cycle was complete, in a sense. I don't think *Tango & Cash* was really a chance for him to perform. I felt that his talent was not taxed, and I don't know that he really cared for the role that much. He probably just walked through it. I didn't see the Jack Palance who I remembered from the old days, so I was a little disappointed in that. On the whole, though, it was great to be next to him.

How did you come to start the Hong Acting Workshop?

I started teaching acting in my house probably thirty years ago, just private classes with people who were interested in taking lessons. Teaching came very easy to me, and through the years I would teach little bits here and there when I wasn't working as an actor. My daughter, April Hong, is also an actress, and in the later years she wanted to help teach too. That's when we opened the Hong Acting Workshop. We taught quite a few classes for kids and adults. Right now, we're planning on starting the Hong Academy of Acting summer camp. The idea is that you would get an intense course in acting, dancing, camera, directing, editing, and voice work, and at the end of the five or six days, you'll come out with a short film of your own, which I'll probably do a cameo in. That excites me to see young people do the whole thing. With the equipment nowadays and the ability to edit their own film, all I have to do is lend my experience to teach them about the craft.

Hong and daughter April Hong

Do you believe people can be taught to act or do they have to have a natural ability?

I think you have to have that natural ability, which is called talent. You have to have talent, and most of the time, you're born with it. It does take a lot of nurturing, and you do that through the correct teachers and advice and experience. If you just have the talent but follow the wrong advice and have the wrong teachers, you're not going to get anywhere. However, even if you just have a medium amount of talent but you have the correct teacher, the correct experience, the correct exposure and the correct publicity, you could become a star. The key is that you have to progress to be the best of talents. Ridley Scott taught me that you have to keep probing into the darkest corner of your mind to find what you are *not* doing, and then do it.

What do you teach your students about preparing for a role?

Through the Stanislavsky method and the Meisner method, you learn how to take on the character. One of the tools for doing that is the "inner monologue." To get a good inner monologue of the character going, you have to study the character's life in the script and then you recreate that character's life by talking to yourself. You keep talking and talking and talking to yourself until the character's thinking and voice become a natural part of you. When you step on the set, you *are* that character. Peter Falk does a lot of that. I watched him, and by watching, I learned a lot from him.

The Big Bang Theory

Is there anything you haven't done in movies or TV that you would like to do?

I would like to have done a lot more straight roles, in the sense of principled people in the American walk of life like doctors and lawyers and teachers and businessmen. Ninety-five percent of the roles I've done are villains, killers, and psychotics. There's always something wrong with the characters I play… Those are the kinds of roles I excel in, the kind of characters that takes something deep, deep in the psyche to create. I can do that well, but after almost 500 roles, there's only been a handful or two of playing regular people. I would like audiences to see me be normal.

What frustrates you the most about the film and TV industry?

I still have to go to auditions. No matter how simple the role, I still have to audition for it. I just got a call to audition for a role as a Korean merchant. I read it, and it's like five lines in the episode. It's very frustrating to have to do that for even a minor role. Maybe they just want to see me to make sure I'm still walking! I think that's what drives me to create my own projects, which I would like to do before I call it quits.

What would you say has been your secret to having such a long and successful career?

I think the main thing an actor has to constantly think about is how to keep the balance in his career. By that I mean you have to balance between sanity and insanity. What is real and what is not real, what is overdone and what is not overdone… You have to land somewhere in the middle because if you go too much to one side, you'll go crazy, and if you do too little, your career just slides down to nothing. How do you keep a balance in the middle so that you don't go and do what some actors have done like killing their wives or killing themselves? A lot of my colleagues have done that. How do you stay in the middle and keep your head above water so that life as an actor doesn't drag you down or boost you up too high? If you can't handle success, you're not going to make it. I think that's the secret… Stay in touch with reality and who you are. For an ordinary person, that's already tough. For an actor, it's even twice as hard.

Godzilla, King of the Monsters! (1956)
   Directors: Ishiro Honda, Terry O. Morse
   Starring: Raymond Burr, Takashi Shimura, Momoko Kochi, Akira Takarada
   American edit of the Japanese creature's film debut has Burr playing Steve Martin, a reporter visiting Tokyo when Godzilla appears and begins wreaking havoc on the city. By inserting Burr into the middle of the action and making it more accessible for U.S. audiences, this version loses some of the subplots that gives the original more dramatic weight, but the "man in suit" chaos and carnage remains intact. And really, isn't that why we watch a movie about a gigantic radioactive lizard?

Chinatown (1974)
   Director: Roman Polanski
   Starring: Jack Nicholson, Faye Dunaway, John Huston, Perry Lopez
   Classic film noir stars Nicholson as Jake Gittes, a private eye specializing in adultery cases. His latest investigation into the extracurricular activities of a married official for Los Angeles' Water and Power Department seems open-and-shut, but as Jake soon discovers, it's just the beginning of a complicated mystery involving corruption, greed, and murder. A near-perfect combination of writing, directing, and acting, *Chinatown*

is a must-see for anyone who values challenging, artistic, and thoughtful cinema. Nominated for eleven Oscars and winner for Best Original Screenplay.

The In-Laws (1979)
> Director: Arthur Hiller
> Starring: Peter Falk, Alan Arkin, Richard Libertini, Nancy Dussault

Sheldon (Arkin) is a mild-mannered dentist whose daughter is getting married to the son of Vince (Falk), a rogue CIA agent who may or may not have been drummed out of the organization for psychological reasons. On the eve of the wedding, Vince pulls Sheldon into a scheme to sell stolen U.S. currency engravings to an eccentric foreign dictator (Libertini). Falk and Arkin play off each other beautifully, and the script is a steady stream of inspired lunacy, making *The In-Laws* a movie that just gets funnier and funnier every time you watch it.

Blade Runner (1982)
> Director: Ridley Scott
> Starring: Harrison Ford, Rutger Hauer, Sean Young, Edward James Olmos

Ambitious sci-fi tale centers on Rick Deckard (Ford), a detective assigned to track down and kill a group of "replicants," genetically-engineered humanoids who defy their programming and come to Earth in search of finding a way to extend their lives. Director Scott has created a visual feast that deftly combines 1940s-era film noir and a bleak (although breathtaking) futuristic setting. After one viewing, *Blade Runner* is a movie that is easier to admire than enjoy, but subsequent screenings will allow you to fully appreciate the thought-provoking, multi-layered story. Nominated for two Academy Awards including Best Visual Effects.

Big Trouble in Little China (1986)
> Director: John Carpenter
> Starring: Kurt Russell, Kim Cattrall, Dennis Dun, James Hong

Truck driver Jack Burton (Russell) pulls his rig into Chinatown and falls into the adventure of a lifetime. When his friend's fiancée is kidnapped, the big-talking but dim-witted Jack must confront Lo Pan (Hong), an immortal sorcerer who needs to marry the girl in order to break an ancient curse. A spirited action/comedy/supernatural martial arts mash-up, *Big Trouble* is a lot of things, but it's mainly just plain fun.

Tango & Cash (1989)
>Director: Andrei Konchalovsky
>Starring: Sylvester Stallone, Kurt Russell, Teri Hatcher, Jack Palance

Rival cops Tango (Stallone) and Cash (Russell) must put aside their differences and work together to clear their names after a criminal mastermind (Palance) frames the duo for murder. This buddy cop film doesn't reach the heights of such predecessors as *Lethal Weapon* and *48 Hrs.*, but it's still an entertaining time-killer thanks to great chemistry between Stallone and Russell.

The Vineyard (1989)
>Directors: James Hong, William Rice
>Starring: James Hong, Karen Witter, Michael Wong, Lars Wangberg

This enjoyably bizarre slice of late '80s cheese stars co-writer/co-director Hong as Dr. Elson Po, a winemaker who produces his own special blend using human blood. The elixir serves to help keep him immortal, but when he starts to run out of the secret ingredient, he invites an aspiring actress (Witter) and her friends to his private island. Oh, and there's also some stuff about zombies, a magic amulet, and naked women chained in the basement. It may not make a whole lot of sense, but cult movie fans are encouraged to take a tour of this V*ineyard*.

The Two Jakes (1990)
>Director: Jack Nicholson
>Starring: Jack Nicholson, Harvey Keitel, Meg Tilly, Madeleine Stowe

This belated sequel to *Chinatown* follows L.A. private eye Jake Gittes (Nicholson) as he takes on the case of Jake Berman (Keitel), a man who wants Gittes to track his wife so Berman can catch her during an adulterous rendezvous. When Berman ends up killing his wife's lover, it plunges Gittes into the middle of a complex puzzle, pieces of which force Gittes to confront his painful past. Trying to follow a classic like *Chinatown* is a nearly impossible task, but if you can temper expectations, *Jakes* is a skillful film that delivers on its own terms.

Richard Riehle

Richard Riehle's career can be neatly divided into two segments: Before Hollywood, where he devoted almost twenty years to doing theater all across the country; and After Hollywood, where he's spent another twenty-plus years racking up nearly 300 film and television appearances. With an impressive body of work that includes roles in high-profile movies (*Glory*, *Casino*, *The Fugitive*), TV shows (*Modern Family*, *Grounded for Life*, *Home Improvement*) and cult favorites (*Office Space*, *The Man from Earth*, *Hatchet*), you never know when or where Riehle (and his trademark mustache) will show up next.

How did you get your start in acting?

It was very bizarre... My sophomore year in college, I was a German major and went to study in Austria. One of the things they told us to do was go to a play or a movie at least once a week to hear the language spoken, so I did that and got very interested in all of the films and the theater stuff. One of the guys that was in the program was a theater major, so when we got back to Notre Dame he sort of coerced me into trying out for the spring musical, and I got cast in it. It wasn't anything I really thought that

I would do for a living, but I needed to get out of school because I was running out of funds. He told me that I could take all the credits I needed for a major in one semester in speech and drama, so I did that. After I graduated, I went back to Wisconsin and back to my job unloading railroad ties at a process plant. I saw an ad for a job at the Milwaukee Rep, so I went and applied for that. I was able to get the job as a stage manager there, and the people at Notre Dame got me a teaching assistantship at the University of Minnesota. By the time I finished my MFA, I thought I'll give this a shot until somebody finds me out. So far, no one has yet!

You made your first film appearance in a 1977 movie called Joyride. *How did that come about?*

I was doing theater up in Seattle at the time and they were casting locally for actors to do the small roles. It was actually not the first time I'd been on a set… I was a stand-in and an extra on *Rooster Cogburn*. That was my first experience and was sort of the most eye-opening for me in terms of what happens on a movie set. There was John Wayne and Katharine Hepburn and a lot of people around them. *Joyride*, being an American International Picture, was a very small, low-budget thing directed by Joe Ruben, who's still working and doing incredible stuff. The stars were sort of young Hollywood people at the time: Desi Arnaz Jr., Anne Lockhart, Robert Carradine and an eighteen-year-old Melanie Griffith. They had one trailer where everybody hung out in-between takes, whether you were one of the Hollywood stars or one of the locals. I played a bartender, and they had a deal with the guy who owned the place that we could serve draft beer while we were shooting. It went pretty well for the first half of the day, but by the end of the day, a lot of the extras were a little too rowdy! They had to weed them out while we tried to shoot the scenes.

After Joyride, *you didn't work in films or TV until the late '80s. What did you do during that time?*

I was pretty much established doing theater at that point. I had been doing it all around the country and it was going pretty well. I was doing what they call the "I-5 Rep." I was working from Alaska down to Arizona and all the theaters along the way. Emily Mann, who had directed a play I did in Seattle, had written a play called *Execution of Justice* and she was going to direct it on Broadway. She called me and said, "I can't offer you a role,

Artichoke

but if you come out and audition—and if the producers like you—you can certainly get into the show." I had never really done the New York thing at that point, so I thought I'd give it a shot. I went out there and I got cast, and it was a wonderful play but it only ran for about two weeks. When it got cancelled, a friend of mine invited me up to Minneapolis to do a season at the Guthrie. I got back to New York about a year-and-a-half later, and in addition to doing theater, I began doing day shots on soap operas and stuff like that. In 1989, [director] Ed Zwick came to New York to cast *Glory*, and I went and auditioned for that and got cast. I went down to

Savannah, Georgia, for about a week to shoot the scenes I was in. *Glory* was the first big film with a recognizable role that I did.

What was it like making the film?

It was incredible. I remember the first time I read the amazing script that [Kevin] Jarre wrote, and I was just blown away by it. The audition was interesting because Ed told me later that the quartermaster was sort of the first villain they run into, and everybody that came in and auditioned played it as a villain. He said I came in and sort of played it as a bureaucrat who was just doing his job and couldn't understand why they were upset. Ed surrounded himself with some great people like Freddie Francis—who won the Oscar for cinematography—and Denzel [Washington], Morgan [Freeman], Andre Braugher, and Jihmi Kennedy, who were the four main guys around Matthew [Broderick]. Ed had also hired a group called A Company, which was a group of African-American actors mainly from New York that went down and did the boot camp with the principals. I thought that was really interesting because Ed put those guys in all the scenes close to the principals, so whenever they looked around, they'd see the guys they had trained with instead of just a bunch of extras. I got there about halfway through the shoot and there was an incredible rapport that had been established, from Ed to the principals to the A Company to all of these extras who were Civil War reenactors who actually camped out and had all their own equipment and clothes. Ed had created this environment where everybody was part of the experience, and I think that really showed in the film.

Would you say Glory *was the turning point in your film and TV career?*

Yes, it was. When I came out to L.A. to do the 1990 pilot season, *Glory* was playing all over. Because it had gotten nominations, including Best Picture, it kind of got me in the door to a bunch of other things. The strange thing is that what I ended up getting was the pilot for *Ferris Bueller* playing Principal Rooney, which is 180 degrees from the quartermaster. NBC was very high on the show and we shot thirteen episodes, and then they decided not to continue with it. I thought I'd be heading back to New York after that, but my agent said, "Stay here and see what develops." It turns out what had developed the following year was not TV at all… Suddenly, I was being seen for films, and I ended up doing seven films all around the country. I

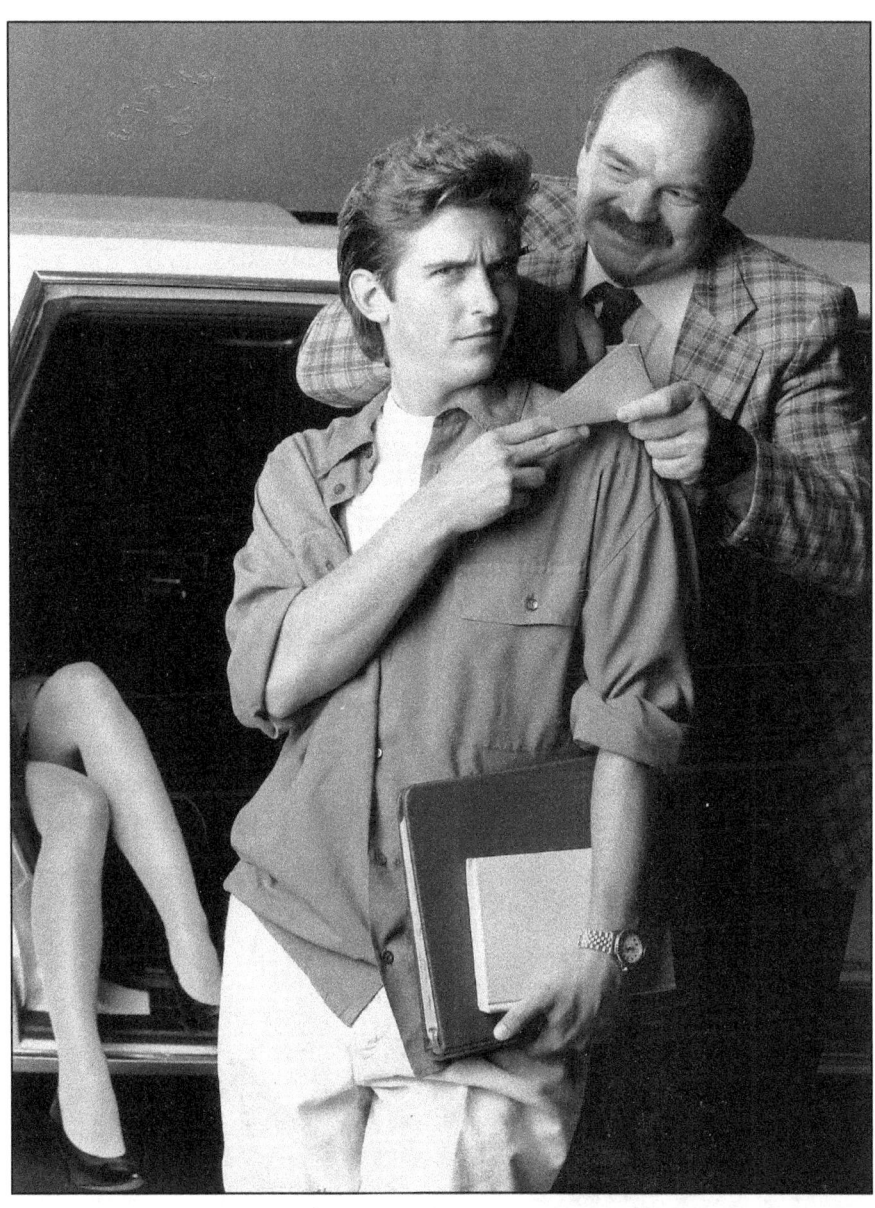

Charlie Schlatter and Riehle in *Ferris Bueller*

think in Hollywood—when you're working—you're desirable, especially if you've got something big on screen that people are talking about.

How did you get involved with Gary Sinise's adaptation of Of Mice and Men?

In-between seasons at the Guthrie, I went down to Chicago and did a production of *Red Noses* at the Goodman. My dressing roommate at the Guthrie was Bob Breuler, and he was a member of the Steppenwolf Company. While I was doing *Red Noses*, I crashed in his basement and got to meet a lot of people at the Steppenwolf. When Gary came out to Los Angeles to hold auditions for *Of Mice and Men*, we talked a little bit about Chicago theater and our backgrounds in the Midwest. I did the first audition and it seemed to go well, and I went back two more times before he cast me as Carlson. I had done the play a couple of times and knew the material very well, and I think that helped a little bit too.

What was it like working with Sinise as both an actor and a director?

Gary is an incredible actor and a wonderful director. I thought it was very interesting to see the relationship between him and John [Malkovich] on the show. They had done the play at Steppenwolf ten years before, and Gary knew everything about every moment of that play. He was incredibly prepared; he knew exactly what he wanted in every shot. We went up to Santa Ynez for a week of rehearsals, and we rehearsed every scene. Horton Foote, who Gary did the adaptation with, was there for that whole rehearsal period, and they made whatever tweaks were needed at that point. We could've done the play at the end of that week—it was so solid

Of Mice and Men

in terms of getting everything down. When we started shooting, it was like John would mess up a line or do something wrong in the first couple of takes and we'd have to do it again. It took me a while to figure it out—and I can't guarantee this is exactly what happened—but I had the feeling that Gary needed a little time to transfer from director to actor, and John was giving him that time by making those little mistakes. By the second or third week when Gary was more into the rhythm of it, he didn't need that extra time, and all of a sudden, John was right on it, every take. They had a very interesting and symbiotic relationship. Gary also invited everybody to come to the dailies every day, and we'd have pizza and beer together. It wasn't so much for us to see the dailies but it was a way to keep everybody involved in the process. It was wonderful.

One of the first blockbusters you worked on was The Fugitive.

That was a really terrific experience. Harrison [Ford] had asked if they could shoot it in sequence because he didn't want to jump back and forth in being Dr. Kimble. [Director] Andy Davis agreed to do that and had worked out the schedule and figured out how to do it economically. They started in Chicago with the murder and the trial, and I came in on the second week as the guard. We put everybody on the bus in Chicago, and then we all moved to North Carolina where we did the bus and train gag. Harrison is amazing… It was between twenty and thirty degrees every night out there, and whether he was on-camera or behind-camera, he was there all the time, which was terrific. He's surprisingly quiet and soft-spoken. The first night that Tommy [Lee Jones] and his crew came on, it was like night and day. Everybody was part of Tommy's process. He wanted all of the people he was dealing with in the scene—his crew, me, the sheriff—to go back to his trailer in-between takes. Not that he had anything to say, particularly, but he just wanted to keep up every-

The Fugitive

body's energy and focus. Andy was terrific, and partly because he shot in sequence, he was able to change the story. The original script was sort of like the premiere episode of *The Fugitive*, three episodes getting him to Chicago, and then the series finale. Once we were in North Carolina and both Harrison and Tommy were there going back and forth, Andy and the writer and the producers realized the story was essentially about Harrison and Tommy, and the story evolved from there.

A couple of years later, you had a part in another high-profile movie, Casino. *How did you get involved with that?*

That was a crazy one… I got a call from my agent on the Monday or Tuesday before Thanksgiving at 10 a.m. He said, "Can you be on a plane to Las Vegas at 1 p.m.?" I said, "I guess so. What's the deal?" He said, "They have to be out of this house on a certain date, they lost the actor playing the role and they need to recast it right away." I said, "Okay," and he said, "Go to the airport and there'll be a ticket waiting for you and some sides. Learn the sides and then you'll meet with them when you get to Las Vegas. Be prepared to stay a week or be on the next plane back. And by the way, there may be other actors on the plane." As it turned out, there was one other actor—a guy by the name of Clive Rosengren, who I had known from grad school—so we flew out and looked at the lines and chatted a little bit. When we got there, they put us in two rooms in the honeywagon and said, "We'll get you as soon as there's a break." A couple of hours later they came and introduced us to Martin Scorsese and [Robert] De Niro, and they said, "We aren't going to be able to do the reading right now but we'll do it at dinner. Just hang loose and we'll get to you as soon as we can." At dinner, they came to the door—I think Clive went first—and then they came and got me and we went to Scorsese's two-banger. Me and Joe [Pesci] and Scorsese and the script supervisor were sitting around the little table in the back, we did the scene and they said, "You guys go to dinner and we'll have a decision by the time the break's over." So Clive and I went and had dinner, and afterwards, we went back to the honeywagon and there was a knock on the door. The guy said to me, "Are you willing to trim your mustache?" I said, "Yeah, sure." He said, "Okay, say goodbye to Clive, we're taking you to fitting." While I was waiting for the Teamster to come pick me up, Joe was standing on the corner smoking a cigar. I had done a film with him called *The Public Eye*, and we shot ten weeks on that. It wasn't that we had become fast friends but we had spent a *lot*

Joe Pesci and Riehle in *Casino*

of time together on mostly night shoots in various parts of the country. So I walked over to him and I jokingly said, "Joe, I know the only reason I'm doing this job is because you put in a good word for me. I just want to thank you." He just looked at me and said, "Yeah… Don't fuck it up."

Did you ever find out what happened to the actor you replaced?

Well, after I went to the fitting, the Teamster was taking me back to the hotel. He asked me what character I was, and I told him I was here to do banker Clark. He said, "Ohhhh, okay." I said, "What do you mean?" He said, "Well, we shot with a guy yesterday who was doing banker Clark and at the end of the day, I took him back to the hotel. This morning, I came to pick him up and he had checked out and disappeared. His agent didn't know where he was, his wife didn't know where he was and nobody seems to know exactly what happened." I don't know if it was too much pressure or tension for him or what, but I thought it was a wonderful experience. The first scene I shot was in De Niro's house on the golf course, and it was 270 degrees of windows. There was a lot of waiting for the light to be right, and Scorsese and Robert Richardson—the cinematographer—would talk film, and just being a fly on that wall was incredible. It was so interesting… I like to say that's when I really realized everybody put their pants on one leg at a time because everybody was just *working*. It was a special experience because of the material and the people that were involved, but nobody acted like it was anything more than just making a film.

One of the films you're best known for is Office Space. *How did that come about?*

I had three auditions within six weeks or so. I came in originally to audition for Tom Smykowski and for the psychiatrist. I had both scenes prepared going in, and I read for both. The first callback, they had me read again for both—which I did—and then the next callback, they had me just reading for Tom Smykowski. [Writer/director] Mike [Judge] called when he finished casting and said, "We're going down to Austin, Texas, my hometown. We'll be on our own, no suits or anything. We're gonna work hard to get this thing done, but we're gonna play hard too. I'll show you a good time, I promise." And he did, it was really great. We made the movie during the basketball playoffs, and every night Mike would take us out to different places around town. After we came back, most everybody sat around and watched the game on the big screen at the local bar. It became a close group of people. A lot of us were there for the whole five weeks, and then some people would come in and there would be this great influx of energy. I remember when [John C.] McGinley and [Paul] Willson came in as the two Bobs, and I was their first guinea pig. Mike let them improv for about an hour going into the scene, and it was hilarious. Then he said, "Okay, let's try it with the words that I wrote." It was equally as funny, but I think allowing everyone the time to kind of find their rhythms and their characters like that was great.

Did it surprise you that the movie has become a cult classic?

Totally. I was in New York doing a play when it opened, so I wasn't able to go to any of the premieres. I didn't actually get to see it until Monday, our day off from the play. I went in and it was a pretty good crowd; everybody seemed to be laughing and having a great time. I was really proud of it and thought the movie had come together very well. I went to work at the theater on Tuesday and told people that we should get together on our next day off and go see *Office Space* because it turned out really well. We went back to the movie theater that next Monday and it was gone. I was a little surprised that all of the reviews across the board—including the New York papers, which I thought might pooh-pooh it a little bit—came out so positive, but it didn't play more than a week or two at the theaters. We just kind of wrote it off at that point, and about six months later, I'm walking down the street and people are quoting lines from *Office Space* to me. By then it was almost eighteen months since I'd shot it, so I was a little taken aback. We thought it was a good film, we thought we had done a good job and we thought it was very funny, but we never realized it was going to have the life that it's had.

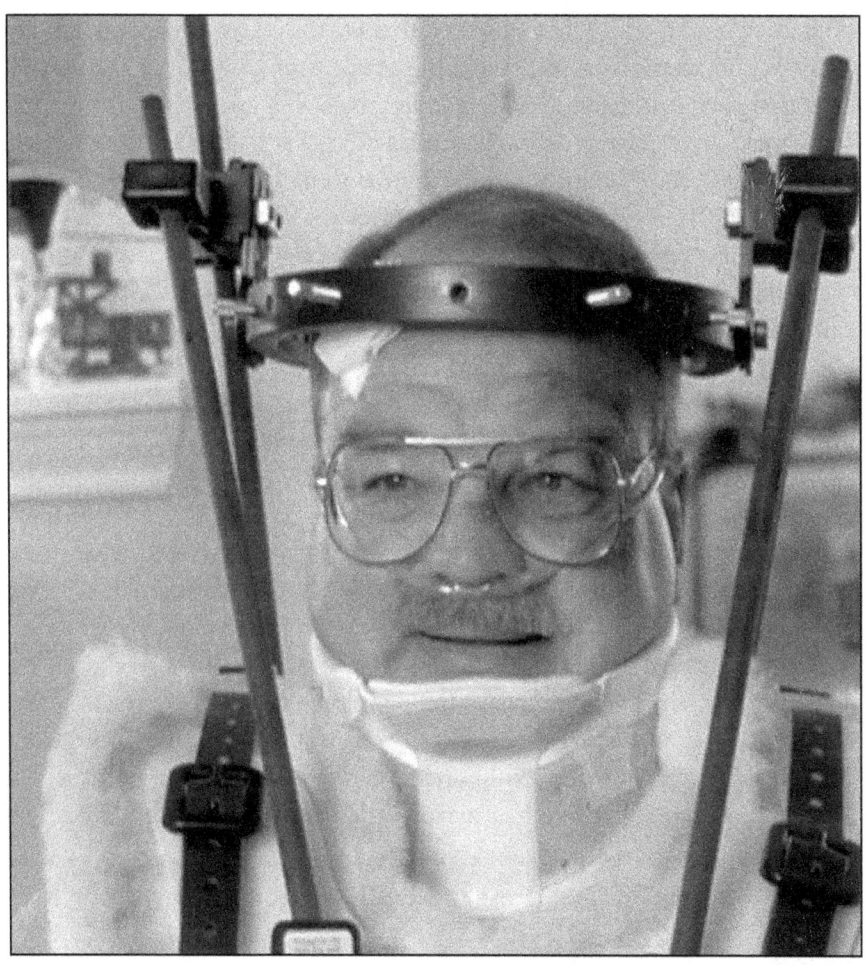

Office Space

Another film of yours that has a devoted cult following is The Man from Earth.

Yes, that was incredible. There was a script that had been floating around since the '60s, I guess, by Jerome Bixby. He had written it when he was doing the classic *Star Trek* and *Fantastic Voyage*, but he never quite felt that he had it exactly right, so he put it away. When he was very sick—essentially on his deathbed—he picked it back up again and finished it. His son decided that to honor his father, he wanted to have it produced. He sent it around to a bunch of the studios and they wanted to do it as long as they could do this, this, and this. He told them that if they were going to do it, they had to do it exactly as his father wrote it. They weren't willing to do that, and after about five years, the script somehow got to [producer/director] Richard Schenkman. He loved the script and went through the same thing with Jerome's son, who insisted that it had to be done exactly as it was written. Richard told him that he thought he could do that, but he was only able to raise a minimal amount of money to shoot it. He got the cast together and he said, "We're going to have to shoot this in seven days. It's mainly one location so I think we can do it. We'll have two cameras going all the time but we're going to have to shoot somewhere between fifteen and twenty pages a day. We're just going to have to get in there and do it." They used this cabin up in Acton, California, and we got up there and just started going for it. I think we had one day of rehearsal, and everybody came in at the top of their game. Poor David Lee Smith, who played the Man, talks forever and is the one who drives it. He literally had pages stashed everywhere. He'd look at them and we'd do another take, and then he'd look at them again… He was just incredible. We shot it straight through for seven days, and I think what hooked everybody was the script. It's so thought-provoking, and I think Richard did an interesting thing in that some ways the people he cast had elements of the characters they played. You could really feel a strong passion about what they were saying, and I think that helped a lot. Another thing was that a lot of us had already worked with each other, and that makes a big differ-

The Man from Earth

ence. In theater, when you have an ensemble or if you're doing repertory, you work with people enough that you kind of have a shorthand and you know what people need so that you can give it to them. I think that helped the whole production.

What was it like working with Brian Cox on the movie Red*?*

Brian is great, and working with him is always a hoot. The first time we worked together was on *Iron Will*. He is so much the man, believe me. He's a terrific actor and making *Red* was a very interesting experience… Lucky McKee, who is a wonderful director and producer and writer, had made this connection with [author] Jack Ketchum before Jack became famous when Stephen King called him "the scariest guy in America." Lucky had somehow gotten the rights to a number of Jack's books, and the first one that I had done a small role in was called *The Lost*. I had read a bunch of Jack Ketchum's stories kind of as preparation, and one day while we were making *The Lost*, Lucky said, "You know, I think you would be right for the role of the lawyer in *Red*." I said, "Oh, yeah, I read that one. That would be great." A couple of years later, I get a call from Lucky. He said, "I'd like to talk to you about doing *Red*. I think we've got Brian Cox to do it, and we want to start shooting." We went out and shot for a couple of weeks and did a bunch of the scenes, and then for whatever reason—I never found out why—I guess one of the producers pulled out and suddenly there was no more money. We had to stop production right in the middle of it. Maybe six or seven months later, I get this call that we're going to finish the movie in Maryland because the person with the money was there. I show up in Maryland and there's somebody entirely different directing it. I have no idea what happened, but we finished up the movie, and when it came out, I thought it seemed almost seamless.

Was it difficult for you to keep the continuity of your performance when you had the long break and the change in directors?

Well, I've had some experience dealing with that kind of thing. I did a double episode of *The West Wing* where I played a police officer from Detroit who the president wanted to honor during the State of the Union address. Chris Misiano was directing those two episodes, and we shot the first part of the scene and it seemed to go pretty well. He came up to me and said, "I'm sorry, I have to go and shoot-out Stockard Channing because she's leaving tonight so I'm not going to be able to do the second half of the scene. Tommy Schlamme is going to come in and do it, if that's okay." I said, "Please… Just tell me what you want me to do." So Tommy came in and did the second part of the scene. In soap operas, it's exactly the same kind of thing. I remember doing a scene on *General Hospital* in which I was the captain of a boat. We started shooting it and we just didn't finish it. So I came back the next day to finish it, and there was another director there. Whoever was directing that day was responsible for finishing what we started the day before. With *Red*, the actual doing of it wasn't much of a problem, but the whole experience was so curious because my connection had been with Lucky all along, and suddenly, I was totally unaware that all of this was happening. I just had to dive in because we only had two weeks to finish the movie.

You've done a lot of horror work in the last several years with Hatchet, Halloween II *and* Chillerama. *Do you enjoy working in the genre?*

I do. I had never done any horror stuff until *Hatchet*, and *Hatchet* came about because of Joel Moore. I had done a short that he produced, and I actually knew him when he was a student up in Gresham, Oregon. I ran into him on the street in L.A. when he arrived here, and I gave him my phone number. One day he called me up and said, "Look, I'm doing this horror film and there's a role that I think you would be right for. Would you be interested in that?" I said, "Absolutely," and so he talked to [director] Adam [Green] and Adam called me and sent me a script. I remember we had this incredible read-through with all this voodoo stuff and candles. Adam is wonderful that way as a director and producer of horror films because he immerses himself and everybody else in the experience. He had an incredible crew doing prosthetics, there were great stunt people guiding us through it, and there was Kane Hodder, who's been involved in the genre forever. Kane didn't want anyone to see his character in the full makeup until we actually started filming, so we were all waiting for his first appearance. As we worked our way up to the cabin, there were lightning flashes and lots of smoke, and there he was. I think some of the screams from the girls were real! There was a lot of energy in that scene because of him waiting to reveal himself and the rest of us having no idea what to expect, and the adrenaline was really pumping because he just pancaked me with that hatchet! We did lots of various shots and close-ups of him driving the hatchet into this prosthetic shoulder that I had because Adam wanted everything done

Chillerama

in-camera—he didn't want any CGI. There was a lot of blood gushing and stuff like that, but I thought it was pretty exciting. One of the things about making horror films is that it's always raining, it's always at night and you're dealing with these horrific ideas, so there's a lot of discomfort involved with it. Because of that, the mood around the set is actually pretty upbeat so you can get through it. Adam was one of the producers of *Chillerama* and he directed one of the segments called "The Diary of Anne Frankenstein." He also did a lot of second unit on the framing stuff. At one point, we had four units shooting the zombies in the parking lot of the drive-in, and we had so much going on that they were literally just dragging me from shot to shot. We filmed it in a working drive-in with four screens, and they had rented out one screen and the parking lot. On the other three screens they were showing movies for the public, so in-between takes we'd sit and watch whatever movie we could see from any of the other three vantage points. Once all of the movies were done for the night, then we'd go up and shoot in their projection booth. It was a lot of fun.

What would you say are the pros and cons of being a character actor?

Kevin Corrigan, Donal Logue and Riehle in *Grounded for Life*

The pro is obvious in that you have a long, long life in your career. I've been here in Los Angeles for over twenty years, and I did theater for almost twenty years before that. I was a character actor when I started; I was never a leading man. I eventually aged into the roles that I had been doing since I began acting. I remember when I was auditioning for *Grounded for Life*, they had already shot the pilot with Stephen Root, but Stephen was on another show and he was on second position on *Grounded*. When it came up, the other show was still going and he couldn't get out of it, so they had to replace him fairly quickly. They had already seen a whole bunch of people and they still didn't have the person that they wanted. I had never gotten in on the original auditions that Stephen had gotten cast in, and I didn't get in on the first round of replacement stuff. It was only on the second round of replacement auditions that I got in the door. They literally brought in anybody who was over fifty years old. Sometimes, it's that large net you can fit in as a character actor that works. I really can't think of any cons… The character roles are often the best, and you usually get a pretty decent payoff for doing less work than the leading man.

Do you still have to audition?

Oh, yeah. It's very unusual that I'll just get an offer, and I actually don't mind auditioning. I'd rather take my chances with me in the room and doing the scene rather than having them make a decision based on what they remember seeing me do. I think that too often the casting people and directors only see you in one limited kind of way and aren't sure that you can do something else. I think it gives me a wider range of things I can try for if I'm willing to go in and meet with them. I recently had an audition for a Disney show, and the producer had no idea who I was. There's nothing wrong with that because there's a lot of younger people in the business who may not know what I've done. I'm not offended if I'm asked to audition… In fact, I'm really happy when people are willing to take the time to see me and let me show what I can do.

How difficult is it to make a living as an actor?

That depends… There are a lot of hills and valleys. I've always kept my nut really small, and I think that helps. I remember when we were doing *Ferris Bueller*, a couple of the younger actors in the cast bought cars and one bought a house. We were thirteen episodes and done, and you never know when your next job is coming. You never know if you'll make enough to qualify for insurance, which is a bigger worry for older actors than it is for younger actors. There are times when you're gonna have to carry yourself over a period of time when there's no work, and there are scary periods when you don't know whether you're gonna be able to make the rent or if you'll be going back to Ramen noodles for a while. In the end, it's all about luck and being in the right place at the right time and being able to produce once you get that opportunity. If you can do that and if you can keep your expenditures down, it's possible to make a living

Producer/director Swamy M. Kandan and Riehle on the set of *The Secret Village*

doing this, but you have to be willing to make a lot of sacrifices to make it work. It's kind of funny… This isn't the most secure business by a *long* shot, but on the other hand, in the last few years of this economic downturn, I think the people working in this business have best been able to get through it. A lot of people who bought into the American dream and have mortgages and car payments and thought they had a job that would take them up to retirement are in a lot worse shape, I think, than people that are going job to job wherever they can get it and filling in the gaps as waiters or bartenders or cab drivers.

What frustrates you about the business aspects of acting?

Finding work. I spent almost twenty years doing regional theater, and I never had an agent. I went from job to job, and often times I'd have eight or ten months of work lined up. Once I went to New York, I couldn't get an audition without an agent. That wasn't too big of a deal because I had come in with a Broadway show, I had a little bit of cache, and I had a pretty good resumé at that point from working in theaters all around the country. I was able to kind of make it go in New York mainly doing theater and occasionally getting some film and TV work. When I came to L.A., it's so totally out of your hands that you don't even know what's going on. You're totally dependent upon your agents being able to line up the auditions for you to get the work. Eventually you'll meet enough people and you'll see enough people over and over again at auditions that sometimes you'll hear if something's happening, but even if you pass that information on to your agents and you don't hear anything back, you don't know if they couldn't get you in or if the casting people didn't want to see you. You never know what the roadblocks are along the way. It's not knowing that's the most frustrating and not having any control over when your next job is coming.

You've had a long and successful career as an actor. Knowing what you know now, is there anything you would have done differently?

I used to teach at the University of Washington and various places briefly, just for a semester here or a master class there. I haven't done it for at least twenty years, but in those days I often would say, "You've got to get the experience. Do the community theater, do the regional theater and take your time to build up your resumé before you go to New York or L.A." It's

different now, partly because I think theater is sort of a dying medium. Unless you're a song-and-dance person, it would be very hard to make a living doing theater. For young actors, you've got to get out there and get your face out in front as early as you can. It's the Emma Stone story: If you're fourteen years old and you do a PowerPoint presentation to your parents saying that you have to go to L.A. now, maybe that's right… I waited thirty years to go to L.A. and twenty years to go to New York, and if anything, maybe I would have gone earlier had I thought about it. On the other hand, I had such a great experience doing regional theater that I don't know that I would've wanted to. All things considered, I'm pretty happy with the way things turned out.

Joyride (1977)
   Director: Joseph Ruben
   Starring: Desi Arnaz Jr., Robert Carradine, Melanie Griffith, Anne Lockhart
   John (Carradine), his girlfriend Susie (Griffith), and Scott (Arnaz Jr.) leave their boring jobs behind in California, and they venture to Alaska with the dream of becoming salmon fishers. Through a series of unfortunate events, the trio winds up becoming outlaws after pulling a heist and taking a young woman (Lockhart) hostage. *Joyride* starts out as a gritty drama before becoming a *Bonnie and Clyde*-esque caper flick, but it's all held together by good work from the young cast.

Glory (1989)
   Director: Edward Zwick
   Starring: Matthew Broderick, Denzel Washington, Cary Elwes, Morgan Freeman
   Excellent Civil War drama centers on Col. Robert Shaw (Broderick), a young man who is given command of the Union army's first black regiment. Shaw is initially skeptical as to whether or not he's right for the job, but with the help of Rawlins (Freeman), a former gravedigger-turned-soldier, Shaw gains confidence and eventually earns the respect of his troops as they prepare for battle. This little-known footnote in the pages of history is brought to stunning life by an excellent ensemble. Nominated for five Academy Awards and winner of three, including Best Supporting Actor (Washington).

Of Mice and Men (1992)
   Director: Gary Sinise
   Starring: John Malkovich, Gary Sinise, Ray Walston, Casey Siemaszko
   In this wonderful adaptation of John Steinbeck's novel, director/producer/star Sinise plays George, a drifter looking for work during the Great Depression with his faithful, slow-witted companion, Lennie (Malkovich), in tow. The duo finds employment at a ranch, an opportunity that leads them to believe they might finally be able to save some money and buy a place of their own. However, the childlike Lennie is involved in an incident that places their dream in jeopardy. Beautifully made and acted to perfection, *Men* is a wonderful cinematic counterpart to the literary classic.

The Public Eye (1992)
>Director: Howard Franklin
>Starring: Joe Pesci, Barbara Hershey, Richard Riehle, Bryan Travis Smith
>Set in the 1940s, Bernzy (Pesci) is a tabloid photographer who makes his living selling shots of victims at crime scenes. He is approached by high society nightclub owner Kay (Hershey) who asks him to dig up some information about a mobster trying to take over her business. When Bernzy obliges, he finds himself in the middle of a conspiracy with a rapidly rising body count. *Eye* offers many pleasures, chief among them Pesci's outstanding performance.

The Fugitive (1993)
>Director: Andrew Davis
>Starring: Harrison Ford, Tommy Lee Jones, Sela Ward, Julianne Moore
>A doctor (Ford) is wrongfully convicted for the murder of his wife (Ward). After a daring escape from the cops, he sets out to find the real killer as a relentless U.S. Marshal (Jones) hunts him down. Based on the '60s television series, Hollywood finally got a TV-to-movie translation right. Exciting action scenes, solid acting and top-notch directing make this a must-see. Nominated for seven Oscars and winner for Best Supporting Actor (Jones).

Iron Will (1994)
>Director: Charles Haid
>Starring: Mackenzie Astin, Kevin Spacey, David Ogden Stiers, August Schellenberg
>Rousing tale of Will Stoneman (Astin), a young lad who enters a grueling 500-mile dog sled race in order to win a cash prize that will save his family's farm. Although not taken seriously by the contest's sponsor (Stiers) or the other competitors, Will's determination attracts the attention of a newspaper reporter (Spacey) who plans on documenting Will's story and riding his coattails to the front page. This being a Disney film, the ending is never really in doubt, but director Haid and a first-rate cast create an exciting film for the whole family.

Casino (1995)
>Director: Martin Scorsese
>Starring: Robert De Niro, Sharon Stone, Joe Pesci, James Woods
>Sam "Ace" Rothstein (De Niro) is sent by the mob to run a casino in

Vegas when he falls in love with Ginger (Stone), a hooker who can't escape the emotional clutches of her pimp (Woods). Things get even more complicated when Sam's hitman friend, Nicky (Pesci), arrives and starts to overstep his bounds, causing trouble for everyone. Scorsese's flipside to *Goodfellas* doesn't quite reach the heights of that masterpiece, but judged on its own merits—as it should be—*Casino* is an extravagantly entertaining film. Stone was nominated for an Academy Award as Best Actress.

Office Space (1999)
    Director: Mike Judge
    Starring: Ron Livingston, Jennifer Aniston, Gary Cole, Stephen Root
    Peter (Livingston) is a complacent corporate drone at a software firm who hates his job. After a botched session of hypnotherapy, he approaches work with a carefree and defiant attitude that inspires his equally unhappy co-workers while drawing the ire of his boss (Cole). *Office Space* is flat-out funny, but anyone who has spent time in nine-to-five cubicle hell will especially appreciate the finer details writer/director Judge pokes fun at.

Hatchet (2006)
    Director: Adam Green
    Starring: Joel David Moore, Tamara Feldman, Deon Richmond, Kane Hodder
    Fun salute to '80s slasher flicks finds a group of tourists in New Orleans embarking on a late-night haunted swamp tour. One of the attractions is the home of Victor Crowley (Hodder), a deformed boy who was accidentally killed, but as legend has it, he wanders the bayou looking for those responsible for his death. *Hatchet* strikes a nice balance between parody and homage, gleefully delivering over-the-top blood and guts with some clever inside jokes for genre fans.

The Lost (2006)
    Director: Chris Sivertson
    Starring: Marc Senter, Shay Astar, Alex Frost, Robin Sydney
    Ugly yet ultimately effective flick centers on Ray Pye (Senter), a sadistic hotel manager who kills two girls just for the fun of it. Four years later, Ray has seemingly gotten away with the crimes, but a detective refuses to give up on the case, leading to a showdown that pushes Ray over the edge. After a tense opening sequence, *The Lost* gets bogged down in a bloated middle section that careens from subplot to subplot until coming

together for a brutal thirty-minute conclusion. It's a disturbing ending, but casual viewers will be tempted to give up before reaching it.

The Man from Earth (2007)
　　Director: Richard Schenkman
　　Starring: David Lee Smith, Tony Todd, John Billingsley, Ellen Crawford
　　John Oldman (Smith), a college professor who is moving on to other prospects, is surprised when his colleagues arrive at his house to give him a going away party. During the festivities, John decides to come clean about his true identity and reveals to his guests that he is actually 14,000 years old. *Earth* is an absolute rarity in today's cinematic world: A high concept sci-fi flick with thought-provoking ideas and philosophical debates instead of glossy spectacle and shiny CGI. Those who are up for the challenge will find ample rewards from this little-seen gem.

Red (2008)
　　Directors: Trygve Allister Diesen, Lucky McKee
　　Starring: Brian Cox, Noel Fisher, Kyle Gallner, Tom Sizemore
　　Gripping revenge drama stars Cox as Avery, a widower whose only companion is his loyal dog, Red. One day, three punks kill the animal for kicks, leading the law-abiding Avery to seek civil justice. When his efforts are blocked, he decides to take matters into his own hands. Usually relegated to supporting roles, Cox finally gets his chance in the spotlight and delivers a powerful performance that carries the film from beginning to end.

Halloween II (2009)
　　Director: Rob Zombie
　　Starring: Scout Taylor-Compton, Malcolm McDowell, Brad Dourif, Tyler Mane
　　Writer/director Zombie's reimagined continuation of the classic slasher franchise explores the damage created in the wake of Michael Myers's killing spree. Laurie (Taylor-Compton), the virginal target of Michael's attack, is now a rebellious teen slowly descending into madness, and Dr. Loomis (McDowell) has cashed-in his credibility to become a celebrity author and egomaniac. Meanwhile, Michael (Mane) is having psychological issues of his own, seeing visions of his dead mother. Give Zombie credit for daring to do something different with

one of horror's most iconic villains, but just because it's different doesn't mean it's good.

Chillerama (2011)
   Directors: Adam Green, Joe Lynch, Adam Rifkin, Tim Sullivan
   Starring: Ray Wise, Lin Shaye, Joel David Moore, Richard Riehle
   When drive-in theater owner Cecil (Riehle) is forced to close down, he plans a last-night screening of four never-before-seen horror films. The first flick, "Wadzilla," is about a giant sperm monster. That's followed by "I Was a Teenage Werebear," a gay beach movie musical; "The Diary of Anne Frankenstein," featuring Hitler as a mad scientist; and "Deathication"—a literal shitfest—that segues into *Chillerama*'s framing device of horny zombies running rampant at the drive-in. If you didn't stop reading after the words "giant sperm monster," then you need to watch this gross, vulgar, juvenile, demented, offensive, and *hilarious* anthology movie.

James Rebhorn

James Rebhorn was an actor recognized almost as much for his wardrobe as his looks. Beginning his on-screen career playing physicians in *The Doctors*, *Silkwood* and *Regarding Henry*, Rebhorn eventually traded in the white jacket for a suit and tie, portraying everything from antagonistic lawyers (*Seinfeld*, *Carlito's Way*) to bureaucratic officials (*Independence Day*, *Head of State*) to adversarial authority figures (*Scent of a Woman*, *How to Eat Fried Worms*). When not working in the narrow confines Hollywood kept him in, he found time to tread the boards in New York theater, returning to his roots in productions that displayed his true range and talent. Sadly, James Rebhorn passed away on March 21, 2014. He will be greatly missed.

How did you get your start in acting?

I don't know that I can point to one single event. I did not have a lifelong ambition when I was a kid to be an actor—it's something that just sort of evolved. I was a senior in college at Wittenberg University in Ohio, and I had a major in political science. I also had taken so many electives in theater arts that I had a dual major in theater arts. I applied to three drama schools, all of which offered degrees, thinking that I would likely teach or at least have that as a fallback option. I got into all three schools, and I went to the one in New York City because it was near the professional theater world. As so often happens, the first jobs you get are because of recommendations from people you studied with or people that you've worked with in school, and that was the case with me. My first job was in Atlantic City playing the leading man role in the shows for a non-union summer stock company. From that, I met some folks who recommended me to commercial agencies, and I started doing commercials. I also continued to work in theater, doing summer stock, dinner theater, anything that I could. Gradually, through luck and through the good graces of friends, I managed to get more and more opportunities to do better work.

Some of your earliest television work was on soap operas. Was it difficult for you to make the transition from the stage to TV?

It really was not a big transition, because in daytime television you very much did it as a play. You wouldn't necessarily do it from the beginning of the show to the end of the show, but each scene would play out entirely, and there would be three cameras operating to capture the scene. In film, you may do the scene but then you re-do it or re-do parts of it, you might do inserts or pick-ups… You don't really play the whole thing out, and you certainly don't play it anywhere near from the beginning through the middle to the end. But in daytime television, they very much try to do it from the beginning and work right through until the end. The first daytime job I had was on a half-hour show called *The Doctors*, and it was kind of like straddling a couple of worlds. By that I mean they were still using cue cards and Teleprompters, and you could just look slightly off-camera and see the words you had to say. I could never do that… I found it tremendously distracting. It took me out of whatever it was I was trying to do as an actor, so I always memorized my lines. By the time I finished my last daytime job—which was many, many years later on *As the World Turns*—those cue cards and Teleprompters were a thing of the past and everybody memorized the script as best as they could.

Was it a good training ground for you?

Well, there's a habit you get into, which is both good and bad. You're working very fast and memorizing things very fast, and because of that you get into the habit of thinking what you're doing is the right thing to do. Actors are generally taught to trust their first instinct—whatever they think is right initially is usually the right choice. Most of the time that *is* the right choice, but some-

Texas

times it's not, and that's what rehearsal is all about: Discovering when you have made the wrong choice and trying to find the right choice. In daytime television there's no opportunity to do that, so while it's great to be conditioned to trust your first impulse, it's a terrible habit to trust it exclusively. I think the craft of young actors can get very damaged working in daytime television because they come to rely on their first impulse and lose the ability and the capacity and the interest to explore other options.

One of your earliest film roles was in Silkwood. *How did you get involved with that?*

I was submitted by my agent, and I went in and auditioned. Back then, casting directors would usually make a verbal pitch for an actor to the director. For *Silkwood*, a casting director mentioned me, and I was asked to come in to meet director Mike Nichols and audition for him. That's changed… Now, you rarely see a director at an audition. Everything is put on tape and sent over the internet to the director in California, or Vancouver, or Mexico, or wherever it is they're filming. I don't think it's a choice most directors make to not be there; I think it's dictated by the financial reality to keep costs as low as possible.

The film was a critical success and earned five Oscar nominations. Did that kind of attention help open doors for you in Hollywood?

Not that I know of… I remember a pilot I did for ABC many, many years ago called *Plymouth*, which was about life on the moon. That came out of the creator of the show having seen me in *Our Town* on Broadway, but that's the only instance I can think of where my work in one job led to another job. I think most of my work has come from developing a resumé

Scent of a Woman

where people might look at it and go, "Oh, I remember him from that." I don't think *Silkwood* directly led to more jobs for me, but it was another credit I could put on my resumé.

Several years later, you appeared with Al Pacino in Scent of a Woman *and Marisa Tomei in* My Cousin Vinny. *When you were making those films, did you have any idea they were giving performances that would ultimately win them Academy Awards?*

I had no idea… In fact, I'm notoriously inept at predicting what's going to be successful and what isn't. It's always a surprise to me when films are received as well or as poorly as they are. I generally do a film because I like the script, and I'm always disappointed when something doesn't get the artistic or financial response that I think it merits. Things may not work out the way I think they should, but that's not my job, it's the director's job. Film is a director's medium, and actors really have very, very little to do with a finished film, and that includes their performances. You may have done a take that you thought was brilliant, but when the director and editor get together to pick and choose what they want to use, they might use a take that you thought wasn't as good as the other one. It's a peculiar anomaly that actors have some kind of power in the medium when the directors actually have the final word on their performances.

I think one of the most overlooked films on your resumé is Lorenzo's Oil. *What was it like making that?*

George Miller was a terrific director, and working with Susan [Sarandon] and Nick [Nolte] was a great experience. I thought the movie was very,

Rebhorn and Peter Ustinov in *Lorenzo's Oil*

very well-written and explored a topic that was important and compelling. It was sort of marketed as a movie-of-the-week, and because of that, a lot of people were afraid to see it because they didn't want to get all weepy in a movie theater. I think that movie should've gotten a much bigger audience than it did... It was very early on in my career, and I think it was probably my appearances in *Scent of a Woman* and *Lorenzo's Oil* that made me recognizable to Hollywood producers and casting directors. *Scent of a Woman* was a huge financial success and *Lorenzo's Oil* was an artistic success, and in both of those movies, my face was on the big screen in good roles. There's no way to prove this, but I think it was from that point on that I became a viable commodity in Hollywood.

When you work on projects based on true stories like Lorenzo's Oil, *do you conduct any research or do you just stick to the script?*

Generally, I'll do research whenever I can but it depends on the circumstances. Sometimes I don't know I'm doing a job until the day before, and when that happens, there just isn't any time to do it. There are other times when it may not be particularly valuable because the director and the writer are interpreting things instead of portraying the real-life events.

8 Seconds

There are times, though, when the producer or director will arrange for you to meet the actual people, and that can be very interesting. For example, I did a film called *8 Seconds*, which was based on the true life story of Lane Frost, a championship bull rider. His parents were on the set, I met them and spent a lot of time with them, and they were terrific. To play the father of Lane Frost was a heavy responsibility that I took very seriously, and it was a real honor and a real gift to spend time with Lane's parents.

What kind of information did you try to get from him?

Well, it was a delicate situation because we were making a movie about the life and death of his son. I thought it would have been almost rude and ill-mannered to probe too deeply about his relationship with Lane, so I didn't try to get information as much as I just tried to spend time with him. That having been said, there were times when there would be factual questions I'd ask him. "Did this really happen like this?" or "Did that happen like that?" Those were little details, but to really understand their relationship required a kind of interrogation that I was not comfortable pursuing. That's why I chose to be more passive during my time with him than aggressive.

When you're playing a real-life person, do you try and pick up their physical characteristics and mannerisms?

Well, Clyde Frost—Lane's father—is not a public persona, so it's not like there's an expectation to do what Meryl Streep did when she played Julia Child. If I were to pick up physical traits and tics from Clyde, I would only do it if I thought it would enhance my work on the character. If it doesn't enhance the character, then it's doing it just for the sake of doing it, and that doesn't serve the story. In *Julie & Julia*, Meryl Streep had an obligation to *be* Julia Child, otherwise people wouldn't have bought into the story. Rarely when I play a real-life character is it someone who has a high public profile, so I don't have an obligation to mimic that person, but if I find it useful and helpful to incorporate a person's traits, I will certainly do it.

The two films you did with director Anthony Minghella, The Talented Mr. Ripley *and* Cold Mountain, *were based on novels. Did you read the books as part of your preparation?*

I actually did. I wanted to know where the inspiration in the script had come from and to see if there was anything in the book that might, in some way, enhance my understanding of the character I was playing. In the case of *Cold Mountain*, my character was a doctor, and it was a very small role. That character didn't even exist in the book, but I understood what Anthony was trying to do in creating that role in the script, and we talked extensively about that. Anthony created such a terrific working environment on his films, and he was a sensational man. I think it's a huge loss for the industry that he's no longer with us.

You appeared on the series finale of Seinfeld. *Were you a fan of the show before working on it?*

Matt Damon and Rebhorn in *The Talented Mr. Ripley*

I rarely watch television. I'm a baseball fan so I watch baseball, but that's about it. If I have a half-hour of free time, I would generally prefer to read a book. Sometimes I'll watch a movie, but I don't even do that very much. I don't think I had ever even seen a full episode of *Seinfeld* until I did the job. After I worked on it, I made a point to watch some episodes, and I thought it was very funny. I'm not trying to make a comment about the quality of television, it's just not a medium that I choose to spend my free time on.

Is it difficult coming in to do a guest role on a long-running show like Seinfeld?

It's certainly a challenge because they all have established relationships. They have a place they've been hanging their hats for years, it's their home, they're comfortable, and they have a repartee with the crew. It's a challenge to come into that situation as a "guest artist" of the week, especially if I've never worked on it before. There are some shows like *Law & Order*—I've been on that six or seven times—and when I go there, I sort of feel like I'm coming home. I know the directors and I know the cast and crew very well, so that's a comfortable place to go back to. But it's true that the longer you're in this business, the more your family expands. It's rare now for me to work on a job where I don't know at least three or four people on that show, whether it's actors, or crew, or writers, or producers.

Would you say that you've been typecast?

Independence Day

Rebhorn, Sean Penn and Al Pacino in *Carlito's Way*

I think everybody's typecast. That's the norm in Hollywood, whether it's film or television. People want to hire you based upon what they saw you do most recently and most successfully. That becomes a snowball effect, and it's very difficult to break out of that. It's very rare that I'm considered for things that *don't* involve me wearing a suit and tie or being some kind of authority figure. *8 Seconds* is a great example… Instead of being a fellow who wears a suit and is a heavy, I'm a cowboy. That was a great change and great fun for me to do. I embrace those opportunities to do something different when they come along, but they are not plentiful. I think all actors struggle with typecasting their entire career, but on the other hand, I also embrace it because it's given me the opportunity to work pretty consistently and to make a pretty good living. I'm very thankful for that.

Is there anything you can do to try and break out of that or are you at the mercy of the casting directors?

We're all at the mercy of other people. I could encourage my agent to get me submitted for things that are very different, or I could take money out of my bank account and produce a play off-Broadway—or off-off-off-Broadway—that features me in a very different kind of role, but it's very difficult to break through that wall, especially in television and film. They are creative mediums, but they're not particularly creative when it comes to casting unless you're already a bankable star. I think of extraordinary actors like Tom Hanks and Johnny Depp and Sean Penn who have the opportunity to do an extremely broad range of characters because they're bankable stars. That's admirable and I applaud them for that, but we're talking about probably a dozen people who get that chance. Everybody else pretty much has to fit into the role they did the last time. Again, I'm not complaining... There aren't many actors who can support themselves in this profession, and I've been very, very fortunate to be one of them.

At what point were you confident that you could make a living as an actor?

I don't think I've *ever* been confident of that! I've always felt that when I finish a job, that's the last job I'll ever have. I think early on that I was just too scared to change careers and do something else. I thought about it, but as soon as I would think seriously about doing something else, a job would come along to keep me going. I never lived very high on the hog, and I still don't. I never hung out in bars, I never went to clubs, I've never been a clotheshorse—I still wear Wrangler jeans and always have—so it was easy for me not to have to spend a lot of money. In some ways, because I was committed to being an actor, I wasn't committed to making a lot of money. I always lived very modestly and very conservatively so that my needs were not great. I've made my living as an actor, and there

Claire Danes, Amy Hargreaves and Rebhorn in *Homeland*

were times when it wasn't necessarily a *good* living, but I didn't have to do anything else to pay my bills and support myself.

Do you still have to audition?

I do, and in some ways, I don't mind that. First of all, it kind of keeps the creative juices flowing, and I like that. Secondly, if I get hired from an audition, then the director and I both know that we're playing in the same game and have the same ideas. If I'm hired without an audition, I think the director and I won't always know if our ideas about what the role is will mesh. The audition kind of gets that concern out of the way, and we all know that we're in the same ballpark. I *do* mind auditioning when I'm not told everything upfront. By that I mean, frequently—and my career has been made of this—I'm the fallback guy… I'm the guy they go to when they can't get a higher-profile actor. That's not a complaint, that's just an evaluation of the way things are, but I like to be told that upfront. I don't want to be told that I'm being seen with a handful of other actors for a role and then find out two weeks later that they've already offered it to someone else. Those kind of auditions irritate me, and I hate the pretense that the audition is something that actually matters when I'm really only being considered as a fallback guy. Just tell me that upfront… I'll still audition, I'll still have a good time, but at least I'll know what the situation is. That kind of thing happens to me a lot, and I think it's just bad manners not to tell people what the deal is going into it.

How do you deal with rejection in auditions?

Rejection is never easy to deal with, whether it's in your private life or your business life. It's difficult, but early on I came to the realization that what really mattered in an audition was that I walk out satisfied with what I did. If I get the job, that's great, but the most important thing was that I was happy with what I did. If I'm happy with the audition and I'm rejected, that's too bad but at least I did what I wanted to do, and they saw that. If I go into an audition and I don't do what I wanted to do or if I don't respond to the director's direction, that hurts me because I haven't done my job; I've failed myself. As long as I can walk out knowing that I did what I wanted to do, the rejection doesn't hurt so much because it just means they wanted to go in a different direction. That's fine… That's an honest rejection, and I just have to go somewhere else to get another job.

118 | Character Kings 2

Rebhorn and Robert De Niro in *Meet the Parents*

You've worked with some of the great actors like Pacino, Robert De Niro and Philip Seymour Hoffman. Do you try and learn from others while you're working with them or do you stick with your own methods and instincts?

Well, I think it would be foolish not to take advantage of learning from the master that you're with, and I'm sure there are little things here and there that I've picked up. More than anything else, you learn by doing and by being involved in the process with these other actors. In film and TV, you don't usually have very long scenes, so it's hard to kind of develop a great artistic relationship with anybody, and if you're watching them, then you're not really doing your job. Rather than looking at it as a learning opportunity, it's more important that you fully engage in the job that you have to do as an actor. If you do that—and if they're doing their job as an actor—then you'll teach each other and you'll make each other better. Despite what the awards shows might have you believe, acting is truly a team sport. You only succeed as your fellow actors succeed, so you have to really engage in that process. That's the most important thing to learn.

What would you say has been your secret to making a living as an actor?

Well, I really do believe that much of what happens in the profession is due to luck. I'm not suggesting that I just cast my fate to the wind... Thomas Jefferson said, "I'm a great believer in luck. The harder I work, the more of it I have." I think that's been the case with my career. I try to work hard at what I do, and I try to be prepared. Because of that, I think I get luckier being in the right place at the right time. I don't know how you enhance that other than by continuing to work hard and being prepared for any opportunity that comes my way.

A lot of people look to get into acting because they think of it as a glamorous profession. What would you say about that?

It's not glamorous at all! Not at all... In fact, I think most of us find the photographs in the magazines, the parties, the openings, the cocktails, and all of that stuff kind of annoying. It's sort of a construct that's evolved over the years to create publicity for something. Most of us would rather just go in, do our work and go home at night. For instance, the other day I worked on the show *White Collar*. I was called to the set at five-fifteen in the morning and I was wrapped at eight-fifteen at night. Most of that time was spent just sitting in a room, waiting for the few moments that I had to act. I literally sat in this ten-by-fifteen dressing room for five hours

White Collar

just waiting! It's long, and it's tedious, and frequently you're doing it under unpleasant circumstances—not by anyone's choice, but that's just the way it is sometimes. It's not glamorous at all; it's mostly very, very boring. The work itself—when you finally get to work—is very exhilarating, but you're always waiting to do the work you were hired for. That's another reason why I stay in New York, so I can keep on doing plays. Theater is great fun because you get to go out there and play something from the beginning to the middle to the end, but it's also very exhausting too. While you're waiting for hours and hours on a film, on a play you may only be working for two or three hours a night, but you're working all the time, and you're usually lifting heavier emotional baggage on stage, so it's much more exhausting. Maybe it's because I eschew glamorous lifestyles, but I think most actors would just as soon do the work and go home instead of all the other stuff that gives the illusion of glamour.

Any other advice you'd give to aspiring actors?

Don't do it unless it's the only thing in the whole entire world you've ever wanted to do, because you have to make tremendous sacrifices. I've seen a lot of people make unhealthy sacrifices, and by that I mean they make sacrifices of their own morality. That can be very tempting and very dangerous when you make deals with the devil in this business. Don't do that… Make monetary sacrifices like how much you want to spend for a new suit or how much you want to spend on dinner in a restaurant. Those sacrifices are easier to make, even in a world like ours where we feel entitled to everything. Be careful about the sacrifices you make with your family. I've made a lot over the years, and some of them I wish I hadn't, but on the other hand I've been able to provide for my family, and I'm very thankful for that. Another thing is to train well… Most of the young actors I've worked with have come out of high-profile schools like Juilliard, NYU, Yale, and Rutgers. My advice would be to go to a good liberal arts college and get a liberal arts degree before you go on and decide to train professionally. This is a broader comment on our society, but I think we're in a rush to train for careers in this country when we ought to be in a rush to train to be human beings. I think a good liberal arts education would serve you much better in the long run. In terms of the business itself, it's changed, and I'm not sure how actors get their feet in the door. Going to a high-profile academy can help, but the opportunities are not as great as when I was starting out. It's much harder these days, so you've

really got to love it, and don't make sacrifices that would be bad for you as a human being. As an actor, our humanity is one of our greatest gifts, and you don't want to shortchange that.

Silkwood (1983)
    Director: Mike Nichols
    Starring: Meryl Streep, Kurt Russell, Cher, Craig T. Nelson
    Based on actual events, *Silkwood* stars Streep as the eponymous heroine, a worker in a nuclear facility who is diagnosed with radiation poisoning. Convinced the company has cut corners concerning employee safety, Silkwood begins to gather evidence that could lead to a scandal for the plant and its executives. An early starring role for Streep, this film demonstrates why she is one of the greatest actresses of her—or any other—generation. Nominated for five Academy Awards, including Best Director, Best Screenplay, and Best Actress (Streep).

Lorenzo's Oil (1992)
    Director: George Miller
    Starring: Nick Nolte, Susan Sarandon, Peter Ustinov, Kathleen Wilhoite
    Augusto (Nolte) and Michaela (Sarandon) Odone are the parents of Lorenzo, a young boy who has been afflicted with a rare—and fatal—nerve disorder. With no substantial research being conducted, the Odones set out to solve the mystery of their son's illness before it's too late. *Oil* may sound like a standard disease-of-the-week TV movie, but this real-life story is a moving and harrowing journey elevated by the terrific performances from Nolte and Sarandon. Oscar-nominated for Best Actress (Sarandon) and Best Screenplay.

My Cousin Vinny (1992)
    Director: Jonathan Lynn
    Starring: Joe Pesci, Ralph Macchio, Marisa Tomei, Mitchell Whitfield
    College kids Bill (Macchio) and Stan (Whitfield) are arrested for murder in Alabama, leaving Bill with no other choice than to call—you guessed it—his cousin Vinny (Pesci), a brash, neophyte New York lawyer with no courtroom experience. This funny fish-out-of-water tale benefits from the great chemistry between Pesci and Tomei, playing his long-suffering girlfriend. Tomei won the Oscar for Best Supporting Actress.

Scent of a Woman (1992)
    Director: Martin Brest
    Starring: Al Pacino, Chris O'Donnell, James Rebhorn, Gabrielle Anwar
    Charlie (O'Donnell) is a prep school student faced with a dilemma:

He can either testify against his friends for pulling a prank on the headmaster (Rebhorn) or he will face the consequences for remaining silent. As Charlie wrestles with his decision over a holiday break, he takes a job babysitting Frank (Pacino), a cantankerous blind war vet who has his own plans for the long weekend. Pacino delivers a tour de force performance in this entertaining film. Nominated for four Academy Awards and winner for Best Actor (Pacino).

8 Seconds (1994)
Director: John G. Avildsen
Starring: Luke Perry, Cynthia Geary, Stephen Baldwin, James Rebhorn

True story based on the life of Lane Frost (Perry), a bull rider who dealt with numerous obstacles on the rodeo circuit en route to becoming the sport's youngest champion. Those include a strained relationship with his wife, Kelly (Geary), an overly demanding father (Rebhorn), and the need to conquer the one bull that has never been successfully ridden by anyone. Director Avildsen (*Rocky, The Karate Kid*) works his crowd-pleasing magic again and comes up with another winner.

The Talented Mr. Ripley (1999)
Director: Anthony Minghella
Starring: Matt Damon, Gwyneth Paltrow, Jude Law, Cate Blanchett

Intriguing film features Damon as Tom Ripley, a working-class nobody who excels in deception as a means for experiencing the finer things in life. After passing himself off as a Princeton grad, Ripley is employed by shipping tycoon Herbert Greenleaf to go to Italy and retrieve his son Dickie (Law), a spoiled rich kid living off his daddy's fortune who refuses to come home. As Ripley uses his skills to get close to Dickie, a cat-and-mouse game ensues that eventually leads to murder. Nominated for five Oscars, including Best Supporting Actor (Law) and Best Screenplay.

Cold Mountain (2003)
Director: Anthony Minghella
Starring: Jude Law, Nicole Kidman, Renee Zellweger, Philip Seymour Hoffman

During the waning days of the Civil War, Confederate soldier Inman (Law) deserts and starts a long journey home to be with his love, Ada (Kidman), a woman of privilege who is struggling to survive on her own under difficult circumstances. While Inman encounters a number of eccentric characters during his travels—including a posse charged with killing deserters—Ada has to get used to Ruby (Zellweger), a spunky tomboy sent to help with Ada's farm. The genuinely touching love story between Law and Kidman is the heart of *Cold Mountain*, but Zellweger steals the show. Nominated for seven Academy Awards and winner for Best Supporting Actress (Zellweger).

Duane Whitaker

After thirty years in Hollywood, Duane Whitaker has accomplished more than most people dream of. As an actor, he played pivotal roles in *Pulp Fiction*, *Feast*, and *Tales from the Hood*. As a writer, Whitaker penned juicy roles for himself in *From Dusk Till Dawn 2: Texas Blood Money* and *Eddie Presley* (which he adapted from his own play). And as a director, he helmed *Together & Alone*, an acclaimed Tinseltown slice-of-life drama that he also wrote and starred in. In his spare time, Whitaker also teaches an acting class, sharing his techniques and tales of survival with the next generation of aspiring thespians. Learn more at www.duanewhitaker.com.

How did you get your start in acting?

I grew up in Lubbock, Texas, and when I was sixteen or seventeen, I had the realization that I wasn't going to be a professional athlete. I was a decent athlete but I wasn't a freakishly *good* athlete, so when I realized that wasn't gonna happen, I kind of drifted into drama in my junior year of high school. I kind of just sat around that year and didn't really do anything, but in my senior year, I realized that's what I wanted to do. I ended up getting a paying job at a dinner theater, and I was really lucky to get it. It was the only paying acting job for hundreds of miles, and we did a little

pre-show, then we did our parts in the play, and we waited on tables in-between acts. That was a really great experience, and after that I started doing everything that was there. I did community theater, I did a melodrama that toured the parks, I did a show at the university... In a three year period, I sort of did everything that I thought I could do there, so I took off and came to L.A. when I was twenty and started hittin' it there.

Your earliest jobs were on TV shows like L.A. Law, Highway to Heaven *and* Murder, She Wrote. *What were those experiences like?*

Those were what I call "check under the hood" parts, just small five-line roles. I was with an agency that sort of specialized in snagging these small jobs, so that's what I was going out for. They were really good learning experiences but, unfortunately, you had to learn as you were watching them. I'd do a part and then a month later I'd watch it on TV and say, "Gosh, I'm moving around too much there," or things like that. Whatever technique I have was developed just by trial and error in doing those small roles. I guess that's the kind of thing you can teach in a class, but it's always a little different... You sort of have to be under fire and do it in a real situation before you really learn it. It's not rocket science and the technical part isn't that difficult, but if you don't know about camera direction or hitting marks, it can get confusing.

Was it difficult for you to make the transition from theater to acting in front of the camera?

It wasn't because that's what I always wanted to do, that's what I was always looking at. I never intended to be a stage actor for life. It was just sort of a step for me because there was really no other choice. I went through a period of about three or four years in L.A. where if I wasn't in a play, I was directing one. I did a lot of theater and was a decent stage actor but it was never my focus from the beginning. I was making Super-8 movies when I was a kid, so I actually started out sort of as a filmmaker before I had even done a play. Film always interested me, and I felt like whatever natural ability I have was more suited for film work, so that was my goal.

You've done a number of films with director Jeff Burr. How did that relationship begin?

I had done a play that I'd co-written and was in called *Who Killed Orson Welles?* I can't remember why he came to that or what the connection was, but we would run into each other in Hollywood. We used to hang out in a bar called Boardners, so we'd run into each other a lot and he told me he'd seen the play. I ended up doing some looping for him on *Stepfather II*. He'd actually promised me a job on *Stepfather II* and then weaseled out, so I think the first official time we worked together was on *Texas Chainsaw Massacre III* when I came in and did a day on that. That film was such a bad experience for him that he went away for a while, and when he came back, he was interested in *Eddie Presley*, a one-man play I had done.

Whitaker and director Jeff Burr on the set of *Eddie Presley*

What was the inspiration for Eddie Presley?

I had been kickin' around the idea of this Elvis impersonator story for years. It was kind of based on when I was a bartender at the Hilton back in Lubbock, and there was this guy who would come through there who had a high-level job—I think he was a junior executive somewhere—and he kind of just chucked it all and became this B-level Elvis impersonator. He wasn't a particularly interesting guy and he wasn't a particularly good Elvis impersonator, but I always thought there was something there that might make a good one-man show. I never really could get a handle on what the hook was, and years later I was in McDonalds on Hollywood Boulevard where I saw this street magician guy just flip out over getting a refill of a cup of coffee. The cops came in and dragged him out, and I thought that was the piece I was missing. I couldn't figure out why the performance Eddie was doing was so important, but he had a meltdown and this was his big comeback gig. The story was really just a metaphor for where my acting career was at the time, and it was kind of my personal *Rocky* about my frustrations. I wrote the play in one night when I was working as a security guard at EMI on the graveyard shift, and the play was literally produced about three weeks later. It just happened to fall into an open spot at the theater company I was with, and one of the guys running the company said, "Let's do this." It was an interesting piece of theater because whatever anybody thought it was gonna be, it *wasn't* that. *Eddie Presley: A Tribute to the King* was the actual name of the play, and people were probably coming in thinking they were going to see some idiot do a bad Elvis act, but it was sort of a confrontational theater piece. It kind of turned around on the audience and asked them, "What have you done with your life?" I'm sure it was an uncomfortable thing for them to sit through, and it freaked a lot of people out. It did get some nice reviews, and one of the best reviews didn't even get published because the paper ended up going out of business! To this day it would have been the best review I ever got as a writer or an actor. *L.A. Weekly* didn't love it and I don't think the [*Los Angeles*] *Times* even reviewed it, but the play was successful in the fact that it did its run and people showed up to see it.

How did it come to be a movie?

Jeff had had a really bad experience with the whole corporate filmmaking thing, and he wanted to go back and make a full-blown independent film

Eddie Presley

where nobody could take away his control. We went for a *long* period of time trying to raise the money, and we literally didn't even get a nibble—nobody was interested. At one point, it looked like we were gonna just sell the project to another company because a fairly big producer wanted to buy it and put another actor in the part. We had that meeting, and the actor kind of talked himself out of doing it. I think we were all very close to just giving up when all of a sudden it kind of came together at the last second.

Was it difficult adapting the material into a screenplay?

It wasn't really difficult because we knew where we ended up. The third act was the performance, so it was just a question of how did we end up there? It was really a case of backward screenwriting, I guess. It was a fairly quick process, and we had what we considered a shooting script ready to go in a couple of months. I would write, and then Jeff and I would get together and go over it. There was a lot of talk after the fact that we probably should have done the film more non-linear, where it's jumping back and forth. That could have been interesting, and hindsight's always 20/20. There's a lot of things with that movie that we all probably would've done differently.

As the writer and the star, did you have a lot of input into the finished product?

I actually did not. I had very little input, and in retrospect, I should've pushed harder for that. It was an interesting situation because Jeff and I had really different ideas. I've done screenplays for other people, and you sort of learn that one person is not gonna see it the same way I do, and they're gonna put their own spin on it. I was an equal partner in the company, so if I really wanted to, I think I could've bullied my way into the editing room more. I think it had more to do with Jeff's bad experience with people telling him what to do, and I don't think he really wanted anybody telling him anything. We would look at different cuts and I would give him my opinion, but that's all it was. I've worked with Jeff more than any other director, so it's not like we didn't get along or anything like that. I just think a lot of his frustrations from *Chainsaw* might have caused him not to be as open as maybe he should've been on the cutting of *Eddie*. I've always said I have real mixed feelings about the movie, but I'm at peace with it. I think it's interesting, and it's a great try if nothing else, but I always felt like we were one or two cuts away from being *really* good. I think there's a better movie in there than what we ended up with, but you never know… I could be completely wrong, but that's always been my feeling.

Are you in any kind of position to go back and re-cut the movie your way for a special edition DVD?

Not really, because it's not my movie. Even now, we have real fundamental disagreements about what we would've done differently. Given the footage we have now, if you told me to cut it and Jeff to cut it, they would be radically different movies. I think one of the problems is that we shot an enormous amount of film… It was an enormous amount for a movie like that, and maybe we made enough rope to hang ourselves in a lot of ways. It should've been a ninety-two-minute burst, and I think he wanted to make it *Once Upon a Time in America*, and somewhere in the middle we kind of got sidetracked. Having said all that, I don't want it to sound like I hate the film, because I don't. There are people who just adore that movie, and over the years I've gotten a lot of emails from people who really connected with it. J.R. Bookwalter put the DVD out on Tempe in 2002, and he did a great job with it. I guess you can always go back and re-do stuff, but as far as I'm concerned, it is what it is.

How did Quentin Tarantino end up making a cameo in the film?

Quentin and [director] Sam Raimi were gonna come in and play the nuthouse attendants just as a gag cameo. I think Sam ended up getting a better deal somewhere else, so Bruce Campbell stepped in. I had never met Quentin, but he was working on *Reservoir Dogs* at the same lab we were at. We'd see Lawrence Tierney in *Dogs* in one room and then see Larry in our movie in another room. Quentin came in for a day to film the cameo, and we mostly just talked about Larry Tierney and what a nightmare he was to work with. We had kind of a common enemy, so we just hung out and talked about that. I ended up running into Quentin about a year later at a coffee shop at two or three in the morning. He was there by himself eating a hamburger, and we started talking. I was wearing a cowboy hat and had long hair and a beard, and I looked completely different from the last time he had seen me. He said, "I'm doing this movie and you're kind of right for this one part. I'll have them call you." The movie was *Pulp Fiction*, and it ended up being a long, drawn-out, painful experience to get that part, but the bottom line was that I ended up doing the job. As an actor, that was a major thing for me to be in that movie.

Pulp Fiction

Bruce Willis and Whitaker on the set of *Pulp Fiction*

I read an interview where you said that Pulp Fiction *opened some doors for you but you never really took advantage of being in the movie. Can you elaborate on that?*

Well, it wasn't the kind of part where people came out of the woodwork to hire the guy who played a hillbilly rapist, but whatever heat I had from being in *Pulp Fiction* did get me some offers that I never would have gotten before. At the time, I was making my own movie and not even really concentrating on acting. Looking back, it seemed like the thing to do at the time, and I still think that was the right thing to do. I'm not a particularly good business person, so from that standpoint, I probably should've tried to take more advantage of being in the movie to get better roles and better representation. Again, hindsight is always 20/20, so you never know.

How did you get involved with writing the script for From Dusk Till Dawn 2?

I had written a script for a friend of mine who was trying to get a job as a director. It was a strip bar movie—a really specific, one location kind of thing—and he took it around and couldn't get anybody interested in making it. It sat in a drawer for a few months, and a director I'd worked with named Dan Golden called me and said, "What have you got?" He had directed some movies for Roger Corman and he said, "Do you have anything that Corman would do?" I told him about this strip bar movie called *Zipper's Clown Palace*, which I thought was a great title that riffed on a famous strip bar here called Jumbo's Clown Room. Dan took it to Roger, Roger wanted to make it, and we were literally shooting it a few weeks later. The movie got finished, Roger changed the name of the movie to *Stripteaser* and I sent the movie to Quentin. Quentin was really amused with the movie and he showed it to Bob Weinstein. At that point they were gonna do two *Dusk Till Dawn* sequels, and Quentin called me one day and asked me if I wanted to co-write one with Scott Spiegel and write myself a nice part in it. I said, "Yes, I do," and that consumed the next two years of my life. The film is called *From Dusk Till Dawn 2: Texas Blood Money*, and since I'm from Texas, I thought if I set the film there they'd send us to Texas to film it. We ended up shooting in Cape Town, South Africa, so that plan kinda backfired!

Were Robert Rodriguez and Quentin pretty involved in the production?

Robert was more involved with part three, but Quentin was really involved a lot in two, especially at the beginning. He had a say in casting

From Dusk Till Dawn 2: Texas Blood Money

decisions, and he contributed quite a bit to the script. In fact, his name was actually on the script at one time, but I think he ended up taking it off due to some Writers Guild thing. At some point, he kind of disappeared to go work on something else, but he was with us right up until we went off to shoot. I wasn't involved in post-production at all, so I don't know how much input he had in that, but he was pretty involved in the early stages of the film.

The original From Dusk Till Dawn *wasn't a huge box-office hit but it has a pretty devoted fan base. Was it intimidating doing a follow-up?*

It really wasn't because I think we realized going in that it was designed to be a straight-to-video sequel. We were shooting on a tiny fraction of the budget the original had, so it was all about trying to make an interesting story within the budget limitations. It was a real movie and we had a little money, but it wasn't like we had George Clooney or anything like that. It was never going to be anything other than what it was, which was a very low-budget, straight-to-video sequel. And for what it is, I think it's pretty good. We weren't trying to make *Midnight Cowboy*… That's one of the difficult things I've had to come to terms with as an actor. I remember calling Jeff Burr at one point and telling him, "You know, we only got one take with this big dialogue scene, but they spent three hours shooting a plastic bat floppin' around." Jeff said, "You've got to remember what movie you're making," and that was a very good point. In genre films, the focus is not necessarily on your work as an actor. I think I've been able to do good work in the genre but that's not what people are really looking for when they watch those movies. Robert Patrick and Bo Hopkins were a lot of fun to work with, and there were a lot of good people in that movie. For a low-budget horror sequel, that's a pretty good cast. The film has followers and detractors, but it made a lot of money, and that was the idea.

You wrote and directed a movie called Together & Alone. *How did that project come to life?*

After the whole *Eddie Presley* thing, I wanted to do something that I could totally control and shoot for no money, just to see if I could do it. I financed it myself with my acting jobs, and I started with the idea of doing a no-budget Robert Altman movie—just a bunch of stories about a night in Hollywood that connect somehow. I wrote it very, very quickly, and I sent the script to a guy named Sean Hughes, who had seen *Eddie* and was trying to get me involved in another movie he was doing. Sean said, "We can shoot this. I have cameras, I've got flatbeds and my friend's got a grip truck with lights… Let's do it." After that, it all kinda started falling into place, so we went out and did it. We shot the movie in eight days—four days with a two-week break, and then three more with a day of pick-ups—and it was totally run-and-gun. I don't even know what the final budget of the movie was, but it was less than $50,000. It was really an experiment to see what would happen, and creatively it's my favorite thing I've ever done. As I was writing it, I didn't even know how a lot of the stories connected. When I got tired of doing one story, I'd go and pick up another one, but they all kind of came together. It was not the kind of movie that would've been easy to get made at any budget, and I never really made any attempt to get it funded because I knew there was no way anybody was gonna put up a nickel for it. It was also a test of whether or not I could direct a movie. Even though I had directed theater, I didn't know if I could direct a movie because I was kind of intimidated by some of the technical stuff. It turned out to be a great experience.

Eddie Presley *and* Together & Alone *are very similar in that they both focus on people struggling in Hollywood. In fact, you recently had an Ameri-*

Thom Draper, Joe Unger and Whitaker on the set of *Together & Alone*

can Cinematheque screening of both films at the Egyptian Theatre. What is it about these kinds of fringe characters that interests you?

When I first moved to Hollywood, it really was a different universe that I stepped into. I met a lot of interesting people, and one of them was a guy named Gene Rutherford. He was an actor who had something of a career, he knew everybody in town, and then he literally had a breakdown—a couple of times—and he kept trying to revive his career. He was a fascinating guy, and he's still the most interesting person I've ever met. Joe Unger's character in *Together & Alone* was based on Gene, and I'd say ninety percent of what that character says actually happened to Gene and was in his own words. I also learned more about acting from him than anyone else. He'd studied with Sandy Meisner in New York, and when I started teaching acting, I sent Gene a letter—he didn't have a phone anymore—and told him what I was doing and asked if he had any insight. He sent me all of these great notes he'd taken in Sandy's class, just real smart stuff. Not everybody I met was like Gene, of course, but I've always been more interested in the less obvious people, guys who are struggling musicians and stand-up comedians, people like that. I really like those guys, and I guess I was one of them to a degree. There were all of these coffee shops in Hollywood with all of these interesting people hanging out, and I had a girlfriend at the time who was a waitress. She had to deal with these people, and she asked me, "What's so interesting about these idiots?" I didn't know why—and I guess I still don't—but I was fascinated with them.

Do you have any plans to direct again?

There's a couple of things I'm looking at doing. It's kind of upsetting to look at the time that's passed where I haven't directed anything else. I've directed a couple of little things like trailers, and I actually directed some second unit on *From Dusk Till Dawn 2*, but it's been frustrating to never be able to get a movie set up like I wanted it. There's a project I've been trying to get made for years called *30 Weight*. In one sentence, it's about a guy who finds a can of oil that's worth a lot of money. *A Simple Plan* with an oil can, if you will… That's a movie that came *very* close to getting funded a couple of times. I also just came up with a thing recently that kind of started in the acting class I teach. It's a very low-budget improv movie that I don't know what to compare it to. It's a very strange little thing, but it should be a lot of fun. I've got a very commercial script that

I'm going to try and sell so I can finance that stuff. It's called *BOXX*, and I've been describing it as a rock 'n' roll ghost story in the '80s. In the best of all worlds, I'd like to direct it, but it's a fairly large-budgeted project so I can't imagine anyone letting me do it.

How did you get involved with Feast?

I had known the Gulager family for years and years. John's father, Clu, was actually in *Eddie Presley*, which was a part I had written for him. He's just brilliant in that, and he's probably one of the best actors I've ever worked with. John was getting closer and closer with this *Project Greenlight* thing, and he miraculously ended up getting the job. I really liked the script, and when I read it, I really wanted that part. John brought me in to read for it, and if you watched the show, John and the casting director obviously had a pretty unpleasant relationship. I think she really didn't want me for the movie mainly because I was his choice. At one point, he told me he couldn't even get me in the room for a meeting, and that pissed me off because I knew if I got in the room, I'd have a chance. I ended up getting cleared by Bob Weinstein or somebody at Dimension. Whoever was mak-

Feast

ing that decision said I was okay, so getting the job was kind of unpleasant, but I really enjoyed making the movie, and I liked the way it turned out. There's some stuff I did that got cut that I wish was still in there, but the movie wasn't about me, so I can't complain. I think the movie works great, and it's a great balance of really scary shit with really funny stuff. That's hard to do, and I think they did a good job with it. Of all the horror movies I've done, that's one of my favorites.

What was it like having the making of the movie being filmed for the Project Greenlight *reality show?*

It was weird because you constantly had people with cameras on you. I basically just hid from them… I figured if they didn't have any footage of me, they couldn't do anything with it. I spent a lot of time in my trailer, and I really didn't talk when they were around me. If you see the show, I'm not in it very much. I would never go out on the set and lay down in a chair to take a nap or something because they could cut to that shot five times and go, "Hey, where's Duane at?" That kind of stuff can be easily manipulated, so I just tried to avoid it.

Did the TV show accurately reflect what it was like making the film?

It's accurate in the sense that they didn't make up anything, as far as I know. It's basically like they follow a script. From what I saw, it looked like they would get together and go, "We're gonna follow this storyline." I wasn't there the whole time because I didn't come in until the second week of shooting, but I didn't see anything on there where I went, "Oh, wow, *that* didn't happen." Sometimes it's out of context or it's out of order of when it actually happened, but I didn't see anything that was made up. I'm sure there are other people who would argue that, though.

When you're hired for an acting job, is it hard to just be an actor when you have all of this experience in writing and directing?

Not really. You just have to think before you say anything because you don't want to step on anyone's toes. I remember I was shooting a movie where we were cheating a shot, and I was pretty sure they had me looking on the wrong side of the camera. The director of photography said, "Look here," and I said, "I'm just asking, and you may well be right, but if this is

this and that's where they were, shouldn't I be looking here?" He was like, "Yeah, yeah, you're right." It's not like I'm some technical whiz, but there are times—especially with younger filmmakers—when I know more than they do, so that can be frustrating. Ultimately, I think I really prefer being the lazy actor who says, "I'll be in my trailer, call me when you need me." When you've done the other stuff, you realize what a great job it is just to be an actor, and that's the only thing you have to think about.

Do you think your experience as a writer and director has helped you as an actor?

Absolutely. It helps you understand and see the bigger picture, but sometimes that can be a disadvantage too. I'm able to see where my character fits into the story, and because of that I may not do as much as some other actor to draw attention to myself. *Pulp Fiction* and *Tales from the Hood* came out not too far apart, and very few people realized I was in both movies. I guess that's a compliment in a way, but it didn't really help me as an actor. I've had people say about me, "Well, he kind of does the same thing every time," but if they watched four minutes of my demo reel, they'd see that's not the case. There's a lot of character actors who've made a living doing the same stuff over and over—and there's nothing wrong with that—but I'd like to think that I have *some* sort of range and can do different things. Generally, though, people aren't going to take a risk on someone like me, and I rarely get the opportunity to do stuff that's beyond my type. I did do a role on *Cold Case* that was kind of atypical… He was kind of a twitched-out sort of guy who's had a bad experience. The description of the character they used was that he's "haunted," which I really liked. Every once in a while I'll get to do something a little different like that, but generally speaking, you're not gonna get hired for something that you haven't already proven you can do.

You've written screenplays by yourself and you've collaborated with others. Which do you prefer?

I prefer to write by myself because the scripts I really love are mine, for better or worse. In those collaborative scripts, there's always stuff that ends up in there that I don't like. Most of the times I've collaborated, that was just part of the deal, but I've enjoyed doing it. I get calls all the time and people are like, "I've got this idea," and I'm like, "You know, I have enough bad ideas of my own." The good thing for me about collaborating is that I'm put on a schedule. The percentage of what I've written that's been produced is very high, but I've probably only written about two percent of what I *should* have written by now, so there's a certain lack of discipline there.

How did you come to start your own acting class?

It started about ten years ago through a weird series of circumstances. There was a period where I wasn't really doing anything, so I thought I'd go and take an acting class just to have something to do. I was never really a big class person, but I started taking my friend Kim Darby's class and was hanging out there a lot. I had a few people there tell me, "Hey, if you ever teach, we'd be interested in taking your class." That started me thinking, and then I ran across a guy that I had known who'd been teaching for years, and during our conversation, he mentioned that he had some space available one night a week. I thought maybe I'd try it for a couple of months and see what happened, and I've been doing it for about ten years now. My joke was that I wanted to keep my acting class a big secret, and I've succeeded admirably! It's a very small class… I don't think I've ever had more than ten people in there at a time. It started out as a curiosity, and I really didn't know if I even had anything to say, but it turned out I really enjoyed doing it. I've learned a ton from it because I'll get up and

Director Thomas L. Callaway and Whitaker on the set of *Broke Sky*

work too. It's good for me and it keeps me honest, and you learn a lot just by watching other people work every week. Early on, I was prejudiced against most classes because I thought whatever quality I had would get beaten out of me if I thought about it and analyzed it too much. I've seen that happen with actors... I've seen really interesting actors that would go off to a class, come back, and they weren't interesting at all anymore. It was all about demonstrating some technique they had learned, which is just bad acting. So I was pretty leery of classes, but I was wrong because there's so much to learn, and you can always get better. I've known a lot of talented people who never went anywhere, and I've known a lot of driven people who shouldn't be working who've starred in fifteen movies. Acting is work, and there's a lot to be said for just hittin' it every week and working on your craft. If I had done more of that, I'd be a better actor than I am. With younger actors now, I think there's this attitude of, "Somebody's just going to discover me and all of that stuff will take care of itself, I don't have to learn how to do it." It's a reality show mentality that being famous is the same as actually having skill, and it's not. Most of the people who are good actors are good because they work at it.

What are some of the things that you cover in your class?

It's not anything radical that I invented, but film acting is different in the sense that most of the interesting stuff happens in-between the lines. Good film acting is about giving what you get from the other person, staying in the moment and reacting. It's not about delivering lines or anything like that. In class, people will get panicked and lost and start looking on the paper, and I always say, "You'll never find the scene on the paper. The scene is between the two people." It's sort of a really simple concept: Know the lines and know where you're going but be open to what the other person is going to do. That's an easy concept, but when you're sittin' on the set and there's 150 people waitin' for you to do the scene, it's not so simple. Some people tend to fall back on what they think will work and lock themselves into that instead of playing the scene and seeing what happens. What you do should be based on what the other person does, and vice versa. Most of the good people that I've worked with do that, and I think it's much more interesting to listen and react instead of just reacting automatically.

How difficult is it to make a living as an actor?

It's extraordinarily difficult, and it's not lost on me that I've been *extremely* fortunate. I don't use the word "lucky" because that sounds like I scratched off a lottery ticket when I've actually created a lot of opportunities for myself, but it's awfully tough and it's gettin' tougher all the time, especially for a character actor. I'd be shocked if you talked to one character actor who said it's easier now than it was ten years ago. There's fewer jobs out there and they're paying less money than they used to. For whatever reason, I've been able to make a living at it for most of my adult life, and that was my goal from the beginning. I wish that my career was a little further along, I wish that I was doing bigger films, and I wish that I was making more money on the stuff that I am doing, but I look around and none of the people I started with are still in the business, period. I think Dan Roebuck is the only guy I met early on who's still very much working, but I can't think of anyone else. When you look at it like that, I've definitely been very fortunate.

What frustrates you about the business aspects of acting?

I think the most frustrating thing for me, personally, is I've never been able to put myself into a position to get good representation. I've never had that, and it's a huge, *huge* handicap. A lot of people would say it's insurmountable, and I went through a period of about four years where I worked a lot and didn't even have an agent. I knew people who were doing things and they were aware of me, so I was very fortunate that they were callin' me to work. I never had a strong agent or manager to pitch me for things, so it's frustrating that I can't get into the room a lot of times to audition. When I do get a chance at something, I'm not brilliant every time—nobody is—but chances are pretty good that if it's something I'm remotely right for, I'm going to be one of the people they end up considering. I never went in for *Walker, Texas Ranger* or *Deadwood* or *Justified* or any of these shows that you think would be a no-brainer for me to do, and that's because I didn't have anybody really fighting for me to get in there. That's frustrating, and part of that is my fault. You know that agent or manager is out there, and you've got to keep grinding away to find them. That's part of being a good businessman—which I'm not—and that's not something I'm particularly proud of, but that was never my focus. My focus was always to do the best work I could do, and I just assumed that everything would take care of itself on that end. Sometimes it does and sometimes it doesn't, but that's one thing I would do differently. I would approach the whole thing more as a business, and most of the people I know who have really great careers have good people behind them. I've never had that, and I've essentially been on my own almost from the beginning. I've managed to work pretty consistently despite that, and once you get to my age, you're more likely to go, "I'm just gonna stick with the agent I've got, at least he hasn't screwed anything up lately!"

What advice would you give to aspiring actors?

Finding good representation is important, but on the flipside, one of the things I think I've done right is to create opportunities for myself.

Write a play and create something for yourself, and if you can't write, find someone who can and develop stuff with that person. If you just sit around waitin' to get picked, you may get lucky or you may not, but having a script can help you get in the door. One of the first people I ever talked to when I moved to L.A. was G.W. Bailey. He was from my hometown, and I asked him for advice, and he said, "The only thing that I know is work breeds work." One job leads to another and another, and a lot of times you have to make that happen for yourself. Find a way to do something instead of just sittin' around. Most of the younger people I know just sit around and say, "Well, we'll see what happens," and you look at them in ten years and they haven't done anything. If you're gonna do it, do it. I never felt I was that driven early on, but looking back—compared to most people—I really was. I was pretty ruthless and would try everything I could to get in any door I could, because I felt like that's what I had to do. I'm not so much like that now… You can get by with that when you're in your twenties but it's kind of obnoxious when you're fifty! But if I hear about a project and I don't have a way in, I'll write the director a letter, and if the casting director won't see me, I'll try and go over their head. Sometimes that pisses people off, but if somebody gets pissed at you for tryin' to get a job, who cares? Try to get out there, and if nothing's happening, make something happen.

Leatherface: Texas Chainsaw Massacre III (1990)
Director: Jeff Burr
Starring: Kate Hodge, Ken Foree, William Butler, R.A. Mihailoff
Michelle (Hodge) and her boyfriend, Ryan (Butler), are on their way to Florida when they pull off a deserted Texas highway for gas and become embroiled in another killing spree led by Leatherface (Mihailoff) and his demented family. Every entry in the *Chainsaw* franchise pretty much tells the same story over and over again, and this one brings nothing new to the table. If you're a fan of repetition, you'll probably enjoy it.

Eddie Presley (1992)
Director: Jeff Burr
Starring: Duane Whitaker, Stacie Bourgeois, Roscoe Lee Browne, Clu Gulager
Compelling character study focuses on Eddie (Whitaker), an Elvis impersonator whose dreams are bigger than his talent. Beaten down by life and living in his van, Eddie is on the edge when he manages to book a

gig that could jump-start his career. When his tape recorder malfunctions and he isn't able to perform, Eddie's attempt to improvise turns into an emotional breakdown. As the writer and star, Whitaker delivers a knockout one-two punch with a great script and a brilliant performance.

Pulp Fiction (1994)
Director: Quentin Tarantino
Starring: John Travolta, Samuel L. Jackson, Bruce Willis, Uma Thurman

Tarantino's influential masterpiece focuses on two mob hitmen (Travolta and Jackson), the wife (Thurman) of their boss, and a boxer (Willis) on the run, in intertwining stories punctuated with shocking violence and dark humor. There's not much more to say about this film that hasn't already been said… It is, quite simply, one of the greatest movies ever made. Nominated for seven Academy Awards and winner for Best Screenplay.

Stripteaser (1995)
Director: Dan Golden
Starring: Maria Ford, Rick Dean, Lance August, Nikki Fritz

A seedy strip club is the site of a deadly hostage situation when a psycho named Neil (Dean) confronts Christina (Ford), a dancer who has become the object of his twisted affection. One of many stripper-themed flicks in producer Roger Corman's catalog, this one stands out from the rest thanks to some great dialogue and Dean's riveting portrayal.

Tales from the Hood (1995)
Director: Rusty Cundieff
Starring: Clarence Williams III, Joe Torry, De'aundre Bonds, Samuel Monroe Jr.

Horror anthology with an inner-city spin finds three gang members (Torry, Bonds, Monroe Jr.) going to a funeral home to retrieve stolen drugs from the mysterious Mr. Simms (Williams III). Every body in a casket has a story, which Simms gleefully shares with his guests. The first three supernatural, socially conscious yarns are a mixed bag revolving around such topics as police brutality, domestic abuse, and bigotry. However, the fourth—and by far the best—tale is a powerful rumination on the similarities between black-on-black gang violence and racially motivated lynchings and murders. *Hood* might be a popcorn movie, but it definitely gives you something more substantive to chew on.

Together & Alone (1998)
  Director: Duane Whitaker
  Starring: Casey Siemaszko, Sarah Bibb, Joe Unger, Thomas Draper
  Engaging drama spends a night in Hollywood with a number of assorted misfits: A once-promising actor (Unger) whose mental instability sunk his career; a guitarist (Siemaszko) who doesn't take his band seriously; and an aspiring filmmaker (Draper) fascinated by the idea of a threesome with his girlfriend and a diner waitress. There's no real plot here, just a series of conversations by interesting characters who dream of overcoming their current struggles by making it big in show business. It's a well-told story that's easy to relate to.

From Dusk Till Dawn 2: Texas Blood Money (1999)
  Director: Scott Spiegel
  Starring: Robert Patrick, Bo Hopkins, Duane Whitaker, Raymond Cruz
  Luther (Whitaker) has just escaped from jail and calls upon his friend, Buck (Patrick), to get the old gang together for a bank robbery in Mexico. After being bitten by a bat, Luther is transformed into a vampire and begins attacking his buddies, while cops, led by the determined Sheriff Lawson (Hopkins), surround the bank. Living up to the first *From Dusk Till Dawn* is a tall order, but *Texas Blood Money* captures the spirit of the original and ranks as a worthy sequel.

Feast (2005)
  Director: John Gulager
  Starring: Krista Allen, Balthazar Getty, Clu Gulager, Henry Rollins
  Patrons at a bar in the middle of nowhere are forced to defend themselves from an attack by monsters. That's pretty much all you need to know about *Feast*, an entertaining throwback to '80s horror/comedies that doesn't pretend to be anything more than a B-movie gorefest (and on that level alone, it succeeds admirably). For those who think such a simple concept can easily be brought to the screen, check out the third season of *Project Greenlight* for a fascinating look at the behind-the-scenes trials and tribulations director Gulager and his cast and crew went through during the making of the film.

Raymond J. Barry

Raymond J. Barry was a latecomer to the Hollywood scene, spending the first twenty years of his career honing his craft in the world of New York theater. After turning his attention to film and television, he delivered memorable performances in such diverse projects as *Born on the Fourth of July*, *Dead Man Walking*, *Walk Hard: The Dewey Cox Story*, *The X-Files*, *CSI*, and *Justified*. Acting is just one of several creative outlets at his disposal, as Barry is also an accomplished playwright, painter, and sculptor. Stay up-to-date with all of his artistic endeavors at www.raymondjbarry.org.

How did you become interested in acting?

I was born into an artistic family on my mother's side. I absorbed through osmosis an appreciation for art. As a matter of fact, I was educated by my mother to believe that art was more important than anything, even money. That was a very unusual education, very unique. Her value system permeated my own without my realizing it. She wasn't didactic but she taught by example. She was a painter and a published writer, and when she was sixty-one, I invited her into my theater company—Quena Company—in New York City, and she began to act. I directed her in four or five plays, we performed in New York and all over the East Coast, and that was a journey that went on for eight or nine years. Back to the original point, my grandfather was a sculptor, my uncle was a concert pianist and my sister was a painter. My family was artistic and I was a jock. I played four varsity sports in high school and I played three sports in college, but I had all of these artistic influences through my family, and it was bound to have an effect. One day, a man named Jim Barnhill—who started the theater program at Brown University, where I had a full scholarship—came up to me and asked me if I would like to be in a play. They were looking for a football player to play the part of Hal in William Inge's *Picnic*. Long story short, I did that play and about five other plays. Jim Barnhill got me into Yale Drama School, and afterwards, I went to New York and studied with Uta Hagen and William Hickey. That's how I began… I was also very shy as a young person, and there was something about being able to get up on stage and express myself that was very appealing to me. It fulfilled a need that I had.

When you worked with William Hickey, what were some of the things that he taught you about the craft?

Well, I was very raw when I studied with Bill. I was very, very afraid and determined at the same time. I had done very little, and I had done nothing on a professional level. At that time, I used to plan ahead too much about what I was going to do, and my work was too intellectual. It was not from the body, it was not free enough, and I was thinking too much. Bill knew it, and he taught me to believe like a child, to rid myself of thought processes that were judgmental and just get up there and believe in the situation in a simple, direct manner and let my sensitivities guide me through the scenes, as opposed to intellectualizing from one beat to another. That, combined with various techniques which he taught—"substitutions," "personalizations," "inner-outers" and "intentions"—all of that was certainly important but it wasn't as significant to me as learning how to play like a child plays in a sandbox once I'm up on stage. He taught me that acting is simple, it's easy… Just do it. Generally speaking, when someone says, "Just have fun," you don't know what the heck they're talking about. When you try to have fun when you're nervous and tense and full of anxiety about what people are thinking, a statement like that usually doesn't have much meaning—it's easier said than done. If anyone

The Serpent

could bring a young actor to that place of innocence, Bill could. When you study with a great teacher like Bill Hickey, what happens is you realize ten years later—and in my case, it might have been twenty years later—what he was talking about. You don't get it right away, and you can't fulfill what they're talking about immediately. Maybe sporadically you can, but not consistently. I was always great the first time I did a scene, but then when I began to go up in front of audiences, I would try to imitate that first time, and you can't do that. You must stay open to the second time

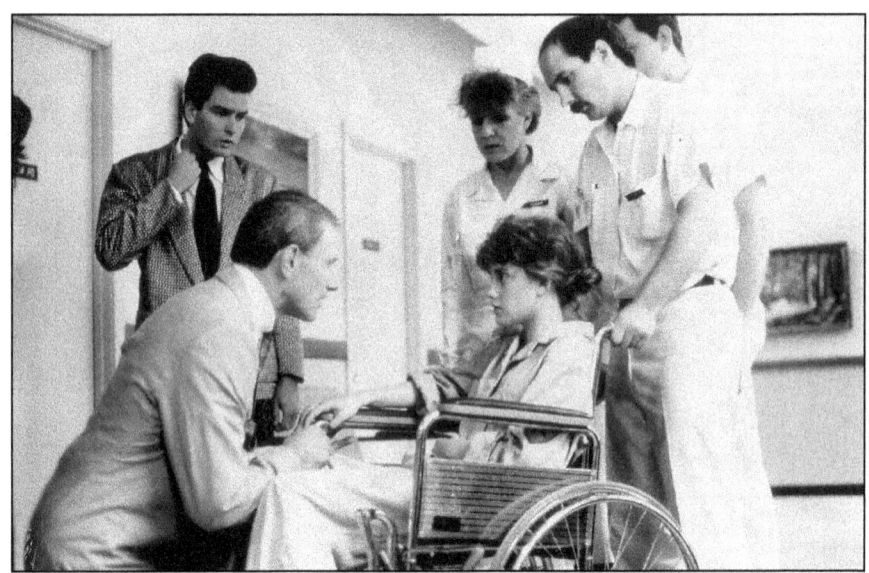

Charlie Sheen, Barry and Keri Green in *Three for the Road*

and the third time because each time is a new time in the moment. I didn't quite understand that as a twenty-one-year-old, but I understand it now as a seventy-three-year-old. It's a fun time when you finally get that.

Two of your earliest film roles were in The Goodbye Girl *and* An Unmarried Woman, *both of which received multiple Academy Award nominations. Did your association with those high-profile films help open some doors for you in the industry?*

No. I was very naïve at that time, commercially. I was a New York theater actor with very little connection to film. The parts I played in *An Unmarried Woman* and *Goodbye Girl* were small parts, and if I had any commercial sense of what was going on at that time, I would have recognized that the two directors who hired me for those jobs hired me because of the way I looked. I wasn't alert enough to that part of acting and casting, and I didn't capitalize on it. If I had been smart enough, maybe I would've gone out to Hollywood and pursued a film career at that time in my life. On the other hand, I had a daughter who I wasn't going to desert, and I was working every day all day long. It wasn't like I was *looking* for work. I had my own theater company, I was doing workshops in prisons, I was working with Joe Chaikin's Open Theater, I worked with the Living Theatre, I did twenty-five plays at the New York Shakespeare Festival, I did

Broadway, off-Broadway, I was directing… I was so busy with theater that I never thought about movies very much in terms of what they would do for my career. In fact, the first time I thought about that was when I did a large role in a Michael Cimino film called *Year of the Dragon* with Mickey Rourke and John Lone. By that time I was forty-four, and it was a large enough role that I got a lot of attention. I realized then that now I should pursue a film career. I had done so much theater that it was time for me to move on, and I came out to Los Angeles. I started working right away on a movie called *Three for the Road* and another movie called *Out of Bounds* with Anthony Michael Hall. Suddenly I was making a lot of money very fast, and I realized I could've been making a damn good living when I was twenty-five if I had moved here earlier. But the real truth is I didn't know how to act when I was twenty-five, and I had to do all of those plays to figure it out. I was tight, I was nervous about myself and I didn't know what the heck I was doing. When I started to act, I was shaped as an athlete, and I felt that the more effort you put into something, the better you were. That's the way it works in sports but that's not the way it works with acting, so I had to unlearn all of that.

Speaking of Year of the Dragon, *how did you get involved with that?*

When I was in New York, I did a lot of part-time jobs. I was a dishwasher, I renovated lofts with a friend of mine, I was a plumber, I worked at the door of the Broome Street Bar, I taught at NYU and City College and Hunter College, things like that. One day, I was digging trenches in the

Barry and Mickey Rourke in *Year of the Dragon*

basement of a building on Broadway, and I made a call to my agent during my break. He says, "You've got to go in and meet Michael Cimino. You're gonna have to read today for this film." I'm exhausted and I've got tar on my hands and all kinds of crap from the work. Long story short, I walked into the office dirty from the job, and I was so tired that I was relaxed. I knew I wasn't going to get the part anyway, so I just read it, and my reading was good. They bring me in again a week later, and this time I haven't been working all day and had more time to prepare, and I do the reading again. It was good, but it wasn't as good as the first time because I'm kind of geared up for it. They bring me in a third time and a fourth time, and then they hired me. When we started shooting about three months later, Michael said to me, "You know, I knew I was going to hire you right away because I liked all of the dirt on your hands. You were a mess, and I liked the way you looked." That's how I got cast.

Oliver Stone co-wrote the script for Year of the Dragon. *Did your work on that have any influence on you being cast in his film* Born on the Fourth of July?

Very much so. He liked my work in *Year of the Dragon*, and he also liked Caroline Kava, who played Mickey Rourke's wife, so he paired us off as the mother and father of Tom Cruise. Oliver also had me read a couple of times, but he knew he was going to cast me. Sometimes these guys know right away who they want, and in the case of Oliver Stone, he told me later, "I knew I was going to put you in this from the beginning because I knew you were right for the role." So, yeah, my work on *Year of the Dragon* had a lot to do with my being cast in the film.

Did you do any research for your role as Ron Kovic's father?

I did two things… The first was that I reinformed myself about the Long Island accent. I grew up on Long Island but I had spent my career unlearning that accent, and I had to get it back. The second thing I did was a technique called "emotional recall" every day in my hotel room. I put myself in a very delicate frame of mind to do *Born on the Fourth of July* because of the subject matter. I felt an enormous responsibility to do well in that film because of my respect for Oliver Stone and because of my respect for the men who went to the Vietnam War. If one of my sons ever came home from a war paralyzed, it would kill me, so I purged myself to arrive

Born on the Fourth of July

at an emotional condition that would be appropriate for that character. In fact, I *became* that character. He doesn't know how to communicate, he doesn't know how to say "I love you" to his own son, and he doesn't know how to fight for his rights. He works at the A&P, he barely gets by, and he doesn't know how to get in touch with his emotions. I tried my best to enter the skin of that man and it was a very uncomfortable shoot for me because of the nature of that character's emotional life. There's a scene in Tom Cruise's bedroom between him and me when he comes back from the war. At one point, I actually broke and came to tears and could barely talk. It's some of the best work I ever did, but boy, did I pay a price for it… It was a bitch.

Have there been any other times when you've so fully invested yourself in bringing a character to life?

Yes. There's a movie I did called *Interview with the Assassin*, and that was an interesting thing. By that time, I was more intelligent as an actor, and I used something that I intrinsically understand about intimidation. It's

Interview with the Assassin

like when you get on a football field and you look at your opponent like this is going to be the day of reckoning, and you're going to win. I played football in college for four years, I played in high school for four years and I played Pop Warner, so I knew how to achieve that kind of almost stupid, macho, animal-like mentality. People who walk around that way with that 1,000-mile stare can very often be dangerous. I know it when I see it, I know how to imitate it, and I knew that's what I needed to enter the skin of my character. Neil Burger wrote and directed the thing, and he really did a good job. Unfortunately, not a lot of people have seen it. I'm proud of the work in it, and I think it's a pretty good film.

You're in almost every scene in Interview. *How challenging was it for you to essentially carry the entire movie?*

I had to memorize 105 pages in five days. Since I was in every scene, I knew I wouldn't have the time to memorize the stuff while I was shooting. I had to come prepared, and it had to be done beforehand, because when you shoot something like that, you're shooting from seven o'clock in the morning until seven o'clock at night, and if you're in every scene, there's no time left over. You come home and you're exhausted. There was something very good about that because I didn't have time to overwork; I had just enough time to learn it. I also had to do another accent, and I had done two movies before that. One was called *The Chamber*, in which I had to use a Mississippi accent, and the other film was *Dead Man Walk-*

ing, in which I had to use a Louisiana accent. On those two films, I worked diligently and painstakingly on the accent—with tapes and everything else—but with *Interview with the Assassin*, I didn't have the time for that, so I combined the Louisiana and Mississippi accents together to make my own speech delivery. The reason I only had five days to prepare was because they had originally hired somebody else to do the job. The guy they hired was a sniper in the Vietnam War, and he had killed twenty-five people. He *was* the character, but he couldn't act, and they didn't realize he couldn't act until they started to rehearse. Suddenly, they panicked and realized this guy can't do the movie. They saw everybody in town and I was one of the guys they pulled in. I was the right age and I was built well; I wasn't out of shape. A lot of guys who are sixty years old have pot bellies and don't look like they could be snipers, but I had the macho look like nobody could push me around. I say that in a healthy way because I'm not violent and I'm not screwed up, but I look like I *could* be. If I want to look that way, I know how to look that way, and they hired me.

You appeared in Rapid Fire *with the late Brandon Lee. What was it like working with him?*

He was friendly. I think he was working too hard as an actor when he didn't have to. He was still at that age when you think you have to break

Barry and Gene Hackman in *The Chamber*

your balls when you don't. He was trying to make too much out of it. He was very handsome and it was the beginning of a brilliant career; he was going to be like his father. Brandon called me after the shoot was over because he wanted to do one of my plays. He wanted to do a play I wrote called *Once in Doubt* because he had seen me do it in Chicago, where we shot the movie. He gave me a call about doing the play and I said, "Go for it, baby," and then he got killed. I would have liked for him to have done the play because I think he would have done it very well.

You also worked with Powers Boothe in that film.

Powers was very cool… He had a very strong presence and a great voice. We got along very well and had some good conversations. He had done a little bit of New York theater and was almost a movie star. I always thought he was talented. I saw him in a movie called *The Emerald Forest* where he was a guy running around the Amazon. It was a very good movie, and I was very fascinated with his work in that.

A few years later, you reunited with Boothe on Sudden Death.

I remember we shot *Sudden Death* in Pittsburgh, Pennsylvania, and the best thing about that shoot was that I wrote a play called *Mother'Son* in all of the time I had to languish in my hotel room. I wrote a whole play, and I also saw the Andy Warhol Museum. Those were the two most significant things I accomplished during that shoot. [Director] Peter Hyams is a very nice man, and he hired me because he loved my work in *Born on the Fourth of July*, but my role wasn't terribly interesting. What held that movie together was the editing… Jean-Claude Van Damme had a problem with the acting part of his role and he couldn't pull it off, so they had to cut some scenes. They had a lot of trouble with the film.

You mentioned Dead Man Walking *earlier. Tim Robbins is known primarily for his acting, but what was it like working with him as a director on the film?*

It was great working with Tim. Since he's an actor, he understands what to say to an actor. There was a scene in the movie that I had to read in my audition, and in the audition, I cried. So when we're shooting the scene, I'm trying to cry again, and he comes up to me and says, "Don't cry. I've

Susan Sarandon and Barry in *Dead Man Walking*

got enough crying in this movie." And that freed me… It meant I had no requirements other than to say the words and mean what I said. He was simple and direct and he knew what he was doing. He's very, very smart. The script was brilliant, and all of my scenes were with Susan Sarandon. I love that woman, and when she accepted her Oscar, she thanked me, which I really appreciated. It was a wonderful experience making that film, and I felt good about my work. It was a difficult part to play and there was a lot of dimension to it. I had a great time with it.

One of your films that's developed a cult following over the last few years is Walk Hard: The Dewey Cox Story.

"The wrong kid died!" Guys and kids come up to me and say that to me all of the time. It *has* become a cult film, and it was a good shot in the arm for me to do that. I had a good time with it, and I worked with Margo Martindale, who played my wife. I also worked with Margo on *Dead Man Walking*, I did a crazy film in Mexico with her called *Bobby Z*, and now I'm doing a TV series on FX called *Justified*, and Margo played on that series for a year. I always love working with her… I also enjoyed working with [writer/producer] Judd Apatow and the director, Jake Kasdan. Jake

Barry and John C. Reilly in *Walk Hard: The Dewey Cox Story*

and John C. Reilly fought for me for that role. I did a great reading, but Sony wasn't sure; they wanted Donald Sutherland. What happened was that I had to read again, and they brought the head of Sony down to witness the reading. I'm so naïve about who's who that I didn't even know who the hell she was. I didn't realize what kind of pressure I was under. They tried to break my balls and I didn't even know my balls were being broken, but I did another reading and got the role.

That seems to be a recurring theme with you. People know from the start they want you for a role but you still have to jump through hoops to get it.

Yeah, I'm not a movie star, you know? I work literally *all* the time, non-stop, and I always do a decent job, but I'm not a movie star. That's because I came out here when I was forty-five years old. I missed the "Tom Cruise" period of my life, but I wasn't ready to come out then, so that's neither here nor there. I'll take what I've got, and I'm happy with it. I could have gone in so many different directions but I actually did okay. I can make myself some money and I'm sending my kids through college. I'm pretty proud of that.

Barry and Timothy Olyphant in *Justified*

When you have to audition, what's your process of preparing for it?

I memorize the words and I go through them 100 times letter-perfect, which may take all day. I do that every day until I have the audition, and in the process of going through it 100 times letter-perfect, I begin to understand what the material is about, and I begin to touch the emotional life of the character, *if* there's an emotional life. It's a very simplistic process but it's also a very arduous process as well. Sometimes I don't have to audition… With *Justified*, they just gave it to me. *Lost*, *CSI*, and *NCIS*, they just gave to me. When there's some dialogue going on about who they should cast, like with *Walk Hard*, then they'll bring me in to see how I read.

You mentioned Justified, *which I think is one of the best shows on television.*

I've never seen one episode but I've heard that it's great. I love shooting it, I love the character, I love the people who make it, and I love how I feel on the set. I'm very comfortable and I'm very fond of [writer/producer] Graham Yost and his commitment to the show. I just really like the gig, and I love the prospect of doing this for seven years, maybe even ten. They'll probably have me killed off at some point, but they've kept me on it now for three years and I'm very grateful. Being a regular on *Justified* is a prestigious position to be in. They guarantee eight episodes out of thirteen every season, so it's not only prestigious but it's also a much more profitable situation for me. I really like the job, and I love the fact that everybody responds not only to the series itself but also my work in it. I have no complaints.

In addition to acting, you're also an award-winning playwright. How did that begin?

Jack Black, Kim Gillingham and Barry in *Back When Back Then*

It began when I lived with a woman named Irlene Smith. She's a wonderful poet, we fell in love and we lived together for about seven or eight years in New York City. I had my own theater company which made original plays, and Irlene would write and read her poetry, mainly at the Nuyorican Poets Café in Manhattan. Through her influence, I felt the impulse to write plays and realized that writing was not necessarily only for intellectuals. I saw guys in the barrios of New York City who had eighth-grade educations and had written plays and poetry. Miguel Pinero was nominated for a Pulitzer Prize and he only had an eighth-grade education, and here I was, a graduate of Brown University with a degree in philosophy, and I didn't write. There was something wrong with this picture... I was enmeshed in the bowels of New York theater and I felt it was time to write my own plays, so I did and I've never stopped. It seasoned me as an actor because I used to be afraid to do monologues in front of an audience, so I put a monologue in at the top of every play for me to do so I would overcome that fear. I got used to playing the lead role because I wrote the parts myself. For example, I wrote and played the part of a homophobic father—Jack Black played the son—in a play called *Back When Back Then*. We did it in Ireland, New York, Colorado Springs, Los Angeles, and Portland, Oregon. I travel with my plays all over, and it keeps me tough. Acting requires toughness... You can't show up on a set and not know your lines; you've got to know your words. You can't be afraid of people watching you; you've got to be used to it. Sometimes I work on my plays for three years. I rehearse them five days a week for two hours a day, and it keeps my mind tough. Acting is blue collar work on stage: You get dirty, you get sweaty and there are no retakes.

As a writer, are you ever tempted to tinker with your scenes on a movie or TV script?

No. I am absolutely, unequivocally religious about saying the words that are written. A writer has a unique skill that too often actors think they have, and they don't. Writers are not actors, nor are actors writers. It's a different kind of skill; take it from me, I know what I'm talking about because I do both. Having said that, during the scene in *Born on the Fourth of July* between me and Tom Cruise in the bedroom, I improvised a lot of those words. Things started to happen emotionally and I just couldn't help myself. It was so real... I was crying, my kid was paralyzed, and I just started to talk, and Oliver kept all of it in there.

We've talked about the creative aspects of acting. Is there anything that frustrates you about the business side of the craft?

There's something very profound about being involved in an art form that liberates you as you spend more time doing it, but at the same time, it also eliminates you from role possibilities because of the age factor. I mean, if I wanted to play Hamlet today, I could kick ass, but I'm too freakin' old. It's too bad, but that's the way life is. I'm okay because I can write my own parts in my own plays, but in terms of film and television work, what's going to be in the offing when I'm ninety? Whereas a painter matures and gets better and better and has freedom of choice throughout his career, an actor doesn't have freedom of choice. It's an interesting quandary.

What would you say has been your secret to making a living as an actor?

The way I look and my memory. I have an excellent memory, so I show up very well-prepared. I'm very disciplined… I know how to work and I work really hard. I'm also at the point where I trust myself in my work and I don't have some inner dialogue about, "Should I do this? Is this good? Is it not good?" I make sure I know the lines, I focus on what I'm doing, and I just go out and do it. Also, I don't do drugs and I don't drink. I'm clean, I have a healthy life, and I show up in shape. My advice to people who want to act would be to stay away from the drugs and the booze and write your own material for the stage to keep yourself tough.

The Goodbye Girl (1977)
    Director: Herbert Ross
    Starring: Richard Dreyfuss, Marsha Mason, Quinn Cummings, Paul Benedict
    Writer Neil Simon gives us a different kind of odd couple in this witty romantic comedy. Mason stars as Paula, a former dancer and mother to precocious ten-year-old Lucy (Cummings) who has just been abandoned by her live-in boyfriend. With no job and no money, Paula is forced to share her apartment with Elliot (Dreyfuss), an actor whose quirks and eccentricities drive her crazy. Dreyfuss is at his best and is matched step-for-step by the equally impressive Mason and Cummings. Nominated for five Academy Awards and winner for Best Actor (Dreyfuss).

An Unmarried Woman (1978)
    Director: Paul Mazursky
    Starring: Jill Clayburgh, Alan Bates, Michael Murphy, Cliff Gorman
    Clayburgh delivers the performance of her career as Erica, a content wife and mother whose world is turned upside down when her husband (Murphy) suddenly leaves her for a younger woman. Faced with an uncertain future as a single mom, Erica embarks on a journey of self-discovery that leads her to Saul (Bates), an artist that simultaneously charms and challenges her. Alternately funny, sad, scathing, and heartbreaking, *Woman* is a product of its time that still resonates today. Nominated for three Oscars: Best Picture, Best Screenplay, and Best Actress (Clayburgh).

Year of the Dragon (1985)
   Director: Michael Cimino
   Starring: Mickey Rourke, John Lone, Ariane, Leonard Termo
   New York cop Stanley White (Rourke) is tasked with ending the gang wars in Chinatown. His first target is Joey Tai (Lone), an ambitious crime lord who isn't afraid to get his hands dirty when it comes to keeping his criminal organization profitable. The film is a beautifully shot thriller with some exciting action scenes and intense drama, but Rourke's character is so unlikeable that it's difficult to root for him, making *Dragon* a good movie with a slightly bitter aftertaste.

Out of Bounds (1986)
   Director: Richard Tuggle
   Starring: Anthony Michael Hall, Jenny Wright, Jeff Kober, Glynn Turman
   Iowa farm boy Daryl (Hall) lands in L.A. and mistakenly grabs a satchel full of heroine at the airport baggage carousel belonging to drug dealer Roy (Kober). With Roy *and* the cops in pursuit, Daryl turns to an aspiring actress/waitress named Dizz (Wright) for help. This forgotten relic of the '80s doesn't pretend to be anything more than an adrenalized action/thriller, and on that basis alone it works.

Three for the Road (1987)
   Director: B.W.L. Norton
   Starring: Charlie Sheen, Keri Green, Alan Ruck, Sally Kellerman
   Scattershot teen comedy has a political aide (Sheen) and his best friend (Ruck) enlisted to deliver a senator's rebellious daughter (Green) to a reform school. The cast is capable, but the script is light on laughs and heavy on the "ick" factor. (SPOILER ALERT: Sheen's college-age character professes his love for Green's underage hellion.) Sheen completists may feel compelled to go down this *Road*, but everyone else should take a detour.

Born on the Fourth of July (1989)
   Director: Oliver Stone
   Starring: Tom Cruise, Raymond J. Barry, Caroline Kava, Josh Evans
   Stone's gut-wrenching companion piece to *Platoon* tells the true story of Ron Kovic (Cruise), a gung-ho, all-American teen who enlists to fight in Vietnam. After being wounded and paralyzed during battle, Kovic returns home to find a nation filled with indifference, leading him to re-

think his allegiance to God and country. Cruise is exceptional and really gets to show his range, but Willem Dafoe steals his scenes in a small role as another disabled vet. Nominated for eight Oscars and winner for Best Director and Best Editing.

Rapid Fire (1992)
Director: Dwight H. Little
Starring: Brandon Lee, Powers Boothe, Nick Mancuso, Raymond J. Barry

After witnessing a murder, mild-mannered art student Jake (Lee) is not only trapped in the middle of a drug war but is also the target of corrupt cops who are supposed to be protecting him. With no one to trust and nothing to lose, Jake decides to take matters into his own hands. Yes, you've already seen this movie a thousand times before, but *Rapid* rises above genre mediocrity thanks to Lee and the solid supporting cast.

Dead Man Walking (1995)
Director: Tim Robbins
Starring: Susan Sarandon, Sean Penn, Robert Prosky, Raymond J. Barry

Sister Helen Prejean (Sarandon) is asked to visit Matthew Poncelet (Penn), a convicted killer on Death Row. As his execution date draws near, the nun finds a connection to the lost soul and becomes his spiritual advisor, much to the dismay of the victims' families. *Dead Man Walking* is a powerful and moving film, tackling the hot-button issue of capital punishment and giving equal weight to both sides of the story. Nominated for four Academy Awards and winner for Best Actress (Sarandon).

Sudden Death (1995)
Director: Peter Hyams
Starring: Jean-Claude Van Damme, Powers Boothe, Raymond J. Barry, Whittni Wright

"*Die Hard* on ice" has Van Damme as a fire marshal who brings his kids to a playoff hockey game where the vice president (Barry) is taken hostage by a disgruntled ex-Secret Service agent (Boothe) who threatens to blow up the stadium unless his financial demands are met. With reliable director Hyams at the helm and Boothe exuding his patented blend of charm and menace, *Sudden Death* ranks as one of Jean-Claude's better cinematic efforts.

The Chamber (1996)
Director: James Foley
Starring: Chris O'Donnell, Gene Hackman, Faye Dunaway, Robert Prosky

Based on the novel by John Grisham, *The Chamber* focuses on an idealistic lawyer named Adam (O'Donnell) who takes on the case of his grandfather, Sam Cayhall (Hackman), a racist inmate convicted of murder awaiting his execution. With time running out and pressure mounting from the state governor and members of the Ku Klux Klan, Adam must unravel the mystery surrounding the killings in order to save Sam's life. Hackman is excellent (as usual) and gets terrific support from an impressive ensemble.

Interview with the Assassin (2002)
Director: Neil Burger
Starring: Raymond J. Barry, Dylan Haggerty, Renee Faia, Kelsey Kemper

Ron (Haggerty) is an unemployed TV cameraman whose neighbor, Walter (Barry), approaches him with a startling claim: Walter was the gunman on the grassy knoll who killed JFK. Intrigued but understandably skeptical, Ron agrees to document Walter's story, which leads them on a journey for the truth that ultimately alters both of their lives. This overlooked and absorbing drama features a captivating "what if" scenario brought to life by Barry's mesmerizing performance.

Bobby Z (2007)
Director: John Herzfeld
Starring: Paul Walker, Laurence Fishburne, Olivia Wilde, Jason Flemyng

Deliriously dense and off-kilter action flick has Tim (Walker), a three-time loser facing life in prison, being offered a chance at freedom by a DEA agent (Fishburne). All Tim has to do is impersonate a deceased drug dealer named Bobby Z during a hostage swap, which goes horribly wrong. Left to fend for himself, Tim must outrun a drug lord's henchmen, the feds *and* a biker gang (don't ask), all the while trying to protect the real Bobby Z's young son. Although it was unceremoniously sent straight to video, the movie is better than a lot of bloated Hollywood junk littering the multiplexes.

Walk Hard: The Dewey Cox Story (2007)
Director: Jake Kasdan
Starring: John C. Reilly, Tim Meadows, Jenna Fischer, Raymond J. Barry

Hilarious parody of music biopics stars Reilly as the titular Dewey Cox, a singing sensation who, over the course of fifty years, travels the well-worn road of success, temptation, loss, despair, and redemption. The humor isn't for everyone, but those who get it will find *Walk Hard*'s combination of big laughs, catchy tunes, and a talented cast led by Reilly worthy of multiple viewings.

Stephen Root

Stephen Root has been a fixture on movie and TV screens for nearly three decades, but he is perhaps best known for two roles: Billionaire station owner Jimmy James on the sitcom *NewsRadio*, and stapler-obsessed Milton in the cubicle cult classic *Office Space*. Instead of making a career out of playing variations of those characters, Root deliberately sought out new challenges, including portraying a gay vampire (*True Blood*), a maverick judge (*Justified*), and a real-life forensic expert (*J. Edgar*). Blessed with the luxury of being able to pick and choose the projects he works on, Root continues to successfully defy audience expectations.

How did you get your start in acting?

I went to the University of Florida, and as a freshman, I didn't know what I was going to do. I just picked journalism, but by the end of my second year, I realized that it wasn't for me. I took an elective class in directing and I kind of got the bug from there. I started taking acting classes, I switched majors, and that was the start.

Aside from college, did you ever have any professional training or was it all learn as you go?

It was learn as you go. The first job I got out of college was with the National Shakespeare Company, a bus-and-truck based in New York City. We went to colleges, junior colleges, and different venues all around the country for nine months out of the year. It was a twelve-person company, we did three Shakespeare plays, we were triple-casting each show, and we did all of the sound and lighting and everything. That was my training… Three years of Shakespeare on the road, and it was all learning on the go. After that, everything else seemed pretty easy!

Monkey Shines

Did you have to do any day jobs while trying to make it as an actor?

I did the requisite bartending and waiting tables. I had a couple of temp jobs… I was in the membership department of the Natural History Museum for a summer. Mostly though, to really pay the rent, it was bartending and waiting tables while I did free shows down below Fourteenth Street in New York trying to get an Equity card and continue upward from there.

Your first movie was George Romero's Monkey Shines. *How did you get involved with that?*

I had finally been doing some off-Broadway stuff and a couple of Broadway shows by then, and I was also doing commercials, so I was known by a lot of casting directors in New York at that time. It was a straight audition for Romero, and the casting director said, "They don't know that you haven't done film work yet, so you *have* to promise me that you won't say anything about it." I said, "Okay… I won't lie, but I won't say anything." That first movie was very much a learning experience for me. I didn't know anything about it other than what I'd seen on commercial shoots, which is a different kind of thing.

Was it difficult making the transition from acting on stage to acting in front of cameras?

Oh, sure, I think it is for everyone that comes from stage. On stage, you're playing to the back of the house and on camera you're playing "real"… as real as you can get. Even if you're a big character in terms of personality and speech, you've got to play it small and real. It took several years of doing that and beating myself over the head and saying, "Stop *acting!*" before I got past it. Whether it's stage or film or TV, you're going through central truth in a character. You just have to vary the level of your face and the projection of your performance. It took me a while to learn to knock it down a few notches for the cameras.

What was it like working with Romero?

He was a nice guy. At that point, George had already done a lot of his really good movies, and he was kind of on the decline in terms of getting support from the studio. My character ended up being the villain of the piece, and I remember the ending being different. We shot something where the monkeys were eating my bleeding flesh that never made it on to the screen, but I think he was trying for a sequel, as most people try to do. I have a singular memory of him when I was doing a scene where I was opening a door. I was so new to it that when I was opening the door, I'm not sure if it was too fast for him or too slow, but he said, "Just open the frickin' door!" That's the kind of stuff that you learn.

Your early work in TV covers a lot of genres: Sitcoms, crime dramas, sci-fi, even a Western. Was it a coincidence that you did such varied work or was it deliberate to seek out different kinds of roles to avoid being typecast?

It was deliberate later. After I had done *NewsRadio*, all I got was sitcom offers, so I stopped taking them and only took film and hour dramatic offers, but that was later on. When you're first thrown into L.A., you've got to build a resumé with whatever job you can get. Even with Broadway, and off-Broadway, and many regional theaters on my resumé from New York, it counted for nothing here in L.A., so you have to start at the bottom, and the bottom is sitcoms and hour dramatics and whatever else you can come up with. The first couple of years I was here, there were a lot

Root (center) and the cast of *NewsRadio*

of times when I was having three auditions a day. Fortunately, I booked some and started to build my resumé.

Speaking of NewsRadio, *Jimmy James was kind of your breakout role. How did you get involved with the show?*

It was a straight audition. They were actually looking for an older actor—somebody in their fifties—to be like Mr. Carlson from *WKRP*. I wasn't in that age range, so I kind of fought to get the audition because I wanted to do my version of that character, which was bent… I didn't want you to know whether he was an idiot or an idiot savant. I came in with that plan, [creator] Paul Simms liked it, and we worked on that for the network audition and the studio audition. We just kept going in that direction and by the time I got to the end, I don't think there were any other Jimmy's left—it was just me. By the time I did my last audition, I felt very secure in that character.

I assume the financial security that came with it was pretty important at that point in your career.

Absolutely! I had a wife and kid, and to have a steady job is the goal when you first get out here. I had done a series a few years before that called *Harts of the West*, and it was an hour dramatic shot way out in Antelope Valley—it wasn't like a downtown Hollywood shoot. That show only lasted a season, so with *NewsRadio*, it was nice to have that security for that long of time and be so close to home. In the middle of *NewsRadio*, I got *King of the Hill*, which started out as a small show and then got much bigger over a couple of years. Financially, that was very beneficial as well.

How did you get involved with King of the Hill?

[Creator] Mike Judge got a hold of me because he knew I'd done a lot of Southern plays and Southern characters. He wanted me to audition but he didn't know what for. I auditioned for Dale but I didn't feel good with it, so then I auditioned for Bill, and that one felt right. Voiceover work is a hard circle to break into, and *King of the Hill* really opened the door for me to do a lot of film work in things like *Ice Age* and *Finding Nemo*. Once you've done voices in three or four movies, the door opens a bit and you get offers for smaller things like Saturday morning cartoons. It's fun to do, but breaking into it is tough.

Since you were already working with Mike Judge on King of the Hill, *did he just offer you the role of Milton in* Office Space?

Strangely, I had to really fight for that role. When we were doing the table read at Fox to see if they wanted to do it, I read the Bobs, I read the hypnotist who dies, and I read one other role. Mike was going to read Milton, but he decided he'd rather listen to it instead of doing it himself, so he gave me very short preparation to read Milton. He showed me the two-minute pencil-sketch video that he'd done for MTV where he did the voice, so he already had an idea of what he wanted to do. I looked at it and told him I wanted to take it farther than that and give him

Office Space

a lisp. That's what I did at the table read, and then I still had to audition after that to actually get the role. At that point in time, I was a TV name but not a movie name.

When it came time to make the movie, did you stick with what you had done in the audition or did you continue to work on the character prior to filming?

Mike liked what I had done in the audition, so then I just started working in that direction. By the time I actually got the role, he was happy with what I was doing. When we were making it, he would give us direction on some specific things but he also let us improvise as well. All of us would throw in our own stuff, and some of it got in and some of it didn't. It was a pretty tightly-scripted movie but there are a lot of good improvs that made it into the film.

Given the variety of work you've done before Office Space *and after, does it bother you that people so closely identify you with Milton?*

No. It was weird for a while because that's all people saw, and you want them to realize that you can do other things. I'm very happy that they like that character and liked my work in the movie, but I also did *The West Wing*, you know? As an actor, it was a little frustrating from a casting point of view because I got offered a lot of weirdo roles, some of which I took and some I didn't. They wanted me to do Milton seven more times, and I wasn't interested in doing that over and over again. For me, variety is the whole point of being a character actor, and I try not to repeat myself, even though sometimes you can't help it. So it was frustrating for a little while but it's heartening now because every couple of years, a new generation of eighteen- and nineteen-year-olds discovers the movie. I think as long as those types of cubicle jobs exist, the movie will continue to be relevant.

You've done so many guest appearances on popular series like 24, True Blood *and* Justified. *When you're cast for a guest role, do you make a point of becoming familiar with the show beforehand or do you just go in and do it?*

I make a point of telling my representation which shows I would be interested in doing. *True Blood* was a great challenge because I was outside of my comfort zone. My wife and I were already big fans of *24*, so that was fun to do. At this stage in my career, what's fun for me is to do TV arcs and then films, then arcs and then films. That's more interesting to me than doing one show, although I might be doing a show for FX called *Outlaw Country*. It's a pilot at the moment, so whether it gets picked up or not one never knows, but I like that network. I did *Justified* for them, and I think the head of that network, John Landgraf, is one of the smartest guys

24

around. I had done a pilot with him years ago that didn't go, but I was very happy to hear he was the head of a network. He's smart and he's good.

Your first movie with the Coen brothers was O Brother, Where Art Thou? *How did that come about?*

That was just another straight audition. I think they knew of my work but I didn't know them, so I just went in and scared them! I rolled my eyes and got the role. They're my favorites to work with. I love them, and anything they want me to do is just fine with me. They're just really easy to work for and I have an enormous amount of respect for all of their films. Some of them don't work, but it doesn't matter because they're all interesting.

When you did Leatherheads *and* The Men Who Stare at Goats *with George Clooney, did those come about because of your work with him on* O Brother?

Yeah. George and I developed a relationship on that, and he said, "We'll find something to do in the future." I was like, "Okay, that's great," and it turned out to be *Leatherheads*. We had a great time on that, and he was a terrific director. Later on, he called me for a very short role in *Goats*. He said, "Do you want to come to Puerto Rico for a couple of days and shoot?" I said, "Okay," and that was a fun little thing to do. I'm hoping to work with him in the future. George and the Coens use a lot of the same people on their films, and I'd be very happy to be included in anything they do.

O Brother, Where Art Thou?

Justified

How important would you say relationships are to sustaining an acting career?

I think they're *very* important. I have an ongoing relationship with Mike Judge, the Coens, George and Kevin Smith, and I've worked with them enough that when a role comes to mind they think I might be right for, they'll give me a call. I don't have to audition for them and I don't have to compete for it. As an actor, it's the best situation to be in. Plus, I get to work with people I really respect and enjoy being around. You can't ask for much more than that.

You mentioned Kevin Smith as a director you have a relationship with. How did you get involved with his film, Jersey Girl?

Kevin just asked me to do it. He was a fan of *NewsRadio* and still is, God bless him. He told me he takes the DVDs with him when he goes on tour, which is very cool. What I liked was that he let me define the character. He asked me, "What do you want to do with him?" I said, "I want him to be the guy who says the most obvious thing. If the sky is blue, I want him to say, 'It's really blue up there.'" And that's what Kevin let me do. I know *Jersey Girl* is a much-maligned film, but I thought it was a cute little comedy, plus I got to work with George Carlin.

I was going to ask you about Carlin.

Oh, he was great. He was very professional and personable, and I remember he would come out, do his scene, and then he'd go back and lock himself in his trailer and write. He'd work on material for his stand-up shows in-between scenes, and he was very disciplined about doing that. But he was so much fun to be around... I remember one day, he gave me one of his books and signed it, "Fuck you. George." That was great!

What can you tell me about your role in Smith's horror film, Red State*?*

I play a Southern sheriff along with John Goodman, who is really great in the movie. It's an "ecumenical horror film," as Kevin calls it, and it's about these church people that you see on TV that protest at soldiers' funerals and things like that. It's not a horror film in the conventional sense, but it's a different take on people who do some pretty bad things. I think it's actually the best script Kevin's written, and I think it's his first grown-up movie. The cast is amazing... Goodman, Melissa Leo, Kevin Pollak, and Michael Parks are all fantastic. I'm really proud to be included with those actors, and I think the film is tremendous.

Red State

Is there a particular project or role you're really proud of that you wished had gotten more of an audience?

Well, there are several movies I would've liked to have not been cut out of! I had five scenes in *White Oleander*, and they took place in the story *before* the story that starts the movie. At one point, the movie was three hours long, so I understand why they cut it, but I thought I did some good work in that. *The Soloist* was another one... I played an *L.A. Times* reporter

Armie Hammer, Leonardo DiCaprio and Root in *J. Edgar*

and got to work with my pal Catherine Keener, but most of my stuff got cut, and rightly so after I saw the movie. That's just the way it goes sometimes.

You've portrayed real-life people like John Lloyd in The Conspirator *and Arthur Koehler in* J. Edgar. *What kind of research do you do when playing a real person?*

When I play characters based on real people, I'll go on the internet and see what I can find out about them. Even if I don't have a physical resemblance to them, I'll try and look for any traits they might have had, like a limp or something. John Lloyd was a drunk and didn't take care of himself, so I used that. Arthur Koehler was the wood expert who basically convicted Bruno Hauptmann of the kidnapping of the Lindbergh baby, and there was a lot of information out there about him that I looked at.

Steve Buscemi and Root in *Boardwalk Empire*

It's all about feeling comfortable in that person's skin, and that's true of whether or not the character is real or fictional. You look for whatever you can use to bring the person to life.

You've done films with a lot of directors who are also actors, like Robert Redford, Clint Eastwood and George Clooney. Is there a benefit for you in working with people who have experience on both sides of the camera?

Yeah, absolutely. As directors, those guys are true artists and they know what they want, but as actors, they also know there's value in experimenting and playing around, and they know good things can come from that. Plus, there's a shorthand that we share. George might be explaining a scene and he'll say, "Go ahead and do that one thing you did," and I'll immediately know what he's talking about. The best directors, whether they're actors or not, are the ones that trust you. When a director trusts that you're prepared and able to do the material at the level they're expecting, it makes you rise to the challenge of meeting their expectations.

You mentioned earlier about being selective with the projects you choose. What do you look for when deciding whether or not to do one?

A great director and a great script. I'm tired of trying to spin straw into gold with bad scripts. I did that for years in the theater when I was starting out, so now it's all about a superlative script. I've been very fortunate in this business to get to the point where I have the luxury of being able to pick and choose what I do. It doesn't happen very often for character actors—or even actors in general—and I'm very grateful to have that opportunity, so I try not to waste it.

What frustrates you the most about the business aspects of acting?

The reporting of residuals continues to amaze me… The studios supposedly track whenever something airs, and you have no choice but to take them at their word. They'll say, "Oh, such and such aired four times." It might've actually aired twenty times, but how do you know? I think there should be some kind of outside agency that monitors that. We're in a brand new age, and I think eventually everything will be available at the push of a button. Somebody will want to watch a show from 1973 and—BAM!—they're instantly watching it. I'm not sure if actors can afford to trust the studios to accurately report that information. For me, that's probably the most frustrating part of the business side.

What advice would you give to aspiring actors?

Don't do it! Seriously, don't do it. Don't do it for the fame and certainly don't do it for the money. Ninety-eight percent of SAG members are unemployed at any given time. It's hard work to get a job, and once that job's done, then you've got to get *another* job. Do you feel like waking up every day and trying to find a job? I'm a sixty-year-old man and that's what I do; I wake up every day and try to find a job. If you don't want to do that, then acting isn't for you. If, however, you feel as though you absolutely *have* to act, then put all of your heart and soul into it and go for it.

Monkey Shines (1988)
    Director: George A. Romero
    Starring: Jason Beghe, John Pankow, Kate McNeil, Joyce Van Patten
    Beghe stars as Allan, a man whose life is changed in an instant when an accident renders him a quadriplegic. His scientist friend, Geoffrey (Pankow), gives Allan a helper monkey named Ella to assist with Allan's needs, but unbeknownst to Allan, the animal has been injected with a serum to make Ella smarter. This produces an unintended side-effect where Ella is able to read Allan's mind and act out his vengeful thoughts against those who have wronged him. This enjoyable thriller benefits greatly from terrific performances by a strong cast.

Office Space (1999)
    Director: Mike Judge
    Starring: Ron Livingston, Jennifer Aniston, David Herman, Stephen Root

Peter (Livingston) is a complacent corporate drone at a software firm who hates his job. After a botched session of hypnotherapy, he approaches work with a carefree and defiant attitude that inspires his equally unhappy co-workers while drawing the ire of his boss (Cole). *Office Space* is flat-out funny, but anyone who has spent time in nine-to-five cubicle hell will especially appreciate the finer details writer/director Judge pokes fun at.

O Brother, Where Art Thou? (2000)
Director: Joel Coen
Starring: George Clooney, John Turturro, Tim Blake Nelson, John Goodman
Typically quirky—and utterly delightful—film from the Coen brothers tells the story of Everett (Clooney), Pete (Turturro), and Delmar (Nelson), newly-escaped convicts in the 1930s South who embark on a journey to Everett's home in order to retrieve some buried treasure. Along the way, the trio encounters a variety of obstacles, including an evil Bible salesman (Goodman), a mystical lawman and the Ku Klux Klan. One of the Coens' most underrated efforts. Nominated for two Academy Awards: Best Screenplay and Best Cinematography.

Ice Age (2002)
Directors: Chris Wedge, Carlos Saldanha
Starring: Ray Romano, John Leguizamo, Denis Leary, Goran Visnjic
A wooly mammoth named Manfred (Romano) reluctantly teams up with Sid (Leguizamo), an overbearing sloth, to return a lost baby to his human tribe. The two are joined by Diego (Leary), a saber-toothed tiger, who offers to help while concealing his true agenda. The story is as old as its prehistoric characters, but *Ice Age* is still an entertaining romp that will appeal to kids and adults of all ages. Oscar-nominated for Best Animated Feature.

Finding Nemo (2003)
Directors: Andrew Stanton, Lee Unkrich
Starring: Albert Brooks, Ellen DeGeneres, Alexander Gould, Willem Dafoe
Pixar hits another home run with this fish tale about an overprotective father (Brooks) searching for his young son (Gould) after the boy is caught by a fisherman and placed in an aquarium. Beautifully animated, smartly written, and wonderfully acted (DeGeneres is a standout as Brooks's scatterbrained traveling companion), *Nemo* is destined to be

a family classic for generations to come. Nominated for four Academy Awards and winner for Best Animated Feature.

Jersey Girl (2004)
   Director: Kevin Smith
   Starring: Ben Affleck, George Carlin, Raquel Castro, Stephen Root
   Ollie (Affleck) is a hot-shot New York PR guy who becomes an unemployed single father. With nowhere else to go, Ollie moves in with his dad (Carlin) and struggles to raise his daughter (Castro) while trying to get his career back on track. *Girl* reps a nice change of pace for writer/director Smith, who tells a genuinely sweet and funny story with characters who are believable and sympathetic.

Leatherheads (2008)
   Director: George Clooney
   Starring: George Clooney, John Krasinski, Renee Zellweger, Stephen Root
   Dodge Connelly (Clooney), a player in the early days of pro football, is watching the upstart league collapse around him. A former college-star-turned-war-hero named Carter Rutherford (Krasinski) comes home to massive adoration, and Dodge gets the idea that having Carter play will boost attendance at the games. Meanwhile, a reporter (Zellweger) starts digging around to find out if Carter's heroic tale is real or exaggerated. This screwball comedy is pure fun from beginning to end.

The Men Who Stare at Goats (2009)
   Director: Grant Heslov
   Starring: George Clooney, Ewan McGregor, Jeff Bridges, Kevin Spacey
   Bob (McGregor) is a reporter in Iraq who meets Lyn (Clooney), a member of a covert military group of psychics led by a hippie commander (Bridges) who longs for a more peaceful, non-lethal style of combat. Although the movie is supposedly based on real events, *Men*'s satirical approach to the material hits the mark thanks to impeccable work from a stellar cast.

The Soloist (2009)
   Director: Joe Wright
   Starring: Robert Downey Jr., Jamie Foxx, Catherine Keener, Tom Hollander

Struggling *Los Angeles Times* columnist Steve Lopez (Downey Jr.) finds inspiration when he meets Nathaniel Ayers (Foxx), a homeless man with a gift for making music. Lopez digs deeper into Ayers' background and discovers a man who trained at Juilliard but dropped out due to issues with schizophrenia. There are moments where *The Soloist* threatens to veer into mawkish movie-of-the-week territory, but the dynamic performances of Foxx and Downey Jr. make this true-life tale hard to resist.

The Conspirator (2010)
Director: Robert Redford
Starring: James McAvoy, Robin Wright, Kevin Kline, Evan Rachel Wood

Captivating film tells the story of Mary Surratt (Wright), the owner of a boarding house where John Wilkes Booth stayed while plotting the assassination of Abraham Lincoln. When the country demands justice for its fallen president, Surratt is brought to trial and represented by a lawyer (McAvoy) who has doubts about the innocence of his client. The resolution to this mystery might be found in history books, but director Redford has made *The Conspirator* a riveting lesson worth learning.

J. Edgar (2011)
Director: Clint Eastwood
Starring: Leonardo DiCaprio, Judi Dench, Armie Hammer, Naomi Watts

Sprawling biography of J. Edgar Hoover (DiCaprio), from his days as a lowly Justice Department flunky to his creation of the FBI, the agency he controlled for nearly fifty years. Always relentless in his pursuit for justice and keeping Americans safe, Hoover also became arrogant and paranoid, leading him to keep private files on some of the most powerful people in the country. DiCaprio gives a commanding performance with excellent support from Dench as his domineering mother, and Hammer as his lifelong companion.

Red State (2011)
Director: Kevin Smith
Starring: Michael Angarano, Nicholas Braun, Kyle Gallner, Michael Parks

Three teen boys (Angarano, Braun, Gallner) responding to a woman's online sex ad are drugged and abducted by a church group led by the radical preacher Abin Cooper (Parks). Soon after, federal agents arrive at the scene, leading to a tense standoff between the heavily armed parishioners and the authorities. Writer/director Smith, who normally specializes in stoner/slacker comedy, reinvents himself with this lean, disturbing thriller.

Tony Todd

Tony Todd is no stranger to mainstream audiences, having appeared in such successful movies and TV shows as *Platoon*, *The Rock*, and *24*. However, he is perhaps best known for his work in the sci-fi and horror genres thanks to memorable roles in three *Star Trek* series and the *Final Destination*, *Hatchet*, and *Candyman* franchises. Refusing to rest on his past accomplishments, Todd continues to challenge himself as an artist by performing in the theater and writing and producing his own film projects, with an eye firmly focused on sitting in the director's chair. Folks can learn about upcoming projects from the man himself on Facebook and Twitter.

How did you get your start in acting?

I discovered it when I was in high school. I was a member of the Boy Scouts of America, and the Scoutmaster thought I might be good at public speaking. He started writing speeches for me, which I did at different chapters all over the Northeast sector, and I really liked it. I was kind of shy, and that helped bring me out of my shell. After doing that, I returned to high school and tried out for a couple of dramatic projects. I got one and that was it, that's when I got the bug. After that I went to college, got my master's, I taught for a while, did some bartending in New York… I paid my dues and did a lot of theater, and everything kind of took off from there.

One of the first films you worked on was Platoon. *How did you get your role?*

That came as a direct result of putting time in and working in New York. I was doing a one-man show called *Johnny Got His Gun* by Dalton Trumbo, and Oliver Stone's people caught a production. They called me in for an audition, and the next thing you know, I'm cast. I was literally jumping in the street like *Singing in the Rain* because it was raining when I got the call. [President Ferdinand] Marcos had just left the country, and the woman who raised me—my aunt—didn't want me to go because she felt it was too dangerous. I told her, "I'll get insurance," and she said, "I don't want insurance, I want you." I said, "I've got to go, I'm not gonna turn down a movie." It was a great project to enter the business with because

Todd and Franklyn Seales in *No Place to Be Somebody*

Platoon

Oliver is such an intense visionary, and he knew what he wanted. We had to go through a four-week boot camp. It was like a theatrical rehearsal for me, but it was the real deal. I remember I literally didn't change my clothes for three weeks. We slept on the ground, and every night they'd set up fake air raids that we had to respond to. I think being in the Boy Scouts helped me to deal with the naturalistic elements, and I was a sergeant in the movie, which had some perks like sharing little airline whiskey bottles with the great Dale Dye as he told me how to instill fear into my men. It was an awesome experience and a great cast to work with.

After Platoon, *you appeared in* Colors, *which was directed by Dennis Hopper, and* Bird, *directed by Clint Eastwood. What was it like working with those men on the other side of the camera?*

Those guys are icons to me. They had already spent years in the business and had great success, and they were both very gracious. The best directors are comfortable in their vision, and they do their best to make sure the actor is comfortable. When the actor is comfortable and relaxed, he can dig deeper into his psyche to fully realize the character. Of course, there are tyrannical directors who like to shake your gourd, but I've learned how to work and relate to both types, so it's all good. I also acted with Dennis in a forgotten film called *Sunset Heat*, so I got to watch him do his thing. And it was Clint who told me, "You're gonna go far." They both taught me that if you always be yourself and find the truth in the dialogue and the character, then you'll be fine.

Candyman

One of the roles you're best known for is playing the title character in the Candyman *series. How did you get involved with the original film?*

I had done a film in Africa called *The Last Elephant* with James Earl Jones, Isabella Rossellini, and John Lithgow. [Director] Bernard Rose saw me in it and said, "That's the face I want for the role." I remember getting a call from my agent saying, "Somebody wants to cast you in a film called *Candyman*." I said, "Are you kidding me? What is that, the Sammy Davis Jr. story?" He said, "No, I'm serious. It's a cutting-edge new horror movie." I never had to audition but I had to meet with the studio execs and Virginia Madsen. Everything went smooth, and the next thing I know, I was in training, which consisted of me and Virginia doing horseback classes together, ballroom dancing, fencing lessons—all of that romantic, turn-of-the-century stuff—to get in the right mindset.

When the movie became a hit, was it an easy decision for you to come back and do the sequels?

Well, because I was a young actor, I had to sign a block deal for the three films. I didn't get as much money necessarily as I could today, but it was more money than I had ever seen in my life. Not only was I happy and more content, but I knew that I was more secure. And around that time, I was also working on the *Star Trek* stuff. It's a tough business, but for the first time in my life, I felt financially secure enough to call myself an actor.

You're credited as a co-producer on the third film, Candyman: Day of the Dead. *How did that come about?*

That was more of a vanity contract. I knew that ultimately, down the line, I wanted to be able to produce and direct my own projects, so that was just a way of getting that credit out there initially, and I still intend to cash in on that. I will say that I was happier with the first two installments than I was with the third. I did, however, come up with some of the backstory of Candyman, the fact that he was an artist. That was my contribution to the creation of the character.

You've said in the past that playing Candyman changed your life for better and for worse. Can you elaborate?

Candyman: Farewell to the Flesh

Well, it was good in that it gave me visibility. I didn't know at the time that it would have such a lasting impact. To this day, people still react to me as if I am that character, which is surprising because I've done quite a few things since then. So, I know now how *permanent* film is. There was a minute where I was really worried because I would get a lot of scripts where I was the bad guy, and I'd get a lot of horror films that weren't necessarily very good. That was the bad part, but I've been able to shake that up by being able to return to the stage. I've been able to do Broadway and great regional theater, which lets directors see me in a completely different light. I'd say one out of every three things I get offered is a horror or sci-fi project, and I respect the genres—I'm not ashamed of them. I just want to do really good ones.

The Rock was your first big-budget Hollywood film. How would you compare it to working on some of the smaller-budgeted movies you had done?

The Rock

It was fantastic! Four months in San Francisco working with Ed Harris, Sean Connery, Nicholas Cage... [Director] Michael Bay wasn't as big then as he is now, but he knew who he was and what he could do. On an independent film, you might shoot seven or eight pages a day. On a big-budget film, you shoot two pages a day... and you eat really, *really* well! You also have lots of toys too. Michael had all of these different cameras and lenses at his beck and call, and I've been on independent shoots where all we had was one HD camera. I know the value of both big-budget and independent films, and I appreciate both types. *The Rock* is one I'm very proud of.

One of the films you've done that has a very devoted following is The Man from Earth. *How did you get involved with that?*

The Man from Earth was written by Jerome Bixby, one of the greatest sci-fi writers in history, and it was the script that drew me to the film. Even though it was very little money, what appealed to me is that we were shooting it theatrically—in other words, it was shot in sequence on basically one set. It was a very rewarding project, and I thought the story was a great story. I know that of the people that have seen it, most of them really

The Man from Earth

enjoyed it, and I'm surprised there hasn't been a television deal for it yet. I know they tried to sell it to the History Channel, and they passed, then they pitched it to Syfy, and they said it was too highbrow. I know eventually it'll happen, but until you get into that market, we're missing a huge block of the population. It's just a great story without any special effects, and it works. I love it.

I do too. You mentioned shooting it theatrically... Did you approach it and prepare for it like you would a play?

Yes and no. It was definitely scripted like a play because it was very verbal, and most of the actors we had came from theatrical backgrounds. In theater, the scripts tend to be better because they tend to be more about the human condition. You also have four-to-six weeks to rehearse the material, spending six hours a day getting to know your cast and your character. Then you add the costumes and sets, and everything comes to life when you bring in the most important element: The audience. You also tend to be a little bigger in theater because you're playing to the last row. Film is a different medium... I remember when I did *The Last Elephant*, the director of photography told me, "If you think the emotion, the camera will find it." I love doing them both, and I try to bring a little bit of my theatrical training to film, depending on how much time you have after getting cast. You have to do certain background work like who the character is, in what ways are you like the character, how are you not like the character, things you want or things you want from the other characters around you, how the character feels about himself and his relationship to the world... If you can get those things, it doesn't matter whether the genre is sci-fi, or a thriller, or a comedy. It's all relative because you're trying to create a human being.

You're the only actor to play two different characters on the show 24. *How did that happen?*

Well, the writers on *24* tend to write off-the-cuff. They have a bible and they know what the overview is, but they don't always know all of the details, and I was really disappointed to learn I was only going to be in one episode that first time around. Anyway, I was just finishing up a movie in Wickenburg, Arizona called *The Graves*, and I got a call from my agent saying the producers wanted to speak to me about *24*. I told him, "I al-

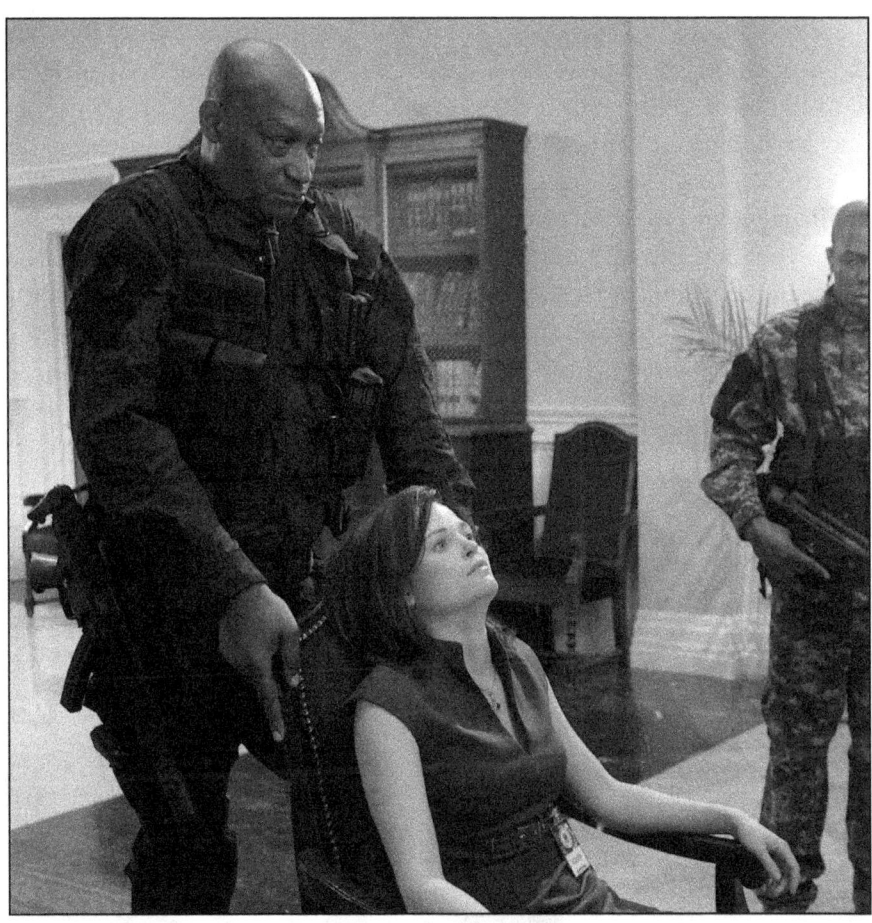

Todd and Sprague Grayden in *24*

ready did it. I thought they didn't use the same people twice," and he said, "They're having some issues." So I went in to meet with Howard Gordon, who wrote an episode of *The X-Files* I was in called "Sleepless," so he and I already had a connection. The next thing I know, I was on a plane to South Africa shooting the stuff for the TV movie, *24: Redemption*, and then invading the White House, which was a very cool thing to do. Working with Cherry Jones was incredible, and I was very happy when she got the Emmy. And let's not forget Jon Voight… I had to tell Jon that one of the first movies that really, really made an impact on me was *Midnight Cowboy*. He told me some stories about that, and it was very cool.

Do you ever get starstruck working with other people you admire?

I used to… I'm a big music fan, and when I first came out to L.A., I pulled up at a stoplight, I looked over and there's Smokey Robinson driving a Rolls Royce right next to me. I was like, "Whoooa… That's Smokey-fuckin'-Robinson!" I'm not jaded yet, so if I met [Martin] Scorsese this afternoon, I'd certainly give him props. I let people know when I respect their talent and their accomplishments. A person's history is everything to me, but how they are as a human being is just as important. Sometimes you can meet your heroes and they disappoint you. I won't mention any names but it can happen, and I try to keep that perspective in mind. I hope when people meet me they're not disappointed.

You're going to be making your writing and directing debut with a movie called Eerie, PA. *What's the film about?*

Star Trek: The Next Generation

Hatchet II

When I said that *Midnight Cowboy* is one of my inspirations, *Eerie, PA* is a direct tribute to that film. It's a non-horror buddy film about two bookies that have seventy-two hours to raise a certain amount of money or else they're going to be dispatched. It's a test of their loyalty to each other and a test of thirty years' friendship and what they have to do to survive. I went to the Eerie Horror Film Festival and just fell in love with the visual quality of the city. It's a dinosaur where you can see the history of when steel was king and the railroads were titans, and yet there are people still there struggling to maintain their livelihood and respect and finding ways to do that. Plus, it's really something how the city embraces sports with such passion. I'm a huge sports nut—basketball, football, baseball—so I can relate to that. We had half of the money set up and then the economy went south, so we're on a little bit of a hold right now, but the movie *will* get made.

Have you always wanted to write and direct or are these relatively new interests for you?

Well, I actually did more writing and directing in school than I did acting. I also have one horror script that I'm writing and another horror script that I'm developing with another producer. Even though this will be my first feature, I know how to talk to actors, and I'm gonna hire a great director of photography so he can cover the technical aspects. I may not know exactly what the name of the lens is that I need, but I know what I want to see, so I'll work with somebody who knows all of that and who has an understanding of the Asian film style because I like that way of looking at the world. Between that and casting—which, as they say, is eighty percent of the struggle in any film—it'll be perfect and it'll be riveting. As I'm going into the next part of my career, I want to do more directing and writing and have more control of the content.

When it comes to financing, has it been difficult trying to raise the money since you're a first-time director?

No, it all has to do with the economy. Years ago, everybody was investing in films because they saw it as a sure bet to make a profit. Today, because of the economy and because certain things didn't make money, there's something like $12 billion less available in funding. Unfortunately, the first ones to lose out are the independent projects, which are ultimately the most creative. I mean, some of the movies in the wind at the big studios are based on games like Battleship and Candy Land. What's next, *Posturepedic: The Mattress Movie*? But that's another side of Hollywood... The side I want to work on is the independent, creative stuff. I know that somewhere out there, there's somebody who wasn't so acutely affected by the loss of wealth that they can feel comfortable with endowing the arts. I'm gonna get it done one way or the other, even if I have to do it with my own money.

You've worked extensively in theater, films, and television. Do you have a favorite?

I love them all, I really do. There's an old adage that movies buy the house, TV buys the furniture, and theater supplies the soul, and there's a lot of truth in that. If I had to choose, it would be theater. There's nothing like performing eight times a week in front of a live audience... nothing. I did a play called *Fences*—which was written by the late August Wilson, who's arguably one of the finest American playwrights ever—at a great theater in Rochester, New York, called the Geva Theatre Center. We sold out 750 seats every night, eight shows a week, and it was extraordinary.

What do you find most frustrating about the business side of acting?

Not being able to act. It's a given that all actors, no matter how successful they are, are going to go through some periods of downtime. I've been lucky because I've never gone more than two months without a job, but during the downtime, you have to learn how to manage your life. I've raised two kids—my daughter just started college and my son is an aspiring musician—and I have interesting hobbies. I paint, I fish, I cook, and I'm an active video gamer. I love to work, but whenever I'm not working, I have a lot that keeps me busy.

Fences

What advice would you give to aspiring actors?

If you really want to act and believe you can do it, don't let anybody shake that faith. If you have even the smallest fraction of doubt—it's okay to feel uncertain, it's okay to feel butterflies—but if you don't think you can do it, then get out of the game. Psychologically, you have to deal with rejection, no matter how good you are or how far you've gotten. You have to develop a tough skin, but you still want to be human and receptive; you don't want to become an asshole. Unless this is something that's a calling or inspirational, then don't do it. However, if you can say that you can't live *without* doing it, then by all means put your best foot forward and let your passions go before you.

Platoon (1986)
    Director: Oliver Stone
    Starring: Tom Berenger, Willem Dafoe, Charlie Sheen, Forest Whitaker

Engrossing Vietnam drama about a young man named Chris (Sheen) who drops out of college and enlists in the Army. As he struggles to survive amidst the chaos of war, Chris becomes a pawn in a power struggle between Barnes (Berenger)—a hardcore killer who wants to win at any cost—and Elias (Dafoe)—a sympathetic leader who just wants to do his duty and go home. Following the macho escapades in films like *Rambo* and *Missing in Action*, *Platoon* is a sobering and terrifying look at war and how it changes the people fighting in it. Nominated for eight Oscars and winner of four, including Best Picture and Best Director.

Colors (1988)
    Director: Dennis Hopper
    Starring: Sean Penn, Robert Duvall, Maria Conchita Alonso, Randy Brooks

Two cops—one a hardened veteran of the street (Duvall), the other a hot-tempered rookie (Penn)—work together in East L.A. trying to maintain the peace in a war between rival gangs. The movie offers some insightful moments about the allure and consequences of gang life, but *Colors* is at its best when focusing on the intense relationship between Duvall and Penn, both of whom deliver sterling performances.

Bird (1988)
Director: Clint Eastwood
Starring: Forest Whitaker, Diane Venora, Michael Zelniker, Samuel E. Wright
Director Eastwood's ambitious biopic of Charlie "Bird" Parker (Whitaker), one of the greatest and most influential jazz musicians of all time who also struggled with drug and alcohol addiction. With a nearly three-hour running time, you would expect the film to be a comprehensive look at a brilliant and tortured artist, but oddly enough, you don't come away with much insight into the man despite Whitaker's impressive performance. Oscar winner for Best Sound.

Candyman (1992)
Director: Bernard Rose
Starring: Virginia Madsen, Tony Todd, Xander Berkeley, Kasi Lemmons
Helen (Madsen), a grad student studying urban legends, comes across the story of the Candyman (Todd), an imposing hook-handed killer. When residents of a Chicago housing project start dying mysteriously, Helen sets out to discover if the tales about Candyman are fact or fiction. Not your standard slasher fare, the film is a surreal (and cerebral) nightmare, made all the more believable by the great work from Madsen and Todd.

Sunset Heat (1992)
Director: John Nicolella
Starring: Michael Pare, Adam Ant, Dennis Hopper, Daphne Ashbrook
Eric (Pare) is in L.A. visiting his old friend Danny (Ant). When Danny gets killed after stealing a million dollars from drug lord Carl (Hopper), Eric is on the hook to find where Danny stashed the money. *Heat* is a middling film noir with a decent premise but a total lack of energy, although Hopper does his best to inject life into the movie.

Candyman: Farewell to the Flesh (1995)
Director: Bill Condon
Starring: Tony Todd, Kelly Rowan, William O'Leary, Bill Nunn

Decent sequel has a teacher (Rowan) and her family being terrorized by Candyman (Todd), leading to an investigation that reveals the origins of the mysterious hook-handed murderer. The original film raised the bar for intelligent horror, and while this movie can't reach those heights, it still does enough things right to warrant a viewing.

The Rock (1996)
Director: Michael Bay
Starring: Sean Connery, Nicolas Cage, Ed Harris, John Spencer

A squad of renegade soldiers armed with biological weapons takes over Alcatraz, threatening to fire on San Francisco unless their financial demands are met. Goodspeed (Cage), an FBI chemical expert, is teamed with Mason (Connery), the only man who ever escaped from the famed prison island. Together, they must infiltrate "The Rock" and stop the attack. This big-budget blockbuster is loud, relentless and often blissfully free of logic, but it's a fun ride and blessed with an absolutely amazing cast. Oscar-nominated for Best Sound.

Candyman: Day of the Dead (1999)
Director: Turi Meyer
Starring: Tony Todd, Donna D'Errico, Nick Corri, Wade Andrew Williams

The third time is not the charm for the franchise as Candyman (Todd), summoned by his great-granddaughter (D'Errico), kills her friends and frames her for the murders. Abandoning all of the creative elements that made the first two films unique, this entry makes a beeline straight into generic slasher territory, resulting in an underwhelming effort that effectively ended the series.

The Man from Earth (2007)
Director: Richard Schenkman
Starring: David Lee Smith, Tony Todd, John Billingsley, Ellen Crawford

John Oldman (Smith), a college professor who is moving on to other prospects, is surprised when his colleagues arrive at his house to give him a going away party. During the festivities, John decides to come clean about his true identity, and he reveals to his guests that he is actually 14,000 years old. *Earth* is an absolute rarity in today's cinematic world: A high concept sci-fi flick with thought-provoking ideas and philosophical debates instead of glossy spectacle and shiny CGI. Those who are up for the challenge will find ample rewards from this little-seen gem.

The Graves (2009)
    Director: Brian Pulido
    Starring: Clare Grant, Jillian Murray, Bill Moseley, Tony Todd
    Sisters Megan (Grant) and Abby (Murray) decide to take one last road trip together before Megan moves to New York to start college. They wind up in Skull City, an old mining town where they're terrorized by a crazed killer who murders tourists for the "greater good" of the community. Although there's not much new in the way of plot or storytelling, *The Graves* gets by thanks to good work from a game cast led by Grant and Murray.

Frank Vincent

After launching his career in show business as a musician-turned-stand-up-comic, Frank Vincent made the leap into film with his long-time collaborator and friend, Joe Pesci. The rest, as they say, is history. With supporting performances in such celebrated projects as *Raging Bull*, *Goodfellas*, *Casino*, *Gotti*, and *The Sopranos*, Vincent has become Hollywood's go-to guy for portraying Mafia figures, finally getting his shot at a starring role as an aging hitman in the award-winning indie drama *Chicago Overcoat*. Check out www.frankvincent.com for news and info on his latest projects.

In the '70s, you did a comedy show with Joe Pesci. How did you two meet?

Joe's a musician—he's a guitar player—and I'm a drummer who had a band that played a lot of lounges in different places. Joe was not working at the time, so I asked him to come with my band, and he did. We had instant chemistry, and in less than a year, we were partners who were rock 'n' rollin' the New Jersey shore. We were doin' really good, and we were doin' a lot of makeshift comedy and ad-libs. Before you know it, we

Vincent, Joe Pesci and musician Ray Capri

wound up taking the instruments away and developed it into a stand-up act à la Dean Martin and Jerry Lewis.

In the first five movies that you made, four are with Pesci. Was that a coincidence or were you guys sort of like a package deal?

We were first asked to audition for an independent movie called *The Death Collector*. We knew the director, and he hired us to do this little movie. Our characters didn't know each other in the movie, so we worked in different scenes. When Martin Scorsese and Robert De Niro were looking for somebody to play the role of Joey La Motta in *Raging Bull*, they contacted Joe, Joe contacted me, I did a screen test for Marty, and we both got hired. Marty's a very clever guy… He understood the chemistry that Joe and I had from working together for so many years. He took advantage of that, and I think that chemistry comes across in what we've done. As for *Dear Mr. Wonderful*, [director] Peter Lilienthal had seen the previous work Joe and I had done, and he also saw an opportunity to take advantage of that chemistry. *Easy Money* was the Rodney Dangerfield movie, and that probably came about because Joe was going to be starring in it. Since he's a very good friend, I think Joe suggested that I meet with the director, and that's how I ended up getting the part.

Did you ever have any professional training as an actor?

No. I studied comedy with a comedy writer—one of the old vaudevillians—for years, and when you work in night clubs and lounges trying to do comedy, that's the kind of training that'll teach you how to have timing and teach you how to make an audience listen. On *Death Collector*, I wasn't scheduled to work for the first two or three weeks of the shoot, but I made it my business to go there every day while they were shooting the other scenes just to get a head's up on the language and the mechanics of it. It's a learnable technique, but it takes time to get it right. Music is really the gift I have, and music is the gift that makes many actors what they are. Music is very relative to timing and phrasing, and you can use that gift in acting.

Raging Bull was your first film with Scorsese. What was it like making the movie?

Being that it was my second opportunity to make a film—and being a complete novice at it—it was unbelievable. I didn't know exactly what we were doing… I knew what the story was and I knew about the characters in the story, but I didn't know what it was going to wind up being. You don't know when you're making the movie what it's going to be when it's all put together. You just go and perform, and then the rest is up to the gods—the editor and the director—as to how they cut the movie. You don't get to see what you did until a year later or whenever it's done. When *Raging Bull* came out, it really didn't make a lot of noise in 1980. It was nominated for eight Academy Awards and only won two. The movie that beat us was Robert Redford's directorial debut, *Ordinary People*. Timothy Hutton should have been nominated as Best Actor, but he went into the category of Supporting Actor and he beat Joe. Joe should've won that.

When the time came for Goodfellas, *did Scorsese just offer you the role of Billy Batts?*

Yes. When the time came, we met and we talked. I wanted to play the role that went to [Paul] Sorvino, but Marty said, "No, I think you'd be better off if you play the Billy Batts role." When Marty says that, that's the

Vincent and Joe Pesci in *Raging Bull*

role you take, and it's a role that's brought me a lot of notoriety and has become something I can't escape wherever I go. Consequently, we started a website called frankvincent.com where I have Billy Batts T-shirts and a bobblehead that we call a "Mobblehead." It's a talking bobblehead of Billy Batts that says, "Go home and get your shine box," "Give those Irish hoodlums a drink," and "Nobody's breakin' up my party." Those are some of the lines from my scene with Joe in the movie, and that scene has brought me a lot of exposure.

From an actor's point of view, what is it about Scorsese that makes him so great?

His attention to detail… A lot of directors are detail-oriented, but Marty wants you to change your tie, he wants you to wear a different color suit, he wants the ashtray on the bar moved. He has that ability of vision to see those things, not to mention his ability to move a story. He also has some great people that work with him like [cinematographer] Michael Ballhaus and Thelma Schoonmaker, the best editor in the world. Marty definitely knows what he's doing.

Ray Liotta, Joe Pesci, Vincent and Robert De Niro in *Goodfellas*

Vincent and Joe Pesci in *Casino*

Does he encourage his actors to contribute their ideas or does he know exactly what he wants?

He encourages you to give him feedback. When you go in for the rehearsal on the set, he looks at the camera angles and figures out what he wants to do. The actors will run the lines together, and he'll say, "What do you think if you did this?" I might say, "Well, what if I did that?" and the other actors will do the same thing. A lot of improvisational lines come out of that process, and Marty keeps the takes he likes best.

Your character in Casino *is based on Frank Cullotta, a real-life mobster who was a technical advisor on the movie. What kind of information did you get from him while you were making the film?*

There was a scene where we had to take a safe out of a wall, and Marty had Frank come over and show us the technique of how to do it. It was something we didn't know about as actors, and we would adjust ourselves based on what Frank did. It was a big help, and he was watching everything. We got a lot of information from him. Frank had taken himself out of the Witness Protection Program, and he was on the set almost every day. There were a couple of other people in Vegas at that time that were not necessarily his friends, and whenever they would come to the set, Frank would have to leave. Sometimes when we were finished shooting for the day, Frank would offer to drive us back to our trailers in his car. We would look in the trunk, open the hood and look underneath to make sure there were no bombs in there!

When you play roles based on real people, do you research their lives or do you just stick with what's in the script?

More or less, I stick with the script because the characters I've played weren't the most prominent characters within the story. [Robert] DiBernardo was a character in *Gotti*, and I met a lot of his family, but I just played it the way they wrote it. There was no sense going any deeper than that because he didn't have that much to do in the film.

I think one of the more underrated movies on your resumé is Cop Land.

Yeah, that was a good movie to make. James Mangold is a good director, and I worked with a lot of people who I know like Harvey [Keitel] and Bob [De Niro] and Sly [Stallone]. It was fun because it was the same kind of theme but with a different director and a different approach, so it was interesting to do. It's a good movie.

Harvey Keitel, Vincent, John Doman and Sylvester Stallone in *Cop Land*

A film of yours that has something of a cult following is The Deli. *How did you get involved with that?*

[Director] John Gallagher is a good friend of mine, and I had done two other movies with John prior to *The Deli*. Anything he's doing that he thinks I might be right for, I'm going to get a phone call. John and I are pretty close and we've done some nice work together. In *The Deli*, Mike Starr, Debi Mazar, and I did a lot of improv in that and had a good time making it.

You also did a play John directed called East of Evil.

Yeah, that was fun. Tony Sirico, Vincent Pastore, and I did that in the Westgate Theatre. It wasn't a big room, it was maybe sixty or seventy seats—a very intimate little theater—and you had to go behind the curtain before the audience came because there was no backstage entrance. We'd be locked behind the curtain as the audience came in, and we couldn't come out because people would see us before the show started. You had to remember to use the men's room before the audience arrived! We had some good laughs trying to work out those little kinds of problems.

Do you enjoy doing plays?

Being in front of an audience is very gratifying because you get instant recognition for what you're doing. Plays are fun, but it's hard work in terms of preparing it, putting it together, and then doing it. It's a whole different world… I've done enough of that live stuff in my life, and it's not something I really relish doing unless it was a real big project that had a lot of money in it.

You're well-known for your work on The Sopranos. *How did you get involved with the show?*

They were auditioning actors, and my agent suggested I go out for it. We really didn't know what *The Sopranos* was… We thought it was maybe a musical show or something. Tony Sirico, Dominic Chianese, and I all auditioned on the same day, and we all read the role of Uncle Junior for [creator] David Chase. Dominic got hired to play Uncle Junior, and they wrote a role for Tony, but David said he didn't want to use me at that point be-

The Sopranos

cause I was too well-known from *Goodfellas*. He told me that he was gonna see me again in a couple of years, and I did go back and visit with him. He said he had something for me that was coming, and I joined the show in the fifth season. David's a genius… From day one to the end, he knew exactly what he was doing. *The Sopranos* is just a marvelous work of art.

When you work on a show like Sopranos *where you have a lot of different directors coming in, is it difficult to adapt to their unique styles?*

Well, some of the directors like Alan Taylor and Tim Van Patten did a lot of episodes, and I worked with those guys a lot. Television is different than movies, and the director is governed by the producers. On *Sopranos*, the writers were also the producers, and they were right there on set. What we did is have a read-through before each show where you sit down with the entire cast and go over all of the dialogue. Then you come in and rehearse with the director, but you can't change anything, you can't improvise. Every word is written… *every* word. You can't change an "uh" to a "the" without permission. The director would decide how the shot's gonna look with the angles and the lighting, but directors on a TV show don't have as much input as they do on a movie.

Was the production schedule as hectic as network television or were you able to take your time to get everything perfect?

Shooting *Sopranos* was more like shooting a movie than a TV show. Each one was shot in two weeks, whereas a one-hour episode of a network crime drama is shot in six days. It was HBO and it was only thirteen episodes a season, whereas *Law & Order* is twenty-three or twenty-four episodes. When I did *Walker, Texas Ranger*, we went over schedule by one day because of weather, and they have to pay you from the minute you wake up till the minute you go to bed on that extra day. It's very costly.

How did you land the starring role in Chicago Overcoat?

The script was sent to my agent. I read it and loved it, so we talked and made a deal. The director [Brian Caunter] came to New Jersey to meet with me and show me the wardrobe for my character, and we signed the contract. When I got to Chicago, on the first day of shooting I saw nothing but twenty-five-year-old kids. I said to myself, "Am I in trouble here?" These were all young kids just coming out of college, but I was amazed at what they could do. They were really brilliant and they did a tremendous job with the cinematography, the art direction, the effects, the storyline… I'm really happy to be a part of it. The movie is absolutely terrific. We were all over Chicago and shot every scene on location. I think the film shot sixty days, and I shot thirty-five of those days.

Chicago Overcoat

Did you feel any more pressure as the star of the film instead of just being a supporting actor?

I don't think I felt a lot of pressure on it, but it *is* different than playing a character and only working for a week. I loved my character so much, and I really enjoyed playing it. I think I like it better being the star instead of a character actor… You have more of a story to tell and you have a big arc. That's different than coming in for five days and spitting out a character that's gonna be in three scenes in three different acts. It's more of a rewarding kind of feeling.

Why do you think Mafia movies are so appealing to audiences?

Well, I think part of the appeal is that the opposite sex loves bad boys. Not just mob characters but the James Deans and all those kinds of guys that you see in movies. They're pretty sexy according to how the culture looks at them. They drive flashy cars, they wear fancy clothes, they have beautiful women and they're out drinking and partying all night. That's an attractive-looking lifestyle compared to the regular average Joe who gets up in the morning and goes to work. The bad boys don't work for a living and punch a clock; they have a different lifestyle, and that's pretty appealing to a lot of people.

Co-writer/director Brian Caunter and Vincent on the set of *Chicago Overcoat*

What would you say to critics who complain that projects like Goodfellas *and* The Sopranos *glamorize the Mafia lifestyle?*

That's a very good question… I did three commercials with Mike Starr for Miller beer for the March Madness basketball tournament. They were really great, and they ended up being taken off the air because the Italian-Americans said it gave them a bad image. That's interesting because there's a lot of people in this world who do bad things. They're bankers and lawyers and doctors who are Italian, Jewish, black, white… They're every nationality you can think of, but the Italian-Americans really have a thing about being portrayed as bad. The truth is that they *did* do some bad things, but they also did a lot of *good* things. I think for them to focus on one small part of the culture is wrong because it's entertainment on the screen. Some things happened which are true, and a lot of it is make-believe. I don't know what all the excitement is about.

You've also been involved with the Grand Theft Auto *video game series, which is often cited as having a negative influence on kids.*

You know, every child has a mother and a father, and the mother and the father are responsible for what the child sees and does. I came off the set of *Sopranos* one night, and there was a gentleman standing on the corner

with a four-year-old kid. The kid said to me, "I love to watch you on *Sopranos*." This child has no right to be watching that show, but that's not my fault, that's his father's fault. If you're raising children and you're letting them play *Grand Theft Auto* before their time, that's wrong. *Grand Theft Auto* is out there as entertainment for people of a certain age. What concerns me is these reality shows on television… What the heck is goin' on with this stuff? I can't imagine what these kids are seeing and the messages they're getting from it. Everything affects everything, and the culture is what it is. I don't know how to solve it… I'm just an actor. I work, and that's what I do.

You've made several mentions of improvising during filming. How do you decide when to do that? Do you get ideas when you're reading the script to change something or do you wait until you're on the set with the other actors to experiment?

What happens is you get to the location in the morning, and you go to your trailer for hair and makeup and all that stuff. When they're ready to shoot something, we go on the set of a particular scene. The director is there with the director of photography and assistant director, and the director says, "Ok, here's what we're gonna do. Frank, you'll be standing over here, and you're gonna talk to Jack over there." I might say something like, "How about if I turn this way when you see me?" You talk about what you're gonna do, what you'd like to do and what the director wants you to do. After you've finished rehearsing that scene, then they bring in the entire crew and you do the scene for them. They look at it and light the scene based on what you did in that rehearsal. It's not a question of whether you want to go in and improvise or not… You don't know that until you get on the location and get into the meat and potatoes of a particular scene. That's usually the way it's done.

Do you still have to audition?

No, I don't audition. I don't think there's any need for me to do that. What am I gonna do at an audition? There's so much footage of stuff that I've done, anybody can look it up. If they don't know who I am and what I do, I'm in pretty bad shape! I'd like to play a cowboy, though... I would audition for that.

What do you look for in a script when deciding whether or not to do a project?

I look for a well-written script with a good story. I look at the character to see if he has an arc that has a beginning, middle, and an end, and what he has to do in the storyline. There's a lot of other things involved, like how much they're gonna pay me, how much time it's gonna take for me to do this and where I have to go to do it. It's not something that you look at for a second and say, "Yeah, I'll do it." There's a lot of things to consider. I have a manager, and she's got to talk about all the technicalities of the back end, the front end, and residual payments. There's a lot of different things that are involved in the business of the business.

Speaking of which, what frustrates you the most about the business aspects of acting?

Writer/director Russell Costanzo and Vincent on the set of *The Tested*

A lot of people will get in touch with my management about a project they want to do. They want to send me a script, but they're not funded yet. They say the funding is coming in one month or two months and we'll start shooting in September, but the funding never comes. You've wasted time reading the script, the project is a no-go because they can't raise the money, and they want your name attached to it to help them raise the money. That's something I don't like to do, and a lot of projects come to me like that. When they made me the offer on *Chicago Overcoat*, they wired me a serious amount of money and it went into escrow, so we knew the project was funded. Until that happens, there's no project—it's all conversation. That happens a lot in this business... People will say, "Let's have a meeting. I'll take you to dinner." Why, so you can say you had dinner with me? I don't want to have dinner with you. If I like your script and I'm interested in doing it, put up some money and we can definitely get together and have a meeting. But this is the way the business is, and that's what's frustrating about it.

What do you think has been your secret to making a living as an actor?

Patience and perseverance… Patience because I started out in the music business and I always tried to put out a good product, which led to more work. I learned that networking is very, very important. When you know people and know what's going on in the business, it keeps you ahead of the game. There's a good possibility of me doing *Boardwalk Empire* because [writer/producer] Terry [Winter] is a good friend and Steve Buscemi is a good friend. It's just a matter of finding something that's right for me. They won't just put me into a scene if it doesn't relate to me; they have to find the right moment. That's the way it is to be an actor… You wait for the work and the work comes if you're worthy of it. As for perseverance, if you really want to do this, you've got to do it. You can't say, "Oh, I'll get a part-time job and maybe on the side I'll be an actor." That's not the way it is. Either you're an actor or you're not. If you're serious about it, that's what your life's dedication should be.

The Death Collector (1976)
   Director: Ralph De Vito
   Starring: Joseph Cortese, Lou Criscuola, Joe Pesci, Frank Vincent
   Jerry (Cortese) is a struggling Jersey boy looking to make some cash working for the local mob. Assigned to collect debts, Jerry's aggressive style leads to trouble when a businessman fails to pay what he owes and the situation escalates into an all-out war. This no-budget crime flick doesn't break any new ground, but it covers the familiar material fairly well.

Raging Bull (1980)
   Director: Martin Scorsese
   Starring: Robert De Niro, Cathy Moriarty, Joe Pesci, Frank Vincent
   Powerful biopic of boxer Jake La Motta (De Niro), a man fueled by a self-destructive rage that made him a ferocious athlete inside the ring and an even more volatile brute outside of it. Widely regarded as one of the best films of the '80s (or any other decade), *Bull* should be near the top of any serious cinematic bucket list. Nominated for eight Academy Awards and winner for Best Actor (De Niro) and Best Editing.

Dear Mr. Wonderful (1982)
   Director: Peter Lilienthal
   Starring: Joe Pesci, Karen Ludwig, Frank Vincent, Ed O'Ross
   Interesting character study focuses on Ruby (Pesci), the owner of a

bowling alley who dreams of making it big as a singer. Life, however, throws roadblocks in his way as Ruby must deal with an unhappy sister, a nephew on the verge of becoming a criminal and mobsters trying to take over Ruby's business. *Wonderful* takes its time meandering from sub-plot to sub-plot, but Pesci's strong performance ultimately keeps the film on track.

Easy Money (1983)
    Director: James Signorelli
    Starring: Rodney Dangerfield, Joe Pesci, Candy Azzara, Geraldine Fitzgerald
    Loveable family guy Monty (Dangerfield) stands to inherit his late mother-in-law's (Fitzgerald) fortune as long as he abstains from the things he enjoys most: Drinking, smoking, gambling, and doing drugs. *Money* delivers some solid laughs from the temptations Monty encounters, but given the premise and Dangerfield's comedic talents, one can't help but think this movie should've been a lot funnier.

Goodfellas (1990)
    Director: Martin Scorsese
    Starring: Robert De Niro, Joe Pesci, Ray Liotta, Lorraine Bracco
    Based on a true story, *Goodfellas* chronicles the rise and fall of gangster Henry Hill (Liotta) and his friends Jimmy (De Niro), a charismatic thief, and Tommy (Pesci), a quick-tempered sociopath, as they do the dirty work for the mob. Simply amazing on every artistic and technical level, calling this Scorsese classic one of the best Mafia movies ever doesn't quite do it justice. It's one of the greatest films ever made, period. Nominated for six Oscars and winner of one (Pesci as Best Supporting Actor).

Casino (1995)
    Director: Martin Scorsese
    Starring: Robert De Niro, Sharon Stone, Joe Pesci, James Woods
    Sam "Ace" Rothstein (De Niro) is sent by the mob to run a casino in Vegas when he falls in love with Ginger (Stone), a hooker who can't escape the emotional clutches of her pimp (Woods). Things get even more complicated when Sam's hitman friend, Nicky (Pesci), arrives and starts to overstep his bounds, causing trouble for everyone. Scorsese's flipside to *Goodfellas* doesn't quite reach the heights of that masterpiece, but judged on its own merits—as it should be—*Casino* is an extravagantly entertaining film. Stone was nominated for an Academy Award as Best Actress.

Gotti (1996)
>Director: Robert Harmon
>Starring: Armand Assante, William Forsythe, Frank Vincent, Anthony Quinn

>Well-made HBO docudrama based on the life of John Gotti (Assante), a career criminal who ascended through the ranks to become boss of a powerful Mafia family. Assante gives a commanding performance as the "Teflon Don," with terrific support from Forsythe as Sammy "The Bull" Gravano. Mob movie aficionados are advised to put this on their "must see" list.

Cop Land (1997)
>Director: James Mangold
>Starring: Sylvester Stallone, Harvey Keitel, Ray Liotta, Robert De Niro

>Stallone stars as Freddy Heflin, the overweight, hearing-impaired sheriff of a small New Jersey community inhabited by New York City cops. When a rookie NYPD officer becomes involved in a scandal, Freddy begins to discover the truth about the citizens living in his town. The impressive supporting players do their jobs well (as usual), but the real surprise in *Cop Land* is Stallone. Abandoning all traces of his larger-than-life, superhuman Rocky/Rambo image, this is easily Sly's greatest acting achievement.

The Deli (1997)
>Director: John A. Gallagher
>Starring: Mike Starr, Matt Keeslar, Brian Vincent, Judith Malina

>New York deli owner Johnny (Starr) has a gambling problem and is in debt to a local mobster. His mom (Malina), a habitual lottery player, gives Johnny ten dollars to place her weekly bet, but he uses the cash to finance his own losing wagers. When his mother's numbers finally hit, Johnny must figure out how to come up with her prize money *and* settle up with the bookie. Starr shines in this amusing slice-of-life comedy featuring an array of cameos from many familiar faces.

Chicago Overcoat (2009)
>Director: Brian Caunter
>Starring: Frank Vincent, Kathrine Narducci, Mike Starr, Armand Assante

>Lou (Vincent) is an aging hitman on the verge of retirement and looking to recapture his glory days with one last job. He gets his chance

when incarcerated Mafia boss Stefano (Assante) orders the murder of witnesses whose testimony could spell big trouble for Stefano's criminal organization. *Chicago Overcoat* is a real find: An under-the-radar entry in an over-populated genre that expertly takes old-school storylines and turns them into compelling drama. The cast is beyond reproach and is wonderfully led by Vincent, who finally gets to display his considerable acting chops in a starring role.

William Forsythe

For over thirty years, William Forsythe has specialized in playing tough guys. From the laughably inept (*Raising Arizona*) to the downright psychotic (*Out for Justice*), his roles have also included chilling portraits of real-life criminals Al Capone (*The Untouchables*), John Wayne Gacy (*Dear Mr. Gacy*), and Sammy "The Bull" Gravano (*Gotti*). It's in films like *The Waterdance*, *Palookaville*, and *Happy in the Valley*, however, where Forsythe excels in depicting emotionally complex characters who are rough around the edges but still have a heart.

How did you get your start in acting?

I was about ten years old, and I was a juvenile delinquent on the verge of probably going in the wrong direction. I was going to a Catholic school, and I had a teacher—a Xaverian Brother—who basically found out about something I did and blackmailed me into doing a play. I guess I owe him a little bit! I graduated early from high school, and at seventeen, I took off for Manhattan. The first day I was there, I went to an audition and got a part in an operetta. I discovered quite by accident that I could sing, so they wanted to hire me for all of these musicals. Somewhere in there,

I just saw that I was going to be heading down a road of some very bad habits, so that's why I focused on really trying to learn the craft. After that, the long process began.

Who did you study with?

When I was seventeen, I started with a pretty amazing teacher named Cynthia Belgrave. She was the perfect first teacher, and after that, I went on and studied at HB Studio and basically sat in on classes of every kind of teacher there was in New York at the time. I spent about three or four years studying with a lady named Pat Randall, who was originally from the Actors Studio, and then after that I studied with Milton Katselas, and I stayed with Milton for over twelve years. A lot of what I've done I suppose you could call method acting, but what basic studying taught me was just how to live and breathe as a character and how to bring it to life in a way that is as real as it can possibly be. I studied for a period of about three years where all we did was sensory work and improvisation. These are very helpful tools, but in the end, you study a very long time to get those things to be working for you, and when I got to Milton Katselas, he just brought it home to me. I was pretty young, and the first thing he said to

James Woods, Robert De Niro, Forsythe and Burt Young in *Once Upon a Time in America*

me was, "I want you to play every scene as the leader. I want you to be the general; I want you to be the president. You're going to play these roles, and I want you to really understand what's inside of you." There's so many different things that you learn, but you have to develop your own personal technique on how to find the truth. That's what all actors really do… Find the truth and find a way to portray that truth that's effective.

One of your earliest films was Once Upon a Time in America. *How did you get involved with that?*

That film changed my life. At that point, I had spent a good nine years studying and doing lots of plays and a couple of films, but that one was really quite amazing. I had a small agent in L.A. and he called me up and said he had something for me. I didn't even know what it was for, but I ran over to the Chateau Marmont and met Joy Todd, the casting director. She just looked at me and she said, "I think you would be very good for this. Go get a monologue, come back tomorrow and do it for me." I still didn't know what I was doing, but I went home, got a monologue together and went back. Right before I was getting ready to go in the room, this other actor came out and he said, "I just can't believe I'm even auditioning for a Robert De Niro/Sergio Leone movie!" That was the first realization I had about what I was doing. I did my monologue and I felt pretty good; I felt like it went well. By the time I got home, I had a phone call from someone who said, "Sergio would like you to come back to the hotel *now*." So I got in my car and drove back, and Sergio Leone was sitting there in a robe looking like Zeus on the mountaintop. He looked at me and said, "When I dreamed of this character, I always saw your face." That was pretty much it… By the time that conversation was over, he told me the part was ninety percent mine. It took about three months to get the other ten percent, but I was the second person cast in the film, after Robert. It was very exciting because Robert De Niro meant so much to me. In fact, years before when *Mean Streets* came out, I saw the movie and I had no idea at the time who Robert De Niro or Martin Scorsese was. I went in and saw the film and I just went, "Oh my God… This is what it's about. This *is* the work." I actually went back to the theater and I applied for a job as an usher. I worked at the theater for about a month and when the movie ended its run, I quit. I saw *Mean Streets* about 800 times! There was just something about it that drew me to a sense of what this work could be.

Forsythe and John Goodman in *Raising Arizona*

A few years later you did Raising Arizona. *What was that experience like?*

It was wonderful. At that point I was a pretty "serious" actor, and then I got on the set and it took a few days to get used to the way we were going about making the film. To be quite honest, it was one of the great experiences I had. I mean, we laughed the entire time we shot the film. I always loved comedy, and to this day, comedy is my favorite of all things to do. Every once in a while, I get the chance to do something that's funny, and I love it so much. Working with the Coen brothers was amazing. You'd see them both sitting there thinking for thirty seconds, and then suddenly they would both turn and start to speak and they would say the exact same thing. They were in tune, and it was a great experience that really opened up another door for me at the time.

That same year, you were part of another terrific cast in Walter Hill's Extreme Prejudice.

I consider that film to be the last of the Mohicans. It's basically a tribute to [director Sam] Peckinpah, and you'll never see another one like that. I think the best image I could have of what it was like to work on a Walter Hill set was when we were filming and the Kentucky Derby was running. We were out in the middle of nowhere and somebody had one of those tiny Watchman TVs with the two-inch screen. I wish I had taken a photograph of it as the entire cast and crew gathered around Walt to watch the Kentucky Derby. That kind of unity you get from a director like Walt is special. After all these years, I've always wished that I would work with him again but somehow it never came to pass, although it almost happened once. Walter is very unique… He kind of represents a Hollywood that we'll never see again.

You were nearly unrecognizable as Flattop in Dick Tracy. *How did that role come about?*

I received a phone call from my agent and he said that Warren Beatty wanted to meet me. I was like, "Cool, I'm gonna meet Warren Beatty!" So I went to the studio, and I met Warren in his office. He didn't really know my work but he had heard things about me, and he gave me this really amazing and charming interview. He said to come back and see him in a couple of days, and when I went back to see him, he had done his homework and seen every movie I'd made. At that point, this amazing little courtship began. He'd ask me to go to dinner and he'd send a limo for me, and I had this pretty amazing week where I met Warren in both L.A. *and* New York. I never read a script because he had no script to hand out, but he said, "I want you to be in my movie and I'd love you to play Flattop." Not having read the script, Flattop was the most famous of all the villains in *Dick Tracy*, so I naturally assumed I would be his nemesis. He neglected to tell me there was a character called Big Boy with Al Pacino

Dick Tracy

playing it! It was a phenomenal experience, I have to say, to work with actors from so many generations. We had guys in that film that made movies in the '20s and '30s. To just sit there and have lunch with Dick Van Dyke, Al Pacino, and Warren Beatty was a fabulous experience.

Was it difficult working under all of that makeup?

It was very challenging, and I had no idea what I was in for. When I went in for the first time, it took four hours to put on. I was under that makeup and I couldn't make facial expressions. I had no control over my face because of all the rubber. I went to the makeup artists, John Caglione and Doug Drexler, before the film started and said, "Do you guys mind if I come every day and we put this on? I have to learn how to speak a second language in here." If you recall, a lot of the other characters that were full makeup had no expressions, it would just be a mask. I worked really hard to make a very subtle face, even though inside I was completely distorting my face. I started to work in the mirror to be able to understand how I could bring that makeup to life. I worked particularly hard on it, and I did it for six months straight. What was really funny is everybody that was wearing makeup all began to look younger! You put that on every day and everybody's face started looking fresh. I owe Warren a lot... *Dick Tracy* was a very special film that came along at just the right time for me.

One of the biggest cult films on your resumé is Stone Cold.

Stone Cold

It is a *huge* cult film! When we made that, Lance [Henriksen] and I used to laugh because we had no script. The script was nothing, it was horrifying. Lance and I would just improvise every scene. That's the only film I've ever done where I was contracted to work three months and we ended up working six. It was like a runaway train. When we finished the film, both of us thought it was going in the toilet. Quite surprisingly, when I go to events and I meet fans, it shocks me how many people love *Stone Cold*. It's an interesting piece on the resumé… There was a guy on the film who was an enforcer for a motorcycle gang, and my objective was to look and get as close as I could to him. I ate huge amounts of food and I was still working out, and I just wanted to have this look that the guy had. By the time we were ready to shoot, we looked like bookends.

Another cult film you've done is Things to Do in Denver When You're Dead. *How did you get involved with that?*

The director [Gary Fleder] and the writer [Scott Rosenberg] liked me, and the part that Treat Williams played—Critical Bill—was originally written for me. I went down and met the guys and I said, "Critical Bill is a great role with the greatest entrance in movie history, but I love this other part." The reason I chose to play Franchise is because there was an amazing monologue that had to do with life and children and regret. I loved the monologue so much that I told them, "Let me play this part and you can get someone else for Critical Bill," and that's where Treat came in. We felt like we were making a pretty good movie, and I thought the film was going to do big box office, but it ended up much like *Stone Cold* and is a cult classic. It's one of the films in my career that people ask me about the most.

Edward James Olmos and Forsythe in *American Me*

I think one of the most underrated films on your resumé is American Me. *What was it like making that movie?*

American Me is just an incredible, special film. When it came out, people feared it; they were afraid of what people would do in the movie theaters. It was so ahead of its time, really pointing out things that were about to become mainstream. I went and had to absorb and live in a culture that was fascinating to me, and to really learn the ins-and-outs and language was unbelievable. When *American Me* happened, I had just finished doing *Stone Cold* and *Out for Justice* and I was huge, weighing in at 260 pounds. [Director/star] Eddie Olmos was giving me this interview, and I looked in his eyes and I could tell he was just being respectful; there wasn't a prayer I was gonna get this movie. Just before I left, I turned to Eddie and I just started speaking to him in the dialect because I was fascinated with it. Eddie looked at me and he goes, "Where'd you learn to do *that*?" The next thing he said to me was, "Can you lose the weight?" I said, "Absolutely," so I ended up dropping sixty-five pounds. There were some crazy things that happened in the process of making the film, and in the aftermath, there were some people killed who were involved with it. It had a very strange afterlife, but I'm very proud that I did that film and very proud of the movie. I think it's truly a classic film.

You've done a few projects with director Rob Zombie, starting with The Devil's Rejects. *How did that relationship begin?*

We had never met before, and he called me up about *The Devil's Rejects*. We had an hour-and-a-half phone conversation where we talked about Robert Shaw and Lee Marvin and all of these amazing, larger-than-life actors. By the time the conversation ended, Rob offered me the part over the phone. Whatever image he may put out, Rob is an incredibly intelligent director. He's smart, he understands what he wants, and he hires all these crazy actors and really puts a lot of trust in them to bring the work to life. You long for those kinds of movies where you feel a sense of family, and I always felt that with Rob on anything I've done with him. I did *Halloween* and an episode of *CSI: Miami* that he directed, and if Rob calls, he's one of the guys that I would show up for.

Your film Happy in the Valley *won four awards at the Monaco International Film Festival, including Best Feature and Best Actor for your performance.*

The Devil's Rejects

You know, the first second I read that script, I went crazy for it. It's really a good-hearted film that takes place in this seedy, greasy world. I just loved it and it rang so true. I loved my character because this was a guy that had known greatness and had been at the top of the game—he had stardom—and now he's kind of been forgotten and reduced to "greasin' up yammies." The character itself had so much room for growth because he is so theatrical and so wild, yet underneath it all is a big heart and a good person. Lee [Madsen] is one of my favorite directors I've worked with in recent years. We were trying to get a lot done for very little, and I think we accomplished it. Some of the things we talk about in the movie are experiences I lived, like how I got to Hollywood and had no connections, how I had every kind of crazy job and did every kind of crazy thing in order to hang in there and get my chance. I love this film, and it's taken a couple of years to see the light of day, but I'm so happy it's coming out because it's a feel-good movie.

You've portrayed such real-life people as John Wayne Gacy in Dear Mr. Gacy, *Sammy Gravano in* Gotti *and Al Capone in* The Untouchables *TV series. What kind of research did you do when preparing for these roles?*

I'm huge into research, and I go in pretty deep. With Sammy Gravano, I really didn't have much time. They basically offered me that part and

The Untouchables

I had about a week or two before filming, but I grew up in Brooklyn in an environment where I was pretty close to that world as a kid. For Al Capone, I went to New York and found two places in Brooklyn where he lived. I walked from his house to his school and began this process of trying to understand from his point of view how it all happened for him. Sure enough, halfway to his school, there was an old building—and I did my historic research—and that building was once owned by [mobster] Johnny Torrio. The guys used to all sit out there and Al, at age nine, would be walking by. I went to the church where he got married, I went to the place where he got his scar... I spent basically a couple of weeks in New York researching Al and his early days, and then I hopped on the train—just like Al did—and I went to Chicago and began my research process there. It was really amazing because there were so many interesting people I was able to meet. A friend of mine knew the wife of one of Al's brothers who lived in the house with Al for years. She was amazing, and people in Chicago embraced my research on Al and opened the door for me. On the other hand, when I played Gacy, I went to Chicago and suddenly I became confounded. I'm kind of a Hardy Boy when it comes to research, and all roads kept leading to a dead end. It was like everything had been whitewashed over, and it got me mad. I thought it was crazy, so I actually stayed a few extra weeks, and I met all of the police, I met all of his lawyers, and there was a gentleman named Barry Boschelli who was a boyhood friend of John's, and the information this guy gave me was *incredible*. I even sat in the cell that Gacy was incarcerated in that first night after he had been arrested. I go in pretty deep when I do a character, and if I have the time, I'll go in as far as I can so I can truly understand who this person is. Mind you, Gacy is a case where I hate to even think about it. I knew when I accepted that part that I was gonna go on a *very* ugly journey, and it was... In fact, that's an understatement. But once I decided to do it, I decided to do it right.

What are some of the traits a good director has that gets the best out of you as an actor?

The good directors obviously know what they want and know what to shoot. The best directors understand that you have done a huge amount of work to prepare for a character and they trust you. They come and they tweak and they play and do things that bring out even more. Somebody once said to me ninety percent of directing a film is getting the right people, and I really believe that to be true. I've worked with so many directors who weren't very good and I've worked with some that I consider to be brilliant, and when you're stuck on a picture and people don't really know what they're doing, it can be a little frustrating.

Do you like working with directors who know exactly what they want from you, or do you prefer those who allow you the freedom to experiment?

Director Svetozar Ristovski and Forsythe on the set of *Dear Mr. Gacy*

When I go in, no matter who the director is, I've done so much work to prepare for it that the last thing you want is Erich von Stroheim ordering you what to do. I think there's a quote from John Hurt where he said, "Don't tell me what to do; tell me what you want," and I think that's brilliant. I have worked with some guys like that, but not very many. I think that when you direct that way, you're not trusting the people you hired. But if a guy's really brilliant and really knows what he's doing and that's his style, then hell, let's go.

Are you in a position to be able to pick and choose what roles you play, or do you still have to worry about paying the bills?

I've made a living as an actor—thank God—for over thirty years. I'm fine as far as that goes, but I'm not a person who has a great love of money. I try to pick the ones that I really want to do, that really excite me, and that's why I've done so many independent films. In that world, however, the business is different these days, and there's a lot of bad films being made. I had this conversation recently with [actor] Michael Madsen, and we were talking about how we're kind of like mercenaries. We show up on the set, we try to bring all of our passion and everything we can do, but at the end of the day, the chance of some films being really good is slim. I think it's important to get up every day and no matter what film you're doing, go in there and give it *everything* you have and not kick back and say, "Well, this is a little film." Personally, I enjoy the independents. For instance, working with Lee on *Happy in the Valley* reminded me of summer stock, where you have people excited about the work. To me, that's thrilling. The last thing I like is being involved with some movies where you can feel that people just phone-in their stuff. I always want to try and do my best.

At what point did you know that you'd be able to make a living as an actor?

The moment I got my Screen Actors Guild card, I knew I was ready. I was one of those guys that spent a lot of time preparing and waiting for my moment. I always knew I would work as an actor, and I always knew I would get work. I don't know why or what it was inside me that made me feel that way, but I always knew. It's funny how I got my Screen Actors Guild card… At the time, I was delivering singing telegrams dressed as a gorilla. I used to juggle and sing while delivering these telegrams, and one day, somebody sent a singing telegram to Gary Owens on the radio. I went in and delivered it to him, and the next thing you know, they used that as a commercial and I went, "Aha!" So I went and complained a little and said they used me on air and I wasn't taken care of, and believe it or not, six months later I was able to join SAG as a result of that. Once I

Happy in the Valley

got in, I knew I would go to work, but it took a year or two to really start to gain the momentum. Sergio Leone gave me the opportunity, as did Robert De Niro because Robert had approval over me. Those guys did so much for me because once I did that film, I entered the big leagues. It took Sergio two years to edit the film and I had to go back home and live in obscurity and take whatever crap I could find to work on, but once the film came out—even though it wasn't a huge financial success—it gave me international exposure and opened the doors for my whole career.

Are there any projects you've done that you're really proud of and wished had gotten more of an audience?

I did a film that I considered to be maybe the best independent film I had ever done. It was called *Sons*, it was directed by Alexandre Rockwell, and Samuel Fuller—Samuel Fuller!—played my father in the movie. We shot this picture in New Jersey, New York, and Paris, France, and I got to be with Samuel Fuller on the beach at Normandy. It was an incredible independent film, and I don't know what it was—maybe because the producer wasn't a particularly likeable guy or whatever—but the film never got any kind of distribution whatsoever in the U.S. It broke my heart because I watched the film again about seven years ago and it's a *wonderful* movie. There's others like that where you can't quite understand why things happen, like *Gacy*. Clark Peterson was an executive producer, and he was

Forsythe, Eric Stoltz and Wesley Snipes in *The Waterdance*

one of the producers of *Monster* with Charlize Theron. That one got a big theatrical release and everything happened for them, and our film had another producer who made some ridiculous deal where he agreed that it would be shown on Canadian TV first, which killed any chance of a proper distribution deal in the U.S. When you've done as many films as I have, there's a lot of crap you've gotta swim through, but there's some really good gems hidden in there that really didn't get the attention. *Palookaville* is a beautiful film and is one I'm very, very proud of. *The Waterdance* is very special, and I ended up getting nominated for a Spirit Award for that. Some people have seen these movies but you always want *more* people to see them.

What frustrates you the most about the business side of acting?

The business side of what we do has never been particularly wonderful for me. That's why I don't live in Hollywood. I choose to be away from the scene and just focus on the thing I love, which is doing the work. The business part of it can be frustrating on many levels… There's a lack of commitment on the part of people. You can work hard on a unique project, and if it goes through large committees, it can become more generic. You spend your life creating all of these characters that shows a lot of range, and it's frustrating to have people look at you only for your most famous bad guy part and not see what you really have done and what you can do. Through time, that's somewhat changed for me, but there are still people who think that way and won't push the envelope and allow me to go do what I love to do, which is create something new. That's why I love films like *Happy in the Valley* because I don't think anyone would have ever cast me in that film for that role if it was a big studio picture. Chances are I wouldn't have gotten that shot, even though I knew the whole time it was something I could really do. Stereotypes and things like that are very frustrating on the business end, and you always try to break that mold. I think I've done it, but it took a whole lifetime.

What advice would you give to aspiring actors?

I give advice to aspiring actors all of the time. I don't know if they want to hear it—some do and some don't—but I think if you want to be serious about the craft, you have to really learn what you're doing. Don't be an actor that sits in Jerry's Deli and *talks* about acting; you have to get up

and *work*. If you're not doing something, you're not acting. Actors are like Olympic athletes, and if you're not in practice, you get worse, not better. It's a long process, and when I first started out, I had various family members and friends say, "What are you doing? You're never going to be able to do this." I was stubborn and said, "This is all I'm going to do and this will be my career." Dig in, work as hard as you possibly can, and try to understand all of the material and all of the great films. I talk to younger actors about classic movies, and they don't know what I'm talking about!

You can't possibly understand what we do if you don't have the knowledge of what came before you. My advice is to study, study, study and learn how to get your instrument loose so that you can reach levels that will even surprise you.

Once Upon a Time in America (1984)
　　Director: Sergio Leone
　　Starring: Robert De Niro, James Woods, Elizabeth McGovern, Joe Pesci
　　Sergio Leone's epic (in both length and scope) follows Noodles (De Niro) and his friends from childhood to old age as they build a criminal empire during Prohibition, only to see it destroyed by greed and betrayal. Clocking in at nearly four hours long, *America* is one of the longest films you'll ever see. It's also one of the most beautiful, visionary, and poetic pieces of cinema ever made. For those willing to invest their time, the rewards are considerable.

Extreme Prejudice (1987)
　　Director: Walter Hill
　　Starring: Nick Nolte, Powers Boothe, Michael Ironside, Maria Conchita Alonso
　　Action-packed shoot 'em up about two former childhood friends: Jack (Nolte), now a Texas Ranger, and Cash (Boothe), a drug czar in Mexico. Their paths are about to collide in a fatal showdown when a group of CIA mercenaries come to town on a top-secret mission. Director Hill has made a career of delivering high-octane, modern-day Westerns with very little fanfare. *Prejudice* is just one of many flicks on his resumé that's worthy of discovery.

Raising Arizona (1987)
　　Director: Joel Coen
　　Starring: Nicholas Cage, Holly Hunter, Trey Wilson, John Goodman
　　H.I. (Cage) is an ex-con married to Ed (Hunter), an ex-cop. When they learn they aren't able to have children of their own, the couple kidnaps one of the quintuplets sired by furniture magnate Nathan Arizona (Wilson). This quirky and surreal comedy from the Coen brothers remains one of their best efforts, with a cast that is absolutely perfect.

Dick Tracy (1990)
>Director: Warren Beatty
>Starring: Warren Beatty, Charlie Korsmo, Glenne Headly, Al Pacino

The comic strip detective is vividly brought to life by director/producer/star Warren Beatty, portraying the titular no-nonsense cop as he battles an assorted cadre of misfit (and misshapen) criminals led by Big Boy Caprice (Pacino). A sumptuous feast for the eyes, *Tracy* features stunning production design and a literal Who's Who of famous actors buried underneath mounds of meticulously crafted makeup. Nominated for seven Academy Awards and winner of three, including Best Makeup, Best Art Direction, and Best Song.

Out for Justice (1991)
>Director: John Flynn
>Starring: Steven Seagal, William Forsythe, Jerry Orbach, Jo Champa

Gino (Seagal) is a Brooklyn police officer whose best friend has just been murdered by drugged-out neighborhood gangster Richie (Forsythe). Of course, many bones will be broken and people killed as Gino seeks revenge. A movie like this is only as good as its villain, and Forsythe delivers in spades, making this one of Seagal's better cinematic vehicles.

Stone Cold (1991)
>Director: Craig R. Baxley
>Starring: Brian Bosworth, Lance Henriksen, William Forsythe, Arabella Holzbog

Dumb but fun action flick has loner cop Joe Huff (Bosworth) going undercover to infiltrate a vicious biker gang led by a psychotic killer named Chains (Henriksen). That's pretty much it as far as the plot goes, but the real entertainment comes from Henriksen, who chews so much scenery it's amazing he didn't gain 100 pounds during production. The best way to appreciate this gloriously insane B-movie is to turn your brain off and just enjoy the crazy.

American Me (1992)
>Director: Edward James Olmos
>Starring: Edward James Olmos, William Forsythe, Pepe Serna, Daniel A. Haro

Brutal and uncompromising portrait of gang life stars Olmos as Santana, a hood who comes of age in prison and becomes a powerful leader behind bars. *American Me* is in many ways the anti-*Scarface*; whereas the Al Pacino classic glamorizes drug dealing and the vast fortunes that come from it, Olmos is more interested in the damage that occurs to individuals and families caught in the crossfire. This isn't a "fun" movie by any means, but it's a well-made and contemplative effort that deserves to be seen.

The Waterdance (1992)
    Directors: Neal Jimenez, Michael Steinberg
    Starring: Eric Stoltz, Helen Hunt, William Forsythe, Wesley Snipes
    Following a hiking accident, a writer named Joel (Stoltz) becomes paralyzed and is taken to a rehab center to begin a difficult new chapter in his life. Joel's ward is populated with several other paraplegics adjusting to life in wheelchairs, including Ray (Snipes)—a self-professed ladies' man trying to reconcile with his wife and child—and Bloss (Forsythe), a racist biker who's counting on a huge financial payday for his injury that may not materialize. Alternately sad, funny and inspirational, *The Waterdance* is a poignant movie with heartfelt performances.

Palookaville (1995)
    Director: Alan Taylor
    Starring: William Forsythe, Vincent Gallo, Adam Trese, Gareth Williams
    Russ (Gallo), Sid (Forsythe), and Jerry (Trese) are three buddies desperate for cash to escape their ho-hum New Jersey lives. With no other viable options, they decide to become criminals even though they don't have the skills—or the brains—to pull off a heist. This low-key comedy/drama is hard to resist thanks to the wonderful work from a talented ensemble.

Things to Do in Denver When You're Dead (1995)
    Director: Gary Fleder
    Starring: Andy Garcia, Christopher Lloyd, William Forsythe, Treat Williams
    Jimmy (Garcia) is a former crook trying to make a go at a legitimate life when his former boss (Christopher Walken, in a scene-stealing cameo) asks him to come back for one last job. Jimmy reunites his old crew, an eccentric group of thugs that includes Pieces (Lloyd), who is literally falling apart from leprosy, and Critical Bill (Williams), a hot-tempered psy-

chopath. When the job goes bad, Jimmy and his gang must try to elude a hitman sent in to clean up their mess. Slightly warped and witty as hell, *Denver* is a real treat.

Gotti (1996)
>Director: Robert Harmon
>Starring: Armand Assante, William Forsythe, Frank Vincent, Anthony Quinn

Well-made HBO docudrama based on the life of John Gotti (Assante), a career criminal who ascended through the ranks to become boss of a powerful Mafia family. Assante gives a commanding performance as the "Teflon Don," with terrific support from Forsythe as Sammy "The Bull" Gravano. Mob movie aficionados are advised to put this on their "must see" list.

The Devil's Rejects (2005)
>Director: Rob Zombie
>Starring: Sid Haig, Bill Moseley, Sheri Moon Zombie, William Forsythe

Sequel to *House of 1000 Corpses* finds a group of serial killers escaping from the law and setting out on a murderous road trip. Director Zombie's homage to '70s exploitation/horror flicks is unflinchingly brutal and sadistic. It's also well-written and well-acted with nasty doses of dark humor. Not for all tastes, but those who can stomach it will find plenty to like.

Halloween (2007)
>Director: Rob Zombie
>Starring: Malcolm McDowell, Scout Taylor-Compton, Tyler Mane, Sheri Moon Zombie

Reimagining of John Carpenter's 1978 horror classic is one part prequel and one part remake, with the first half being an origin story of Michael Myers as a bullied kid growing up in a dysfunctional, white trash family. It's surprisingly creepy and effective, which makes the second half—a virtual note-for-note recreation of Carpenter's film—rather tedious by comparison. Writer/director Zombie walks a tightrope by trying to cater to fans of the original and those looking for something new, and he makes a film that is fifty percent successful.

Happy in the Valley (2009)
>Director: Lee Madsen
>Starring: William Forsythe, Shaun Sipos, Zoe Hall, Dee Wallace

Stewart Fox (Forsythe) is a once-great photographer who is drowning in drugs and alcohol, reduced to doing porn shoots to pay the bills. Convinced he is still relevant as an artist, Stewart dreams of publishing his autobiography, and he hires student Wade (Sipos) to document his efforts. Reminiscent of *Boogie Nights* (and I mean that in a good way), the movie tells an interesting story about an assortment of oddly damaged characters who are each seeking their own path to redemption and happiness.

Dear Mr. Gacy (2010)
>Director: Svetozar Ristovski
>Starring: William Forsythe, Jesse Moss, Emma Lahana, Cole Heppell

Jesse Moss (Moss) is a student with an ambitious idea for his term paper: Get inside the head of convicted serial killer John Wayne Gacy (Forsythe). Through a series of letters and phone calls, Jesse is convinced he has the upper hand against the charming and seemingly docile prisoner, but that's just part of Gacy's twisted game. Unlike most films featuring mass murderers, this chilling thriller revels in psychology instead of blood and guts, with Forsythe giving an absolutely stunning performance.

Jeffrey DeMunn

As a classically trained actor, Jeffrey DeMunn began his career in the theater, but it didn't take long for Hollywood to come calling. Now in his fourth decade in the industry, DeMunn has portrayed a multitude of characters, ranging from honorable lawmen (*The Blob, The Green Mile*) to unlikeable lawyers (*The Shawshank Redemption, Law & Order*) and everything in-between, including an award-winning performance as a serial killer in the HBO movie *Citizen X*. Although busy with film and television projects, DeMunn still finds time to return to the stage, sharpening the skills that have made him one of the most versatile actors in the business.

How did you get your start in acting?

It was in college. I did only one play in high school, I had only a single line to say in the play, and I forgot to say it! When I got to college, I was going to become an engineer and a lawyer and do legal work for an electronics firm. I found the studies so difficult and boring that I leapt into the theater just to have something to do, and I haven't left since.

Did you have any trouble making the adjustment from the theater to movies and television?

Yeah, I had problems. I know that some people have a great facility for moving from one to the other, but it took me a number of years before I started to understand how to work in front of the camera. I'm not even sure I can come up with words to describe what became clear to me, but it became clear on *Citizen X*, which was an HBO movie that I did in Budapest. It was on that project that I said, "Ahhhhh... I see." Up until that time, I would watch people with such power in front of the camera, and I just didn't know how they were doing it. I didn't know what the secret was… That experience was a great help, and I've tried to maintain some of what I learned there in my work since then.

How did you get involved with Citizen X?

That was sort of a last-minute thing. I think a negotiation with another actor had broken down, and they needed to find somebody for the part. I was up in the woods in Canada at the time staying at this little log cabin place and going canoeing every day. One afternoon, I decided I'd use the one pay phone at the place to call down to New York and see if there was anything I should know. My manager was like, "Oh, thank God you called. We've got a script here. Can we get it to you?" Of course they couldn't get it to me, so I was standing in this little phone booth in Canada while my manager was reading sections of the script to me. I had to make a decision without actually having read the whole thing and just a bare description of what would be involved. A week later, I was in Budapest.

You were nominated for an Emmy and won a CableACE award for your work in Citizen X. *What was that like for you?*

It was thrilling, but to be honest, that's an aspect of the business I'm not really comfortable with. It was fun because they flew me out to California, I got to stay at the Four Seasons, there's parties and stuff… It was thrilling to do, and I was *awfully* glad to get home! It was nice for a while, but I certainly wouldn't want a steady diet of that intense limelight.

Besides Citizen X, *you've done a lot of other projects where you've portrayed real-life people. What kind of research do you do?*

I hit the books. Even if I'm not playing a real person—if I'm going to play a Texas Ranger, for instance—then I'll go to Texas and meet a couple of them and hang out a little bit. Whenever I've been asked to do that kind of support, I would. It helps to hit the books and read and get anything I can get. Sometimes, however, you'll learn about and become familiar with a person that is *not* the same person that's in the script, but you still have to do the job. That's what you're hired to do. You've been hired to do the individual that's written in the script and the emotions the writer has given him. You might hit something in the script that's not easily digestible, and you go, "Wait a minute, I read that so-and-so reacted in a different manner than that." Ultimately, you absorb as much as you can and keep whatever is relevant. The rest of it, you just let it fall away and let it go.

Citizen X

Speaking of Texas Rangers, you played one in The Hitcher. *What was it like making that film?*

It was a terrific experience. The director, Robert Harmon, contacted me about playing the hitchhiker. I started reading the script, and I couldn't believe how violent it was. I got to the part where the guy found a finger in his french fries, and I went, "My God, I can't do this," so I had my manager call Robert and say, "Thank you very much, but…" Robert got in touch with me later on closer to filming time and he said, "Look, will you get together and have lunch with me?" I said, "Sure," so we did and he said he wanted me to do something in his film and asked if I'd be interested in playing the Texas Ranger. Then he asked me if I'd watch a short film

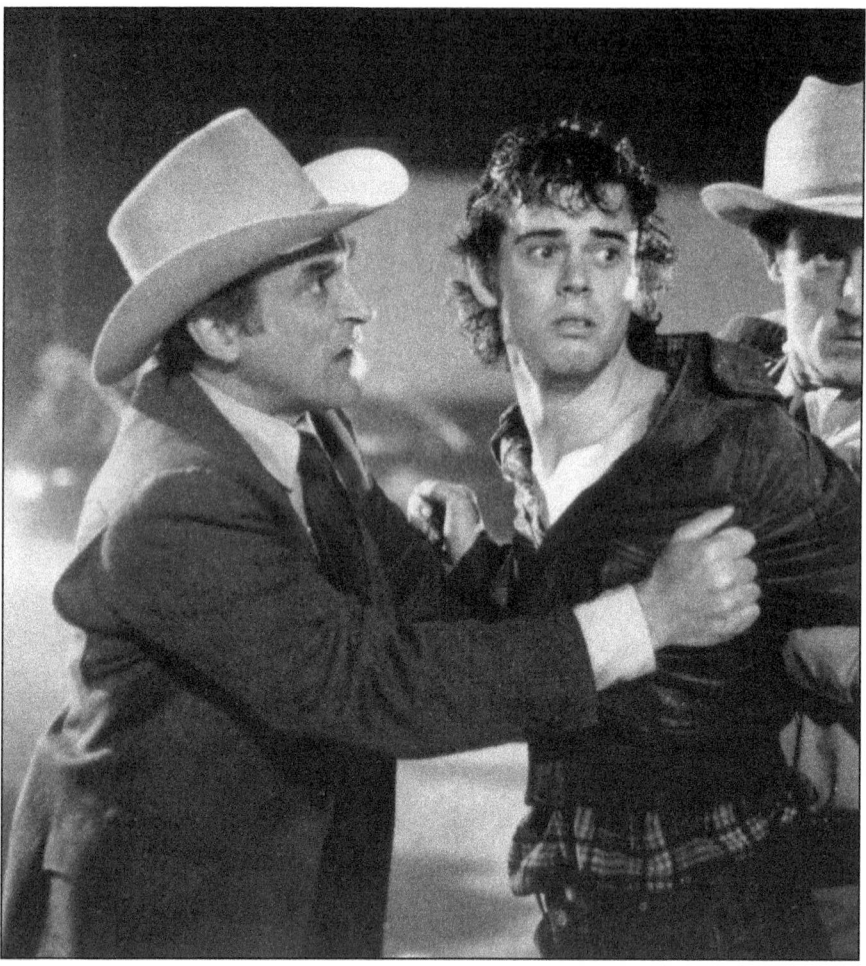

DeMunn and C. Thomas Howell in *The Hitcher*

that he'd made. I told him I'd be happy to look at the short, so he set up a screening. I watched it, and it was just a *brilliant* half-hour of filmmaking, absolutely brilliant. Everything about it said this guy was a talent, and I called him right away after watching it and said, "Oh, yeah, I'll work with you. Just tell me when to show up."

The Shawshank Redemption was the first film you did with director Frank Darabont. How did you get involved with that?

I just got a call and an offer. I had no idea why he wanted me, so I just assumed maybe he had seen me in something. As it turned out, Frank had been one of the writers on the remake of *The Blob* that I had done, and I guess it was because of that that he called me to come do *Shawshank*. It was two days of work, it was great to be there, and it was the beginning of a friendship with him that is still very vital and wonderful. I remember we were taken through both prisons in Mansfield, Ohio. The old one is where they filmed, and right across the road is the new prison. We went through the new prison with all of the inmates in there, and I remember walking out thinking that I'm always gonna stop completely at every stop sign and I'm never gonna do *anything* bad! It was a harrowing and horrific place to be in.

You've also done The Green Mile, The Majestic, *and* The Mist *with Frank. What is it about him that keeps you coming back for more?*

We have a wonderful working relationship, and I would go back anytime he wants me. He has such zest and excitement about what he does, and he loves it—he *loves* movies. You look at something like *The Majestic* and that's his tribute to movies. Everything he does is a tribute to movies. There's a tribute in *Shawshank*... He grew up adoring them, they infuse all of his work and he carries all of that history into his films. He has such a deep love and understanding of American films, and each of the things that he makes is an act of love and respect towards those films. I find that very exciting.

The Mist *garnered a lot of attention for its controversial ending. What's your opinion of it?*

I love it. I think the whole movie reflected what Frank was feeling about our country and human kind. I felt that the ending was very much in fol-

The Shawshank Redemption

lowing with the idea that we are blind and stupid in ways that lead us to do bad things to others and inflict damage to ourselves. It's certainly not the same mindset that Frank brought to *Shawshank* or to the *Mile*. He was in a dark place, and the movie reflected that.

I read an interview with Frank where he said you came up with one of the elements for the ending.

David Morse, Tom Hanks and DeMunn in *The Green Mile*

Yeah, I did. There's a scene early in the movie when the woman leaves the store and says, "Isn't there a gentleman here who will see a lady home?" and nobody dares go outside. This woman has to get back to her kids and she basically says, "Well, the hell with all of you," and out the door she goes. We shot that, and about a week or two later, I was meditating one morning and it occurred to me that she's got to show up again... She's got to be there at the end; we've got to see the woman that nobody would help. I mentioned that to Frank and he liked it, and she pops up at the end in the truck with her kids.

You've done a number of episodes of Law & Order *over the years. How did that relationship begin?*

I can't remember if I had to audition or not, but I know that for one episode, they wanted someone to basically be an Alan Dershowitz-type. This was back when Michael Moriarty was doing the show, and I went and did it. They decided to bring me back to do another one, and they wanted me to be the same character. It just sort of grew from there... You don't make a lot of money doing *Law & Order* but that show has sustained two generations of New York actors. It's a way for a New York actor to be able to make a couple of bucks and still do an off-Broadway show. *Law & Order* has been wonderful for the acting community in New York, so for that reason—if it's at all possible—I'll go and do it whenever they ask.

The Mist

Is it difficult for you to keep the character consistent when your appearances are so sporadic?

You know, I never really thought much about it. The character is kind of a jerk, and he represents some pretty sleazy people, but maybe I don't keep it that consistent. I think that sometimes I've been a lot nicer than other times. Sometimes I've been a real sleazy lawyer who went for the jugular, but there was one episode in particular where I was so ashamed of my client, I couldn't get away from him fast enough!

You've never been a regular on a TV series. Is that something you're interested in or do you not want to be tied down?

Well, it's not something I would have a great desire to do. There was a pilot I did with Joan Tewkesbury called *Elysian Fields*, and that show I would have done. It was a *really* good pilot. While we were shooting in New Orleans, I thought I'd get myself a little place there to live and it would be great. The script was so interestingly written and so funny and human. But no, it doesn't particularly interest me to do a series. I know that there's a great deal of money to be made in doing that, and there's a consistent

Kris Kamm, Frances Fisher and DeMunn in *Elysian Fields*

paycheck involved, but I've been able to keep myself busy enough doing a variety of other things. I think I've enjoyed that more.

In the early days of your career, did you ever have to do any day jobs to help pay the bills?

One time, I got $25 for running a follow spot for a gospel singer. It was one of those situations where I was standing around and somebody came up to me and said, "Can you run a follow spot?" I said, "Oh, yeah," like it was no big deal. This thing was an unwieldy, scalding hot piece of metal that I had to aim at that poor woman 300 feet away and try to keep some light on her. It was horrible, but I got my $25 for it. Other than that, I've been able to get by through acting.

At what point did you realize you could make a living as an actor?

I went to theater school in England, and when I got back to New York, my first job was with the National Shakespeare Company, which was a non-union touring company. There was a road manager there who said a very wise thing to me. He said, "You've gotta give yourself ten years. After ten years, maybe think about doing something else, but don't struggle over it every year." It generally takes about ten years to get some momentum going for yourself, and when I hit that ten-year mark, I was still working, I had some momentum going, and I had some credits behind me. By then I had kids and some pretty serious responsibilities, but I felt my shoulders drop a little bit, and I thought I'd be able to do this.

Do you still have to audition?

Oh, yeah. Sometimes I'll have to audition for some pretty inexperienced people. I remember one audition where I told someone I had just finished working on an Ibsen play, and I was asked if the playwright had been there! You can tell when you're auditioning for someone who knows what they're doing because there's a sense of respect for the situation and a sense of what's involved in acting. Some of these people have no real background in acting, and yet they're making those choices, making those decisions. Auditioning is still part of the process for me, but thankfully it's not as much as it used to be.

When you do have to audition, how do you prepare for it?

You know, I had a bit of an epiphany when it comes to auditioning… Way, way back in the dark ages when I was starting out, I taught acting for one term at the University of Vermont, and I loved it. I wouldn't want to do it forever, but it was fun for one term. I was young enough to think that I knew everything, and there was no question I couldn't answer except the one about how to audition. Students would ask me what the key to auditioning was, and I just didn't know what to tell them. During this time I was reading *Zen and the Art of Motorcycle Maintenance*, which is a fascinating, very dense and interesting book. The author talks about how if you're going to climb a mountain—if you're literally going to climb a mountain—you don't start out at ten in the morning thinking about getting to the top of the mountain. You take a step, and then you take another step and then another step. Eventually, whatever time it is, you'll get to the top of the mountain. If you start right away thinking you've got to get to the top, you're going to be exhausted, it's going to be a horrible day and it just doesn't work. I remember I woke up one morning with that question the students had been asking me nested in with that image of the mountain from the book, and I realized that's how you audition… You just do the material and that's all. You don't try to get the job, you don't try to make the director or the casting director like you, you don't try to impress anyone… Just do the material, just take that one step. When you're finished doing the material and you say that last sentence, leave. You don't stay and try to be pals, you're done. That was kind of a light bulb going on for me, and it's helped me ever since.

Once you get a role, do you have a specific process of preparing for it?

There are a few general things I do, but for me, it's really a question of trying to figure out what will make the most sense for the exploration of that particular character. If I'm going to play a police officer, I might visit some police departments. I might read up on Detroit if he's a police officer from Detroit. Like I mentioned earlier, I might go down to Texas and meet some Rangers. Or I might not do any of that… I just sort of go by my instincts and follow them as to what kind of research is best for that role.

The Walking Dead

Do you ever read reviews of your work?

No. Somebody once said, "The dangerous reviews are the good ones." Those are the ones that can really hurt you. A reviewer might say, "When such-and-such actor picks up the crystal goblet and looks at it, it's the most moving moment of the play." You'll never be able to pick up that crystal goblet again. You just won't... Every time you reach for it, you'll be thinking, *Here it is, the most moving moment of the play*. At that point, you're out of it, you've lost your concentration, and you've lost your focus. Instead of concentrating on the scene, you're thinking about somebody who has nothing to do with the play and what they wrote about it. I think that's dangerous... Also—and I don't mean to disrespect anybody—I don't think there's a lot of good reviewers around anymore. In the past, there were some pretty terrific reviewers who loved theater and understood directors and actors and choreographers. They brought passion to their work. Now, most of the people are just critics, and they have no body of knowledge to draw from. They're just giving opinions, and everyone's got an opinion. If you start listening to any of that you're in big trouble, plus you'll probably get your feelings hurt.

Of theater, movies or TV, which medium is your favorite to work in?

I love doing all three. It's the best when you can do all of them because each feeds the other. You can learn something from one that you can use in another. In terms of what hits closest to the bone, it's theater. Theater is my taproot, and every year I try and do something on a stage. Theater is hard… It's really, *really* hard, but I know it's good for me. It's just a very unique and fulfilling experience, so I try to keep myself going back and doing it.

Is there a particular kind of role you'd like to play but haven't had a chance to?

I've always been interested in playing kind of a backwoods, uneducated person. I'm not sure it would be good for my career to do that, but I was inspired by a film called *Tomorrow*. It's a stunning, *stunning* bit of acting by [Robert] Duvall. I think it's his best work, better than all the others. When he talks in that movie, you can see the words start somewhere down in his bowels, and they slowly come up. When they eventually come out of his mouth, I thought, *My God, that's beautiful*. Aside from that, there's not really a particular type of character that's been niggling at me, and if there is, I won't know it until it happens. When it happens, I'll go, "Oh shit, I've *always* wanted to do this!"

Have you ever had to do a project you didn't want to do in order to help pay the bills?

Oh, yeah. Not so much now, thankfully, but when my kids were growing up and in school, I had to keep the money coming in. There were times when I would get on the airplane to go to the next job, and I'd open up the script to see what it was I'd be doing. There was a greater necessity there than the ar-

Jonathan Spivey and DeMunn in *Death of a Salesman*

tistic aspect of my life. I had a family and I had to keep my nose to the grindstone. I had to keep my ass in gear, get work, do it—and do it well—and then when that was done, I had to go find another one. It was all about the kids.

What advice would you give to aspiring actors?

Only do it if you have to... If you're in it for the celebrity or the money, don't expect a lot to happen. There has to be a pretty deep-seated drive to keep you going in what can be a choppy business to work in, especially now. I don't know *how* people are doing it now because it's become rough out there for young actors. I suppose the other thing I'd say is get to New York, which is a bit of a Mecca for acting. That's not to say you can't get your chops in Chicago or Seattle or San Francisco... I did a play two years ago in San Francisco, and there were some *wonderful* actors out there. These guys were gladiators, doing five shows a year. They're doing one show while they're rehearsing the next one at a different theater, and they were working and battling through it—not making a heck of a lot of money at all—because they love it. Whether it's New York or San Francisco or wherever, if you're gonna do it, do it because you love it.

The Hitcher (1986)
    Director: Robert Harmon
    Starring: Rutger Hauer, C. Thomas Howell, Jennifer Jason Leigh, Jeffrey DeMunn
    Jim Halsey (Howell) is driving on a cross-country trip when he encounters a hitchhiker named John Ryder (Hauer) and decides to give him a lift. As their journey progresses, Ryder begins to reveal his evil nature, and Halsey becomes trapped in the hitcher's deadly game. This tense psychological thriller shines thanks to Hauer's chilling performance.

The Blob (1988)
    Director: Chuck Russell
    Starring: Kevin Dillon, Shawnee Smith, Donovan Leitch, Jeffrey DeMunn
    Excellent remake of the 1950s sci-fi classic about an alien creature that lands in a small town and begins feasting on the residents, growing larger and more ferocious in the process. A teenage rebel (Dillon) and a clean-cut cheerleader (Smith) join forces to try and stop the gelatinous creature before it consumes everything in its path. Unlike most remakes, this isn't a product conceived merely to cash-in on title recognition. This is a full-fledged *improvement*, with director Russell and co-writer Frank Darabont taking the same idea and turning it into a bigger and better movie. If only others in Hollywood these days had the same objective...

The Shawshank Redemption (1994)

Director: Frank Darabont

Starring: Tim Robbins, Morgan Freeman, Bob Gunton, James Whitmore

A mild-mannered banker (Robbins) wrongly convicted for the murder of his wife is sentenced to life in Shawshank prison. Since this movie has been shown on cable every day for the last ten years, chances are you've already seen it and know how great it is. But if you've only watched it once, you haven't experienced everything it has to offer. If you're reading this book at home, put it down and find out the next time the movie will be on. If you're sitting at Barnes & Noble perusing this for free, take it up to the register, pay for it, *then* go home and check the TV Guide. *Shawshank* is the rare movie that keeps getting better and better with every viewing. Nominated for seven Oscars, including Best Picture, Best Actor (Freeman), and Best Screenplay.

Citizen X (1995)

Director: Chris Gerolmo

Starring: Stephen Rea, Donald Sutherland, Max von Sydow, Jeffrey DeMunn

Based on a true story, forensics expert Viktor Burakov (Rea) is appointed to investigate a series of murders in Russia. Soviet officials, refusing to admit that a serial killer exists in their country, dismiss Burakov's theories and go to great lengths to hamper his inquiry. Undaunted, Viktor dedicates the next several years of his life to apprehending the killer. This fascinating bit of history is vividly brought to life by an incredibly accomplished cast.

The Green Mile (1999)

Director: Frank Darabont

Starring: Tom Hanks, Michael Clarke Duncan, David Morse, Bonnie Hunt

Paul Edgecomb (Hanks) is the head guard on Death Row when his life is changed forever by the arrival of prisoner John Coffey (Duncan), a man who's been convicted of the murder of two young girls. Since this is a Stephen King tale, you know there's more to Coffey than meets the eye. After *The Shawshank Redemption*, *The Green Mile*, and *The Mist*, Darabont cemented his status as one of the premiere adapters of King's work. Nominated for four Academy Awards, including Best Picture, Best Screenplay, and Best Supporting Actor (Duncan).

The Majestic (2001)
   Director: Frank Darabont
   Starring: Jim Carrey, Bob Balaban, Martin Landau, Laurie Holden
   1950s period piece features Carrey as Peter Appleton, a screenwriter who's accused of being a Communist. A drunk-driving accident leaves him unconscious and without memory, and he winds up in a small town where people believe he's a long-lost local boy who was killed in World War II. Sure, Darabont's homage to Frank Capra is a somewhat sappy, melodramatic affair, but if you're in the mood for an entertaining, nostalgic salute to old-time Hollywood, this is the movie for you.

The Mist (2007)
   Director: Frank Darabont
   Starring: Thomas Jane, Marcia Gay Harden, Laurie Holden, Andre Braugher
   After a storm, a mysterious mist descends on a small Maine town. David (Jane) takes his son and neighbor (Braugher) to the local grocery store for supplies, but the building becomes a makeshift refuge as deadly creatures begin to attack anyone who dares to venture outside. Inside, things aren't much better, as a religious zealot (Harden) begins to turn the townsfolk against one another. Based on a Stephen King novella, *The Mist* easily ranks as one of the best adaptations of the author's work, with an ending that is absolutely stunning.

William Atherton

William Atherton got his start in Hollywood in the early '70s as a leading man under the tutelage of some of the best directors in the business: Steven Spielberg (*The Sugarland Express*), John Schlesinger (*The Day of the Locust*), and Robert Wise (*The Hindenburg*). In the '80s, Atherton redefined his career by playing smarmy supporting characters in such favorites as *Ghostbusters*, *Real Genius*, and *Die Hard*. In the decades that have followed, the multifaceted thespian has stayed busy performing in a variety of projects, including *Lost*, *Law & Order: SVU*, and *The Citizen*. Fans can stay in the know at www.williamatherton.com.

How did you get your start in acting?

Well, I did everything kind of by the book, and it was much easier for me than it is for kids now. I went to Carnegie Tech—which became Carnegie Mellon—and I went there for four years and graduated. This was the late '60s, and it was a particular time in the culture when theater was really important. So many great and talented people came from Carnegie that you kind of had a *bona fides* when you went to New York: You could meet people, you could get into an audition and you could get someone to an-

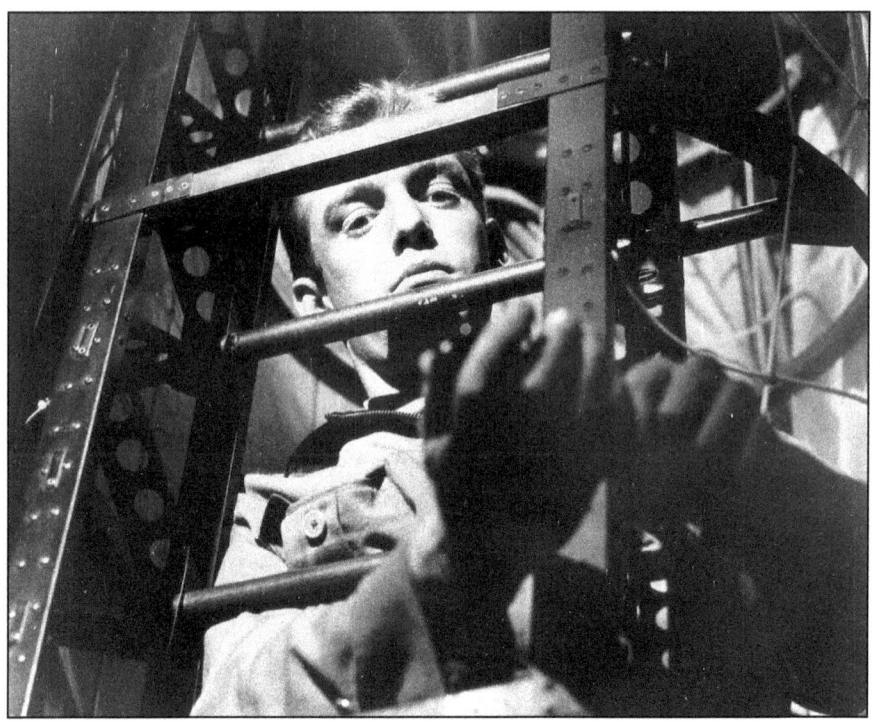

The Hindenburg

swer your telephone call. In New York, I would read plays in a class taught by John Ford Noonan, who was an important playwright. From that class, I met John Guare. John had a new play he was working on called *The House of Blue Leaves*, I auditioned for it, got the role of Artie Shaughnessy, and that ran for a year off-Broadway. About four months into the run, I met David Rabe, who wrote *The Basic Training of Pavlo Hummel*. I played Hummel, and then it all happened after that. It was all luck… I just met the right people and was very lucky.

Your first film was The New Centurions. *How did you get the job?*

The New Centurions happened because of George C. Scott. He was on the board of the Public Theater, so he had seen *Hummel* and everything else. There was a part in the movie for Stacy Keach's partner, and George said he wanted me to play it. In those days, all of the studios had big offices in New York, and they had to go to New York for money and for talent. For actors, the idea was that you didn't want to go to California on your own; you wanted to go to New York and have the studios *bring* you to California. That wasn't really on my radar at the time because the theater is where I felt at home, but George C. Scott was very powerful in those days, and I did the film the minute I left *Hummel*.

When you made the transition from the stage to the screen, was it easy for you or did you struggle with it?

The thing that made it easier for me was that I was working with terrific people who taught me, and I could watch them. I'd watch George, and then I'd watch him again on *Hindenburg*. Between that was *Sugarland [Express]*, and I had Vilmos Zsigmond as a cinematographer. He taught me enormous amounts about film and what to do. And there was Steven Spielberg… It was like falling into a vat of genius!

What was it like making Sugarland Express?

To me, it was like a wonderful interlude, because movies weren't really on my horizon in those days. They brought me to California, I did lots of

Atherton, Goldie Hawn and director Steven Spielberg on the set of *The Sugarland Express*

screen tests and everything, and I looked at it all as kind of like this exotic realm of exotic creatures. I thought it was interesting, but I figured they'd get tired of me and throw me home pretty soon. Then [producer Richard] Zanuck asked me to do the film, and I said, "Oh, okay, fine." The first time I met Steve, I was just overwhelmed by him. I'd never met anybody who loved the movies more and had such a wondrous feeling about it. It was the kind of rare warmth that only true talent has, and he welcomed me and Michael [Sacks] and Goldie [Hawn] and everybody else into that. We did the movie in Texas, and we didn't have any kind of tendrils of Hollywood around us. We all lived in a Holiday Inn in San Antonio and Del Rio and Houston, and it was great because we could just concentrate on doing the work.

The Day of the Locust *was your first big Hollywood film. What was that experience like?*

It was very long. It took a *long* time to make that movie. I went to L.A. in September, I didn't finish until the latter part of April, and I worked every day. It was difficult… Every year, somebody asks me to go somewhere and talk about that movie. Some film school somewhere wants to talk about

Karen Black and Atherton in *The Day of the Locust*

that movie because it keeps going, and it *is* haunting in many ways. I think most of it has to do with Conrad Hall, the cinematographer, because there isn't a frame that isn't beautiful. It's like looking at a Monet in every frame, and it's extraordinary in that sense. The thing that was interesting was that we met everybody who was still around that had done anything in the '30s. Paul Stewart was there, Madge Evans—who was a silent screen star—did a small part, Buckwheat did a small part… It was like all of Old Hollywood was converging on this picture, and that made it fascinating. We went to all of these real locations to shoot, and it was just so cool. In the scene where Natalie Schafer plays the madam, we shot that in Gypsy Rose Lee's house. It was incredible! But it was a tough picture because it was a tough subject, and it was a little all over the place. I'm not the enormous Nathanael West fan that others are. I felt it was a somewhat narrow short story and kind of dark, but I think it was artificially dark. I had this opinion at the time, but who the hell was I, you know? There were really great people involved like [director John] Schlesinger and Conrad Hall and Donald [Sutherland], but my personal feeling was that the movie was snobby. There was a humanistic point of view that I felt was narrow, and it was a little too dark and a little too precious. I think it all comes from the material… If you work on something for a long time and the material doesn't *really* get to you, it has an odd effect on everyone. You really start to wonder what the hell's going on. Sometimes people have done movies where they don't know what the hell's going on, and all of a sudden, it's *Midnight Cowboy* or something else great. As a subject, I think it had some things wrong with it, but people love this movie… Whenever I'm asked to talk about it, I say, "Look, people like this, people dislike this. You can ask me anything you like, and I won't be offended if you dislike it. I'm here to answer questions as impartially as I can with as much goodwill as I can." It was a big event and a culturally-discussed thing at the time, so I approach it like that.

When you're working on a movie that's based on a book, do you read the source material or do you stick with the script?

I do both. The book gives you a sense of place—it gives you a sense of story and character. Everything else changes… They're two different things, and in my opinion, people make a mistake comparing them. A movie's different than a book, it's a different animal. There have been good movies from bad books, and there have been bad movies from good books.

African Queen is a far more impressive work as a film than it was as [C.S.] Forester's story, and I think *Gone with the Wind* is a better movie than that book. I recently saw the Swedish picture *The Girl with the Dragon Tattoo*, and I thought it was a fabulous movie. There have been very few negative reviews, and my feeling is that any negative review came from somebody who read the book and didn't like how it was interpreted. In a way, I think that's kind of unfair because movies have different rules.

Have you ever worked on an adaptation where you felt the script was lacking certain elements of the book?

I felt that about [*Looking for Mr.*] *Goodbar* from the beginning. The movie is supreme because of Diane [Keaton]—and she makes it work—but it's a very New York story, and they wanted to make it more of a general Metropolis story about good girls going bad. That was not the book... The book was very specifically New York, and at that time, singles bars like Tuesdays & Fridays and Maxwell's Plum were beautiful places, and people dressed up to go there. Now, weird things could happen if you went home with the wrong person, but essentially, *Goodbar* came from a New York world that isn't represented in the film. That specificity is lacking, and I think it hurts the picture. When [director Richard] Brooks asked me to do it, I really didn't know what the hell I was going to do. He asked me about doing the part that ultimately went to Richard [Gere], and I said, "No, I'm not right for that. I just don't think that's me." There was the other part of the guy who really liked Diane, but he was written to be dull, and I couldn't see how a girl would be interested in him. I told Brooks, "The only thing I can do is to make him a little strange. There has to be some-

Looking for Mr. Goodbar

Atherton, Annie Potts, Harold Ramis and Rick Moranis in *Ghostbusters*

thing in him that's a little off that keeps the interest going," so that's what I did.

One of the films you're best known for is Ghostbusters. *How did you get involved with that?*

Right after *Goodbar*, I did a tour of George Abbott's *Broadway* with Gilda Radner. She was a big star from *Saturday Night Live*, and I met some of the guys when they came to see the show. I had an awareness of them, and they had an awareness of me. Years later, I was in L.A. for a couple of weeks, I talked with Danny [Aykroyd], and then I met them all. I thought it would be fun but I couldn't compete with them. I had done a lot of comedies, but I went to [director] Ivan [Reitman] and I said, "These are the comic geniuses of our time. I can't sit here and try to be funny. Would it be all right if I played a male Margaret Dumont, where I just don't think any of it is funny?" He said, "Sure," so that's what I did and it was hysterical. It was just one of those choices that you make as an actor, and I had a fabulous time doing it. I had a great time with Bill [Murray], I had a great time with

Atherton and Gabe Jarret in *Real Genius*

everyone, and we improvised a great deal of it. We shot most of it in New York, which was really cool. After all those years of living in New York, I had never made a movie there. I knew it was going to be a big movie, but I didn't know it was going to carry half of the Western economy for the next five years! We were just having fun and it became enormous.

Your next movie, Real Genius, *wasn't as big as* Ghostbusters *but it's gained a huge following over the years.*

Yeah, it's been around forever, and people ask me to talk about it a lot too. The success of that picture is due to Val [Kilmer] and Martha Coolidge, the director. Martha was fresh off *Valley Girl*, and there's nobody who can deal with smart and sexy kids like she can. We worked a lot on the script… The Neal Israel script had some great stuff in that, and then Peter Torokvei jazzed it up, and I worked with Peter on it a bit. But Martha set the tone, and she's responsible for the popularity of the movie. On movies, it's all about the director. Of course you have to have a good script, good actors and everything else, but you have to have someone that brings it all together, and Martha is the reason why that picture works so well.

You're also well-known for your work in the first two Die Hard *films. How did that role come about?*

[Producer] Joel Silver had known of me, and I think he was a fan of *Real Genius*. He had produced *Weird Science,* and in the '80s, there would be a topic for summer movies and the studios would all have movies on the same topic competing with each other. Along with *Real Genius*, there was *My Science Project* and *Weird Science*, and they all came out in the same summer. Joel just asked if I wanted to do *Die Hard*, and I said, "Okay." That was another case where all of a sudden, you realize it's an enormous movie. The first *Die Hard* is a terrific movie, it really is great. It's the best action picture ever, and it's the paradigm for everything else. "*Die Hard* in space," "*Die Hard* on a bus"… Somebody told me there was an actual pitch meeting where a guy went in and said, "I have a great idea. It's '*Die Hard* in a building.'" I understand the concept of being so five minutes ago, but I thought that was interesting!

Before you started filming, did you do any research into TV newscasting?

I went to the Columbia School of Broadcasting in Hollywood. There was a ticker tape, and I would just practice reading it as it came off to get the cadence and a feel for how the things were written. That's the only thing I did, but I did it for an hour or two a day for a while. I wanted to make it seem real to me, and when you're an actor, if it's real to you, hopefully other people pick up on that. It was fun to do, and the more ridiculous things were that I had to read, the better. In the back of my mind, I felt

Die Hard 2

that I couldn't make a mistake. My character, Thornburg, couldn't make a mistake, so he had to be careful about it and businesslike about it. There was really no agenda there… It was only in *Die Hard 2* that there was more of a personal agenda with me and Bonnie [Bedelia]. I had a good time with the first one because I could play this consummate professional who didn't give a shit about anybody and wanted to get the story out. I think people have identified with that character because they believe that's how it really is, and I think they're probably right.

After Ghostbusters, Real Genius, *and* Die Hard, *you seemed to be the guy people loved to hate.*

I didn't really mind that. The thing that has been nice is that I began as a leading man and then I was lucky because I morphed into something else as an actor. That kept me going… The kinds of parts that I was offered as time went on have had more depth, more meat to them. Ironically, playing the bad guys and doing the funny stuff gave me a little more heft because people thought I might be able to do different kinds of things. It wasn't just staring sensitively into the sunset, which a lot of us WASPy guys had to do in the '70s. It changed, and ultimately I'm grateful that it did go that way because it made it possible to do other kinds of parts.

You've done a lot of TV work over the years but you've never been a regular on a show. Is that something you're interested in, or do you not want to be tied down to one project?

Well, I don't do huge campaigns for one thing or another. I'm asked to do things, and I'm grateful that I can choose what I want to do. I was recurring on the last season of *Life*, and that was a really great time. The episode of *Lost* that I did was fun. In a way, it's the best of all possible worlds because I can go in and have a lot of fun doing something, but there's no great responsibility on me for keeping the thing going. When I'm done, I can go do a movie… or not. Television is *very* difficult physically. The hours are long, it's very intense, and there's no time. When people can make it work and succeed under those circumstances, I have an enormous amount of respect for them.

You've talked about working with a lot of great directors. What are some of the traits a good director has that brings the best out of you as an actor?

Michael Emerson and Atherton in *Lost*

Somebody asked Sean Penn—he had directed a film at the time—how he got a performance out of someone. He said, "Never believe that the director gets anything out of anybody." The actor is given the position to show what he can do. That has been my experience with most of the directors I've ever worked with. Nobody drew anything out of anybody that they didn't already have, and usually it had to do with how clear the director was regarding what the scene was about. The best directors are very clear about what the scene is about, and when they're clear and they impart that to you, then you do your job and give it back to them. That's the way it works… There isn't any Machiavellian, Svengali thing that I've ever seen, and I've been doing this for forty years. You have to do your homework and the director does his homework. Generally speaking, I have seen some directors that are not really clear about what they want, and they expect the actor to do something miraculous for them. When you're doing a play, you can come up with something over a couple of weeks' rehearsal, but when you're doing a movie, that can be very difficult. The best directors I've worked with are the ones who made everybody feel comfortable and were clear about what would be good or fun to play. When they're unclear, that's when things get odd.

At what point were you confident that you could make a living as an actor?

Never! You know, there's the story about Dustin Hoffman after he did *Ishtar* where he said, "My God, I'm never going to work again." Obviously, all kinds of wondrous things happened for him after that, but in the arts in this country—not being state-supported, the studio systems being non-existent—it's always kind of pillar to post. I've been very, very lucky.

The Citizen

I think after a certain amount of time, there's a kind of terror when you're twenty-two, there's another kind of terror when you're fifty and a different kind of terror when you're eighty. You just hope that people remember your work and things go on. That's really the world you elect when you're an actor.

When you were starting out, did you ever have to do any day jobs to help pay the bills?

Not when I started acting. Most of my stuff was off-Broadway—which paid very, very little—but in those days when you were off-Broadway, you were still reviewed by *Time* and the *International Herald Tribune*. The world was somewhat different then, and it was about fame, not money. With fame, if things went well, you knew that money would eventually follow. As an actor, I made enough to live on, but when I first went to New York, I had all kinds of jobs: I was a waiter, I was a bartender, and I was a super in a building on the Lower East Side, which was one of the toughest neighborhoods in New York. I would have to get the heroin addicts out of the halls and put locks on the doors so the tenants wouldn't be terrified. For a farm boy from Connecticut, it was a whole new world. It was interesting and it was fun, in a way… and I was lucky it didn't last too long!

With all of the credits on your resumé and all of your experience, do you still have to audition for roles?

No, not really. Most of the time, the role is offered to me. There are some things I'll audition for and some things I won't. Every actor is different, and it all depends on where you feel you are in the business at that time, what you feel will be respectful of you, and how you respect yourself. I often think the audition process is overblown and not terribly efficient nowadays. I don't think it's that useful, but that's just my opinion. Every situation is different, but there are certain, specific things where it makes sense to, and other times when it doesn't. It's a business call.

Speaking of business, what frustrates you the most about the business aspects of acting?

Well, I kind of step back from the business side. I try not to get into that too much because it's kind of lost time on Earth. You're an actor looking for a job and if you get it, fine. If you don't get it, you don't get it. There's no point in making an issue about it, and you've got to be careful that your ego doesn't take over and that you start to feel you're the sensitive one adrift in this morass of money and crassness. You've just got to say, "Fuck it," and go on. That's the only sensible approach to it, I think. That part of the world you really have no control over, so I try not to let myself fall into that.

Do you read reviews of your work?

I do, especially if I was doing something that meant a great deal to me. People say they don't, but they always do. My late, great friend Lynn Redgrave—I did a couple of things with her that got great reviews—she never read the reviews until the show closed. She would always read them later but was afraid to look at them while the show was still going. A good buddy of mine told me that when it comes to reviews, you're never *that* good and you're never *that* bad, so just move on. That's kind of how I approach it.

What would you say has been your secret to making a living as an actor?

Luck... I really do feel it isn't any more profound than that. There are all kinds of theories one can give to one's self to make yourself feel better or more in control, but it doesn't mean they're true. I've been lucky, and you

Atherton and Lynn Redgrave on the set of *Centennial*

have to approach things with a certain kind of gratitude no matter what happens. It was taught to me in New York many years ago that gratitude really is a part of art. You have to be thankful for the situation, make the best of it and hope that another one comes along. If you get too upset by it, go do something else. There isn't a law that says you have to be an actor.

What advice would you give to aspiring actors?

I would say one thing is to be as erudite as possible. I remember somebody saying to me years ago that actors have the biggest libraries, and I've found that to be true. Read as much as possible, read difficult literature… Somebody said you should read at least fifty pages of difficult literature a day if you're not working. It keeps your mind going and it also gets you away from yourself and into other worlds. Read the classics, read Moliere and Chekhov, not just Shakespeare. That's what has always made me feel the most at ease because you're able to bring something with you to the part. A lot of material these days isn't terribly wonderful or challenging for a young actor, and what passes for drama is somebody being in a bad mood. There's a dearth of real conflict, so you have to prepare yourself

and come in with your own weight. When you walk into a room, you want to bring as much as you can with you.

The New Centurions (1972)
    Director: Richard Fleischer
    Starring: George C. Scott, Stacy Keach, Jane Alexander, Scott Wilson
    Roy (Keach) is an idealistic rookie cop partnered with the cynical, about-to-retire veteran Kilvinski (Scott). The film hits a lot of predictable plot points: Roy's enthusiasm about the job destroys his marriage, he abuses alcohol after being shot in the line of duty, and he finds new meaning in life when he begins a romance with a good-hearted robbery victim. Despite the melodrama, *Centurions* succeeds thanks to good work from a solid ensemble.

The Sugarland Express (1974)
    Director: Steven Spielberg
    Starring: Goldie Hawn, Ben Johnson, Michael Sacks, William Atherton
    When a woman (Hawn) learns that her baby is going to be adopted by a foster family, she breaks her husband (Atherton) out of jail and the couple hits the road in a race to reclaim their child. Along the way, they take a cop (Sacks) hostage and become the focus of an epic pursuit by Texas police. This was Spielberg's feature debut, and although he's gone on to helm many other bigger, better and iconic films, *Sugarland* is an interesting and often overlooked start to a brilliant career.

The Day of the Locust (1975)
    Director: John Schlesinger
    Starring: Donald Sutherland, Karen Black, Burgess Meredith, William Atherton
    Ambitious adaptation of Nathanael West's apocalyptic novel centers on Tod (Atherton), an aspiring art designer in 1930s Hollywood. Tod has eyes for his neighbor, Faye (Black), a cunning movie extra who dreams of becoming a star and has no problem manipulating men like Homer (Sutherland) into taking care of her in the meantime. At times heavy-handed but generally hitting its target, *Locust* is a cautionary tale where the characters are cloaked in a glamorous facade that ultimately begins to crack, exposing the savages that live beneath the surface. Nominated for two Academy Awards, including Best Supporting Actor (Meredith).

The Hindenburg (1975)
Director: Robert Wise
Starring: George C. Scott, Anne Bancroft, William Atherton, Roy Thinnes

After Nazi officials learn of bomb threats made against their famous airship, Colonel Ritter (Scott) is ordered to travel aboard the Hindenburg and keep an eye on the passengers as the Zeppelin makes its ill-fated transatlantic flight from Germany to America. The film begins as an engaging mystery but quickly gets bogged down in a mass of red herrings and underdeveloped characters. Nominated for three Oscars, including Best Cinematography. Winner of two Special Achievement Academy Awards for Sound Effects and Visual Effects.

Looking for Mr. Goodbar (1977)
Director: Richard Brooks
Starring: Diane Keaton, Tuesday Weld, William Atherton, Richard Kiley

Based on the bestselling novel, *Goodbar* stars Keaton as Theresa, a devoted schoolteacher by day who cruises singles bars at night. Her road to sexual exploration becomes increasingly dangerous when her self-destructive behavior starts attracting the wrong type of men. The film is not without its flaws, but it's worth watching just to see the bravura performance by Keaton. Nominated for two Academy Awards, including Best Supporting Actress (Weld).

Ghostbusters (1984)
Director: Ivan Reitman
Starring: Bill Murray, Dan Aykroyd, Harold Ramis, Sigourney Weaver

Three parapsychologists (Murray, Aykroyd, Ramis) lose their cushy jobs at a university and go into business as ghost removers. The venture is mocked by the public until an ancient demon is awakened and begins threatening the citizens of New York. I could say more, but this is *Ghostbusters*, and everyone has already seen this and knows how awesome it is. If for some reason you haven't, I have to ask: What's *wrong* with you? Nominated for two Oscars, including Best Visual Effects.

Real Genius (1985)
Director: Martha Coolidge
Starring: Val Kilmer, Gabe Jarret, Michelle Meyrink, William Atherton

This '80s teen classic tells the story of Mitch (Jarret), a high school science whiz who's recruited by distinguished college professor Jerry Hathaway (Atherton) to work on a special project. Mitch is teamed with fellow genius Chris (Kilmer), a prodigy who prefers to spend his time mastering the art of goofing off. When they learn their research is being used for nefarious purposes, the duo sets out to teach Hathaway a lesson he won't forget. Smart, witty, and endlessly quotable, *Genius* is required viewing for anyone who loves great comedy.

Die Hard (1988)
    Director: John McTiernan
    Starring: Bruce Willis, Reginald Veljohnson, Bonnie Bedelia, Alan Rickman
    New York cop John McClane (Willis) travels to L.A. to visit his estranged wife, Holly (Bedelia). During her company's Christmas party, terrorists seize the building and hold everyone hostage, leaving McClane as the only one who can save the day. Often imitated but rarely duplicated (not even by its own sequels), *Die Hard* set the standard for Hollywood action films for the next decade and made Willis a superstar. With a clever script and great set-pieces, the flick is still exciting to watch after all these years. Nominated for four Academy Awards, including Best Visual Effects.

Die Hard 2 (1990)
    Director: Renny Harlin
    Starring: Bruce Willis, Bonnie Bedelia, William Sadler, Dennis Franz
    The best sequel in the *Die Hard* franchise finds John McClane (Willis) at an airport awaiting his wife Holly's (Bedelia) incoming flight when a rogue military group led by Col. Stuart (Sadler) takes over the operations, demanding that a drug lord be freed. If his conditions aren't meant, Stuart threatens to crash all of the fuel-starved planes circling the runways, including the one carrying Holly. Later series installments turned McClane into a superhuman parody of his "everyman" self, but this one continues the feel of the original and gets it absolutely right, making it a truly worthy follow-up.

Mike Starr

Mike Starr has moved effortlessly between big screen box-office hits (*Dumb and Dumber*, *The Bodyguard*), critically-acclaimed dramas (*Goodfellas*, *The Natural*), and popular TV shows (*The Office*, *NCIS*). Although often cast as either a crook or a cop, Starr has made each character uniquely his own. Whether as the gentle giant henchman in *Mad Dog and Glory*, the quirky mob muscle in *Miller's Crossing* or an evil serial killer in *Millennium*, Starr's ability to turn stock parts into memorable ones ensures we'll be seeing his work on screens both big and small for many years to come.

How did you become interested in acting?

There's a few things that happened to me… I remember one of the critical points was when I saw *On the Waterfront*. I must have been about fifteen years old, and it just had such an effect on me. I started doing impersonations of Marlon Brando and Rod Steiger and Lee J. Cobb with all of those great lines. That's when I started to realize about the power of film, and I remember thinking it would be great to be part of an event like that and tell a story that affected people. Another thing is that I lived in a housing project, and Joe Papp—of the New York Public Theater—would bring all sorts of plays into working class neighborhoods so people could be exposed to the theater. I was around the same age—fifteen or so—and I know that's my first, real live performance of professional actors that I saw. Roscoe Lee Browne did a play by Ben Jonson, and I was sitting there in the stands in a school park where we played ball. It just really excited me, and I was lucky enough to tell Roscoe Lee Browne years later what an effect he had on me. I went up to him in a bar in the Hollywood area, and he was very gracious. James Earl Jones was also in one of the plays I saw, and I got to talk to him because my first film ever was a movie in Japan called *The Bushido Blade* and he was in it. I wrote a paper in college on him and I told him I had done all of this research, and he said, "I'd like to read that someday." And then, on top of that, Cleavon Little did what they call a "rock" version of *Hamlet*. He walked through the audience and looked at the kids and said, "Hey, did you ever read Shakespeare?" and then he'd start doing his speech as Hamlet. Afterwards, I remember I went to the Good Humor ice cream truck and there he was, standing there. I asked for his advice, and he just took time telling me about acting and where to get started. He gave me tremendous advice.

Is that when you seriously considered becoming an actor?

I thought I was gonna be a Poly Sci major at Hofstra and maybe just do productions as a hobby. My brother, Beau Starr—who's been in a lot of films—was with the New York Jets at the time, and he invited me out to practice one day with my dad. Well, I didn't know he was gonna ambush me with one of the heads of the drama department and one of the stars of the drama department! My brother was like a stage mother… He was insistent I was gonna be an actor, and it seemed like the furthest thing from my mind. They had what was called a "Core Program," and I couldn't see myself with fifty actors and actresses. I don't know what prejudice I had towards studying acting, but it just seemed strange to me at the time. It was kind of like, "People *really* go to school for that?" But the head of the drama department said to me, "If you're any good, you'll get a scholarship." Well, that was free tuition, and I wasn't getting a lot of offers like that, so I gave it a shot and absolutely fell in love with it. They were very kind to me and I learned so much. It was just such a great experience, and I still have close friends from that department that I stay in touch with. I wound up getting a scholarship and I stayed four more years.

Starr and Gregg Almquist in *Of Mice and Men*

What happened after you left school?

After I was married with my first child, I remember I was working in a gym and making $100 a week. I had a drama degree and I thought, *Geez, I'm supposed to be pretty good at acting, I was at a really good school, why am I not doing that?* So I set about trying to figure out how to break into the business. I went out and did showcases, I did theater, and I was fortunate to have a friend from Hofstra named Gary Epstein—who's a successful agent—and he got me some commercial auditions. A lot of people I worked with at the gym helped me and covered for me so I could go do those things. At one point, I thought about taking a job as a counselor at what in those days would have been called a reform school. My father-in-law got me the job, and I figured I'd do that for a while because it seemed at the time that a lot of the character actors didn't really work until they were in their mid-thirties or early forties. That was the impression I got—

that you matured into it—so I was about to take the counseling job when all of a sudden, I started getting all of these acting jobs. That's when I thought maybe I could do it.

One of your earliest film roles was in William Friedkin's Cruising. *How did you get involved with that?*

I was working on a beer commercial and I met Dan Lauria, who played the father in *The Wonder Years*. He said, "You know, I'm doing a play about the formation of the crime syndicate in the '20s, and you'd be great as Dutch Schultz." Well, that play got a lot of attention, and I wound up being seen by [casting director] Lou DiGiaimo, and he put me in *Cruising*. I'm not sure but I think an actor dropped out, and I was just fortunate that Lou saw me and thought I'd be a good fit playing one of the cops. I had no idea what I was getting into, but it was a fascinating experience—it's a book in itself. I had basically spent five years in university trying to reach the last row of our 1,100 seat theater, and now I had to learn how to just play something realistically on camera. I have to say that Friedkin was one of my first teachers because he would just look at you and say, "You're in a Zen zone, there's nothing else out there." We had protestors, crowds, we had everything going on because it was a very controversial movie at the time and people were afraid of what it was going to inspire and bring about. Because of him, I really learned a way of just "being" without enhancing too much under the microscopic power of the camera and shutting everything else out and just being there in the moment. I wouldn't say that I'm always successful at it, but I learned it on that film. Making that film had a big effect on me, and I also learned a lot about behavior on a film set from Joe Spinell. Joe taught me a lot about being able to improvise or suggest yourself into a scene. I guess it was a very blue collar way of getting more work on a film! He was such a great guy, what a character he was… We stayed friends until he passed away. He was a great influence on me too. It's interesting how sometimes in life it just seems that everybody's there to help you, and sometimes there are saboteurs. I kept getting warned that when you do a play or do a film, there are some people that don't have your best interests in mind and you have to learn to protect yourself. I really didn't know what they were talking about, but you can start seeing it the more you work. As crazy as the situation was on *Cruising*, I had more helpers and more people rushing to do the right thing by me. It was quite an event to be a part of.

A few years after Cruising, *you were in the Robert Redford film,* The Natural. *How did that come about?*

That was wild… I went to the audition knowing I'm not a baseball player. I just thought this is Barry Levinson, who directed *Diner*, and he's not gonna forget me, so I went in and clowned around and had fun. Mickey Treanor—who was an ex-cop and the brother-in-law of another famous ex-cop, Sonny Grosso—wound up playing the trainer. I met Mickey on *Cruising* and he was there during the audition, so I was talking to him and we started telling funny stories. Lou DiGiaimo was casting again, and the next week during the final callback, I heard that Barry Levinson said, "Where's that big funny guy that was with Mickey?" Lou said, "That was Mike Starr, but he's not a baseball player," and Barry goes, "I don't care, we'll put him in somewhere." So I wind up on the set of *The Natural* and I'm with all of these baseball players. Line drives are whizzin' by my head and Barry Levinson says, "Hey, hey, hey… Get off the field, I don't want you getting hurt. I brought you here to just kind of be the designated ad-libber. I'm going to need you to ad-lib, create a character and a reason why you're here." I didn't come into the movie in the greatest shape, so I talked to my brother and he said, "How about if you're one of those guys who's eating his way out of the league?" I said, "Sure," so I would kind of hang around and look lethargic and laid-back, like I was just about at the end of my career. I thought of the name Boone because my son's middle name was Boone, and we named him after Richard Boone whom I met on *Bushido Blade*. We had a lot of professional players and college players who had never been on a film before, and I was one of the only actors in that group. We had a lot of fun, and people wanted to be a part of it.

What was it like working with the cast?

Wilford Brimley really took us under his wing. He was so great to us, and I know he's had issues with people in his career and has a certain reputation, but he took us in and he made us a team. He gave me a hard time one day and said, "Why are you ignoring Redford?" Robert Redford would come and we would stay away from him. We'd all shut up when he was around. I had been in the business a few years, and I just wanted to be respectful, you know? I didn't want to be one of those guys who was like, "Hey, Bobby, how you doin'?" But Wilford said, "You guys are having fun and I know he's a big star, but you're supposed to be a team." Kenny Grassano, who was the pitcher in *The Natural* and a phenom for the Cardinals, he and I went over one day and started talking to Redford, and he was the greatest. It seemed to break the ice, and he started hanging around with us. One of my big thrills is that Robert Redford sat down and told me about his idea for Sundance. He was really a wonderful person, and you could see that he and Barry had a tremendous working relationship. It wasn't like he was trying to direct the movie, but there were suggestions Redford made that are some people's favorite moments in the movie. Richard Farnsworth was just an icon, and getting to hang out with him was one of the greatest experiences of my career. I had just seen *The Grey Fox* before getting the job, and I was just so thrilled to be around him. Wilford was good friends with Robert Duvall, so we got to spend time with him. Duvall was one of my idols, along with Gene Hackman, so getting to watch him work was tremendous. When we did the home run at the end, I just sold out; I bought into it completely. I know we're doing a movie that's planned out and scripted, but we got so excited as we watched it. I felt like I was at a real game, and with each foul ball, I really felt the exhilaration. And then when we celebrated on the field with all of those fireworks going off and the lights crashing, it was just a magical experience.

How did you get involved with Goodfellas?

I remember I was doing a play in L.A. that Arthur Penn was directing, and my friend Frank Renzulli—he wrote a lot of *The Sopranos* but was an actor at the time—he said, "Boy, you should read this book *Wiseguy* because they're going to do the movie." I read the book and I wrote [casting director] Ellen Lewis a letter. I had never done that before, but I wrote a letter that said, "I know actors may say this, but I really think I can fit the look and feel of this character and I would really love an audition." So I wrote that letter, but the second part of the story is that while I was making *Funny Farm*, I had four callbacks for Martin Scorsese's *The Last Temptation of Christ*. I came down to the wire for the part of Peter, which Vic Argo—a wonderful guy who was so loved and respected as an actor and a person—wound up playing. During those callbacks when I was just one-on-one with Scorsese—and I *don't* advise doing this—we started telling each other funny stories and trivia, and I ended up doing impersonations of different people in biblical movies! It was just one of those things where I went with my feelings at the time. I can't believe I did it, but we just laughed so much that by the time I had the audition for *Goodfellas*,

Ray Liotta, Robert De Niro and Starr in *Goodfellas*

we just had a great time with it. He's one of my all-time favorites, and I don't think I'm going out on a limb saying that. When I got on the set, I felt so comfortable with him that it seemed like I would say all of the right things, so when it came time to improvise, he trusted me. In the scene where I talk about Air France, we rehearsed it and really had it down so that by the time we shot it, it really does look fresh and improvised. It was so cool and so much fun… I played Frenchy, who's a real guy named Bobby McMahon, and from what I knew about him, I just wanted to play this guy like he was shot out of a canon. It was just a feeling I got, like I should just burst onto the scene. From what I heard, he wasn't a violent guy but he was a really joyous thief—he just loved doing it. He had this really youthful enthusiasm and exuberance about it, which some people think may have worked against him when all of the deaths came down. When we did the scene, Robert [De Niro] said the word "security," and it just came to me to say, "You're lookin' at it." Bobby is a cargo supervisor and in the book, it's really interesting how they did get the key, but there wasn't enough time to tell the whole story in the movie. The security guard at the airport looked up to Bobby because he was a wannabe military guy, and Bobby had authority. That kind of stuck with me, so I just said, "I'm the commandant." It just came to me and after the scene, Martin said, "Cut. Mike… Commandant?" I said, "Well, it's 1968, *Hogan's Heroes* was the big show at the time and that generation grew up with movies like *Stalag 17*." He goes, "I love it! Keep it in!" I give credit to the actors and to Scorsese for setting up an atmosphere where I was able to do that.

You had a memorable role in the Coen brothers' gangster movie, Miller's Crossing.

Miller's Crossing was a dream come true, it really was. I had met them for *Raising Arizona*, and I guess I made an impression on them. I had wanted to work with them so bad, and they brought me in and it just clicked. They were just such good people to work for and so kind. In that great scene we did with Gabriel Byrne, I decided to just start dancing in the woods. We're looking for a dead body, we may kill Gabriel's character, and I'm dancing! I found out later on the Coens gave an interview where they said, "We knew Mike Starr knew what we were about when he started dancing in the woods." I don't know what that means but I think it was complimentary! I got to sing in the movie too, but after we shot it, the boys called me up and said, "We have a different song for you to do." When you see the movie, they picked a song that worked out much better, but the problem was it didn't match my mouth, so people sometimes think that someone else sang for me. I had five days to learn this song, and I studied Italian but I'm not Italian by blood. I asked one of my friends in the neighborhood—he was from Southern Italy and this song had a real extreme dialect from the North—and he helped me with it, but I was still struggling. I was doing a movie in Toronto, and I was being detained by customs for not having my work permit. I've got five days to learn this song and I'm sitting there with my tape and Walkman. This little woman who worked for customs comes up to me and says, "What are you doing?" I said, "I'm just trying to learn this song." She said, "Let me hear it," so I let her listen and she says, "This is my father's town." I'm being detained for two hours, and she taught me the whole song with the dialect. I came into the studio five days later and I sang it by heart! That tells you how blessed and lucky I am, that some wacky thing will come along that you think will be a problem and it turns into something good.

Goodfellas *and* Miller's Crossing *came out within a month of each other in 1990. Do you think those back-to-back releases helped type you in people's minds as the "tough guy" or the "Mafia guy"?*

I don't know what people think of me sometimes. I could tell you stories where my friends were in meetings for a comedy or a lighter show and someone would say, "Yeah, Mike Starr's wonderful but he's a Scorsese actor," or they'd say, "I don't know if he does comedy." Then I can have

Bill Murray, Robert De Niro and Starr in *Mad Dog and Glory*

something happen where I might be up for a killer or a serious political guy and somebody who's seen *Dumb and Dumber* will say, "Well, Mike Starr is known for his comedy." It's like, *what*? It's so hard to know what people see you as. When I did *Mad Dog and Glory*, we were doing readings down at Robert De Niro's place in Tribeca, and the character was so unique and not a cliché. He wasn't a connected crime guy; that's what he did and that's what he got paid for, but he loved movies and he wasn't an inherently violent person. That's what I would hope I'd be known for, that I play characters of certain working-class backgrounds or mob or police or whatever, and I try not to be the cliché. One thing that people have said to me is that sometimes I'll play characters that might be thought of as evil, and that a heart came through—that I was a good guy who just happened to be doing bad things. More and more, I think that's what I want to play. If people call me for the stock characters, I hope that in those characters I can try to find a person who's really good and who's aspiring to higher things.

You were in Cabin Boy, *a movie produced by Tim Burton that's developed something of a cult following over the years. Did working on that lead to your role in Burton's* Ed Wood?

Cabin Boy

It did. *Cabin Boy* was a great experience with a lot of cool people. [Director] Adam Resnick was a writer for [David] Letterman and wrote the show *Get a Life* with Chris Elliott. I think Tim Burton was a big fan of the show and asked Adam if he wanted to do a movie. Adam just didn't have that "special" movie in mind, so they were kind of trying to come up with stuff, and I think he decided to do a wacky version of *Captains Courageous*. Usually when people tell me they like it, my standard comeback is, "What year of college were you in and how much pot were you smokin'?" Anyway, one day I was telling funny stories with Adam and he said, "Tim Burton is coming to the set and he would really love you. I recommended you for his next movie, this thing about Ed Wood." Tim comes and meets me, and I not only got that but I also wound up getting *James and the Giant Peach* with [director] Henry Selick because of that meeting.

You played real-life producer George Weiss in Ed Wood. *Did you do any research for the role?*

Yeah, they gave us a book about all of the people, so I read that and I even got to meet his widow on the set. Most of it, though—as it should be—was in the script and in the dialogue. [Co-writer Larry] Karaszewski wrote such perfect lines: "Do you have a script?" "Fuck no, but we've got a poster.

We open in six weeks." I kind of felt that a guy like that wasn't gonna be thoughtful and laid-back and really be measured in his actions. I've met producers like that, so I kind of knew where he was coming from. It's interesting… The response I got from actors and the film community about that role was very complimentary. There are things where I've tried to act my ass off, but I didn't do anything heavy in this; I just did what was there in front of me. It was all on the page, and people really responded to it.

Thanks to shows like Entertainment Tonight *and the tabloids, we know all about Johnny Depp, the movie star. What can you tell us about working with Johnny Depp, the actor?*

He's such a kind, down-to-earth person, and just watching him come up with this character was so great. I have to tell you, *Dumb and Dumber* was coming out around that time, and I was getting interviewed and people kept asking what it was like working with Johnny Depp. They kept trying to get me to tell all these bad stories about him, but I guarantee you he's probably one of the nicest guys you could meet. He treats people right and cares about people's feelings and is absolutely the furthest thing from a diva. We had the greatest talks, and there were a couple of times where he gave his phone number to friends of mine and said, "Tell Mike to call me." To my detriment, it's just one of my things that I feel funny about getting in touch because I don't want people thinking I want something from them, you know? "Hey Johnny, what about your next movie? Is there anything I can do?" That's probably a reverse mentality for show business, but I wasn't brought up like that. It would've been better if I did get in touch with him because he's such a great person. I remember one day, Johnny was with the wardrobe designer, and he said, "I think I want to open my collar for this scene." The designer said, "No, Johnny, I don't think that works," and Johnny was like, "Awww, come on." The designer said, "No, Johnny, you should really have it buttoned," and Johnny said, "All right." I couldn't believe it… I mean, I've watched people ruin movies with their ego and their insistence on doing things their way, but here was a guy who was just willing to do what was

Starr and Johnny Depp in *Ed Wood*

right and not throw a tantrum or overrule people with his power. One day, Tim Burton comes up and says, "Guys, we're really moving fast. We're supposed to shoot this next scene tomorrow, but do you think you can do it after lunch?" Johnny looked at me and said, "Is that okay with you, Mike?" Fortunately, I always learn all of my stuff early on, so I said, "Yeah, I'd love to." The way Tim Burton and Johnny worked together was great. It was like we were making an indie film or doing something in college. It wasn't like, "Oh, no, I have to prepare. We've got to call up this person and get this ready; I don't know if it will affect the process." It was just like, "Let's do this! Fuck it, let's go for it. This is great, it's working, let's keep going." I can't say enough good things about Johnny… We'd just have heart-to-heart talks about me and my family or his upbringing and childhood. It was just sharing stories and observations. He's such a class act. I have nothing but super memories of him and the way he worked.

You've mentioned Dumb and Dumber *a couple of times. I can't even imagine what that must have been like to work on.*

I have to say that the outrageous guys were the Farrelly brothers. They were ridiculously funny, and it was hard to keep a straight face. I had my

Starr and Karen Duffy in *Dumb and Dumber*

own relationship with Jeff Daniels, who was quiet on the set and kept to himself, but not in a bad way. When it was time to work, he was there instantly. Jim [Carrey] would fool around a lot and break my balls, but it was fun and he was very kind to people. I would have really cool conversations with Jeff, and I watched hockey with Jim. You'd see all different sides of people on that set. Karen Duffy, to me, was really the star of the movie in a lot of ways. She had her own big following on that set. I feel sad about what happened with Charles Rocket and how that ended… He was a real classy, cool guy to be around. With the Farrelly brothers, it's like you feel everybody on the set is a personal friend, and they just bring you into it and make you feel a part of it.

Was the movie pretty tightly-scripted or was there a lot of improvising that went on?

As I remember, most of it was scripted. In the scene where I die and Jim's on top of me, he would start ad-libbing stuff like, "This will go a lot easier if you learn to relax," and Jeff would come up with comical moves. There would be little extra things, like when I'm dying, Jim got an idea and said to me, "Why don't you pump twice with your legs and then kick me across the room," and then he came back with the venetian blinds in his hand. I remember being surprised by the world's most annoying sound that Jim screamed in my ear, but most of it came from the Farrelly brothers' script. I think there was a strong framework and structure of comedy where they could play around and add things.

I think one of the more underrated movies on your resumé is The Ice Harvest. *What was it like making that film?*

I knew John [Cusack] before the film. When I lived in Chicago, my wife worked at the University of Chicago Hospitals and we have a close mutual friend, so I got to know John. I didn't know Billy Bob [Thornton], but I had read for [director] Harold [Ramis] a few times in the past and had a bunch of callbacks, so there was a good, positive relationship I had with him. Harold told me from the beginning, "Look, this may take away from your screen time, but I think I want to put you in the shadows as a mysterious character so when you pop out of that case, it's really going to be effective." I agreed, and when I saw the film, I knew he was right. I think that technique worked great for the comedy—well, *dark* comedy—and

Starr and John Cusack in *The Ice Harvest*

I got to have input. Harold loved the timing when I'm cursing John out, and he says, "You just said you were going to kill me," and I come back and say, "I didn't mean it." We tried it different ways so that the humor worked great. John was very aware on the set and considerate of other people's screen time and what works for the film. He's not a guy who thinks it's all about himself. Billy Bob Thornton, I can't begin to tell you what a joy he is… I spent a lot of time with Billy Bob, and he's just really great. When I was with both John and Billy Bob, the repartee between them was tremendous. The movie did well on DVD, and one of the producers told me that it's really getting a following, which is good because I think it *is* underrated.

In addition to some of the directors we've already talked about, you've also worked with other respected filmmakers like Woody Allen, Brian De Palma, and Spike Lee. What is it that separates them from the rest of the pack?

I think for the most part they just have their own original style. I also think that there's a respect for the greats who came before them, and those guys are well-schooled on them. The way Spike did *Jungle Fever* and *Do the Right Thing* was totally original. You might say that it was similar to this or that, but he had his own unique take on things. Look at something like *Scarface* and the kind of following it has. There's a thousand different versions of that story or that type of story, but what did De Palma do that made it so great? Brian De Palma is special, he brings his own vision to it and comes up with ideas that people are still talking about and quoting. Those guys all seem to know how to use music perfectly too. I cried watching Scorsese's *Hugo*. The story is just overflowing with heart and respect. I mean, he put scenes with [actor] Harold Lloyd in it. There's a tendency to think everybody's got to be thirty years old to make films, but when you look at *Hugo* or Woody Allen's *Midnight in Paris*, they come from years and years of experience and knowledge and education, and it's like, "Wow!" They're the total package.

What traits does a director have that gets the best out of you as an actor?

That's a good question that I think is really important for people interested in any aspect of film or theater. I once had a director tell me, "We hired you. You're not auditioning for me anymore. You're here for the job because I know you can do this." When a director treats you with respect that hopefully you've earned and deserve, when they trust that you're going to deliver, that's the best. I was lucky to work with George Roy Hill on *Funny Farm*. I had this really over-the-top idea that in this scene I was going to yell and scream at Chevy Chase. He suggested to me, "How about if you have just had enough, and it's all you can do to stay in control, but you're not going to blow up at him. You're going to be really measured when you talk." I was so thrilled that he said that, and I told him that I wanted to do an Edgar Kennedy "slow burn." Kennedy was a character actor in the '40s who would be the foil for the Marx Brothers, and George Roy Hill said, "Yeah, let me see it, Mike." He knew his vision and he had such a great eye that he knew what worked, but he let you know if you were hurting yourself by making faces that didn't work. I think the bottom line is respect… Brian De Palma would simply say, "I need you in this spot here, the camera is going to be here and I need a little nod of the head that you don't like what this is. Just indicate it." That's not someone telling you how to act, it's him telling me what visual he needs. If Scorsese needs something eight seconds shorter or if there's something specific he doesn't want in the story, he'll let you know, but he'll also give you the benefit of the doubt to try something. They know what they want but they also like to be surprised by you, knowing that you're going to bring something. They say that much of the success is in the casting, so when you

EZ Streets

hire somebody that's willing to be part of the team and bring everything he can to his part of the story—and when the director gives you the respect to be part of the process—that's the greatest.

In addition to films, you've done a lot of television work over the years on popular shows like Law & Order, The Office *and* Frasier. *Do you have a preference for either format or do you like maintaining a balance between the two?*

Every now and then I change my mind. In film, you only have one shot to do the character, whereas in TV, you get to really reinvent or enhance your character when you're on a series. I've done some shows that didn't run that long, but I've been able to see how characters can settle into themselves, especially in comedies. I'm addicted to *Seinfeld*, and it just gets better—you see new stuff every time. *Frasier* was an absolute dream... They had it down so well—and this was only a couple of years into it—that when they say "clockwork," it was just perfect. I could see that as a great way of life for a while, but I think it's nice to change venues every six weeks or two months as long as you're not out of work, you know? I think the ideal thing is to do a series and in your downtime do a film or two, or a really good play. It's nice having that steady check that comes with a series. Some guys might complain if they're doing an action show sixteen hours a day, and I understand that it can get exhausting. You hate to say that when people are out of work or in the coal mines, because it *is* nice money, but you can see how—from an acting standpoint—there's a danger of putting things on automatic pilot and getting into bad habits. I've been told that by people who do it, so you really have to try to keep checking yourself. I recently did a soap opera, and I loved doing it. Some of the veteran actors came up to me and were very respectful and complimentary because I didn't just come in and make fun of it and run through it. I just treated it like I was doing a play or a film. I think that's the key… If you really love what you're doing and you treat each job with the same passion and joy, you'll be okay.

You had a memorable role on the cult series Millennium. *What was it like working on the show?*

I didn't know the show, and I had a friend named Bobby Moresco who I had done a great show with called *EZ Streets*. He was one of the producers on it, and he had suggested me for the role. That was really cool and fun… The director, Thomas J. Wright, had worked with [Alfred] Hitchcock and worked on *Apocalypse Now*. People might think a television director just walks around and doesn't care and does whatever the leads say, but that's not the case with Tommy. I mean, he worked with Hitchcock and all of these great people, so you knew you were in good hands. Lance Henriksen actually gave me research on the character. He gave me all of these articles written by profilers, and they really helped me. Lance told me that I was the first guy where the serial killer was featured, and that was interesting to me. Since I didn't know the show, I didn't know what he was talking about at first, but he said a lot of times it was about him going after the killer, and I don't want to say the killer was incidental, but he or she didn't get a lot of attention. I didn't know I had all this responsibility, and I'm glad I didn't know; ignorance is bliss. I just loved doing it and playing that character. At one point, they were going to bring me back but they went a different way. I wanted to do a bunch of them.

Was it a challenge for you to take on such a disturbing character? Did it get you out of your comfort zone?

I did feel after a couple of days that this was strange and creepy stuff, but it all goes back to the basics of acting. You go through the actions—and each actor justifies his own ways—but you don't comment on it: "Watch me be really creepy now! Watch how dangerous and scary I am!" Hopefully you're motivated out of some organic source that's in the material, so you just do what you have to do and everything else will follow. I hope I fool the audience and they really think I'm like that, but I certainly don't sit there and say to myself, "I love to hurt people," and I certainly didn't walk around and keep pictures of people who I wanted to kill. Some actors might approach it like, "No one better talk to me on the set because

Millennium

I'm a killer and I'm carrying a knife, so don't get near me." That can be very psychologically dangerous for some people to do, and you can get lost in it. I don't mean to knock the way other people work, but after all it *is* about make-believe, and I think it's healthier to stay detached. I was exposed to that kind of thinking one time, and I used to torment myself psychologically. I was doing a production of *Of Mice and Men*, and the veteran character actor Bob Darnell said, "You're gonna kill yourself. Eight shows a week? Jesus Christ, don't do that to yourself," and he was right. That's why I think some people wind up having nervous breakdowns and strokes. They get *so* involved and psyche themselves up *so* much. I don't think that's psychologically healthy or a good thing spiritually, but it's a decision actors have to make. Some of the most brilliant performances may have been motivated by techniques I don't believe in, but if that's what you have to do, I'd rather not do it, you know? I don't think it's worth it for the art.

Are there any projects you've done that you're really proud of that you wish audiences would take a look at?

Well, we talked about *The Ice Harvest* and *Mad Dog and Glory*... I did these A&E movies with Gene Wilder called *Murder in a Small Town* and *The Lady in Question*, and I couldn't wait to get to the set to act with Gene Wilder and Cherry Jones and our director, Joyce [Chopra]. It was just such a beautiful experience. They're like Agatha Christie mysteries, and I really felt like they didn't get enough attention. They were talking about doing one every month, but Gene really wanted to keep the quality high, so it didn't happen. Just to be with Gene Wilder and hear his stories... He's not a rambunctious guy by any means, but it was so interesting to hear his observations and discuss acting with him. I mentioned Bobby Moresco and *EZ Streets*, and that show was created by Paul Haggis and dealt with Irish mobsters, politicians, and the police. We were two years before *The Sopranos*, but it was CBS. I don't mean that as a bad thing but it wasn't HBO, it wasn't cable. It was a very complex show, and Joe Pantoliano—who played my boss and friend—would say on the set, "This is not going to be a success. You can't watch this show and walk out of the room to go get a beer. You have to pay attention to all of the details." For whatever reasons—and I heard all the arguments from all sides—we didn't get a chance to finish out the season and put a cap on it. We got dropped before the last episode was even shown. We were limited by the network but we were one of the first to have scenes like me and Joe taking severed

Starr and Gene Wilder in *Murder in a Small Town*

hands out of a freezer. It wasn't exactly stuff that you expected to see, especially since we followed *Touched by an Angel*. We had reviews that your mother would write, as they say, but I think it was just bad timing. I don't think they knew where to put us, and at one point they moved us and put us against *Law & Order*, which at the time was *so* popular. It was tough and we just didn't get seen. I would have loved to have had the chance to finish up the show properly.

What advice would you give to someone thinking about becoming an actor?

You know, people ask me for advice, and I try to give the best I can without being glib. It's hard to read how serious those people are about *really* wanting to be actors. Some of them just want to be famous, or they just want to make money. That's not my business, but it's hard to tell their resolve. I've had people all the time say, "Oh, I want to act, I want to act." I'll tell them to maybe try this or try that, and they're like, "Nah, I don't want to do that. I just want to make some money on the side." And then you have people where acting is like oxygen to them. I heard Morgan Freeman interviewed on Charlie Rose, and Charlie Rose asked him, "What would you tell people about having something to fall back on?" I think Morgan said something to the effect of, "I wouldn't suggest anything to fall back on because if you *can* fall back on something, you *will*." I was lucky enough to work with Morgan, and I heard the stories that he went through. Failure wasn't an option for someone like him. It's hard to give advice, though, because at my age, I'm kind of out of touch with exactly how to go about it these days. Someone can do all the right things and be really wonderful, and then another person can just walk around behaving funny in a candy store, and somebody will see him and want to put him in a movie. It seems like such a different game.

What's been your secret to making a living in the industry?

Divine guidance and luck! I think you have to be flexible, and it's important to learn speech, and it's important to be skilled, but I think you really have to find out what's so special about yourself and bring *that* to the stage or the screen. I remember I got a commercial one time, and they told me, "Well, we've seen all the handsome guys, the tough guys, the funny guys, the rugged guys, the cream puffs… We want someone who can do all of it. We think you can look dangerous or be dangerous and also be very sweet and loveable." I got that job, and I learned something about the business and what I may have. I realized there is something that comes across… You start learning what you project, as opposed to what you *think* you project. And if you don't like what you project then change it. Find out what works for you because it *is* a business. Knowing what sells or gets you that job is important, especially in the beginning. That's how you'll keep working, I think. This is going to sound really silly to some people, but I get along with people well. There are problem people on sets, and eventually if they can do without them, they do. Doing your job and behaving properly and being disciplined goes a long way. I know that for a fact because I've had people tell me, "It was between you and so-and-so, and we heard good things about you but some not-so-good things about

them." I think that knowing they'll have to live with somebody for three months helps influence their decision, and people like to have somebody there that will work hard and they can count on to deliver. Always educate yourself and observe yourself and see how you can improve without being neurotic about it. It's all about self-awareness and knowing what works best for you.

Cruising (1980)
   Director: William Friedkin
   Starring: Al Pacino, Paul Sorvino, Karen Allen, Richard Cox
   A fascinatingly flawed movie, *Cruising* stars Pacino as Steve, a straight cop who goes deep undercover into New York's seedy S&M community to search for a serial killer. As the body count rises, Steve's assignment—spending night after night in gay bars as bait for the murderer—begins to take its toll on him, both physically and psychologically. As a police thriller, the film flounders, but it *is* a harrowing character study of a man trying to live two lives in two very different worlds.

The Bushido Blade (1981)
   Director: Tom Kotani
   Starring: Richard Boone, Toshiro Mifune, Sony Chiba, Timothy Murphy
   In 1854, Commodore Perry (Boone) is in Japan to sign a treaty that will open the country's borders to U.S. influence. A gift intended for the American president—a legendary sword known as the Bushido Blade—is stolen by Japanese nationalists who oppose the deal, leading to a bloody battle for the prized weapon. The story has the makings for a good film, but the talented cast is hampered by a weak script and uninspired direction.

The Natural (1984)
   Director: Barry Levinson
   Starring: Robert Redford, Robert Duvall, Glenn Close, Kim Basinger
   Mythic tale of Roy Hobbs (Redford), a baseball phenom whose pro career is cut short before it ever gets started. Sixteen years later, he attempts a comeback, trying to hold his personal demons at bay as he struggles to fulfill his destiny. Redford shines in this unapologetically sentimental film, but in my opinion—and I admit to being a little biased—it's the work of the impressive supporting cast (Duvall, Close, Wilford Brimley, Rich-

ard Farnsworth, Robert Prosky, Darren McGavin) that makes this movie a winner. Nominated for four Academy Awards, including Best Supporting Actress (Close).

Funny Farm (1988)
   Director: George Roy Hill
   Starring: Chevy Chase, Madolyn Smith, Kevin O'Morrison, Joseph Maher

Andy Farmer (Chase) is a New York sportswriter who gives up life in the big city and moves to the country with his wife, Elizabeth (Smith), to write a novel. It's not long, though, until their idyllic dream of small town happiness comes crashing down after a series of unsettling incidents. Unlike most Chevy Chase vehicles, *Farm* is a more subtle, restrained comedy that won't make you laugh out loud, but you'll have a smile on your face from beginning to end.

Goodfellas (1990)
   Director: Martin Scorsese
   Starring: Robert De Niro, Joe Pesci, Ray Liotta, Lorraine Bracco

Based on a true story, *Goodfellas* chronicles the rise and fall of gangster Henry Hill (Liotta) and his friends Jimmy (De Niro)—a charismatic thief—and Tommy (Pesci)—a quick-tempered sociopath—as they do the dirty work for the mob. Simply amazing on every level, to call this Scorsese classic one of the best Mafia movies ever doesn't quite do it justice. It's one of the greatest movies ever made, period. Nominated for six Oscars and winner of one (Pesci as Best Supporting Actor).

Miller's Crossing (1990)
   Director: Joel Coen
   Starring: Gabriel Byrne, Marcia Gay Hardin, John Turturro, Albert Finney

A gangster movie that could only come from the minds of the Coen brothers, *Crossing* stars Byrne as Tom, the right-hand man to boss Leo (Finney). As Tom deals with the consequences of his secret relationship with Verna (Hardin)—Leo's girlfriend—he is approached by a rival crime kingpin who wants Tom to kill Bernie (Turturro), a sleazy gambler who happens to be Verna's brother. In a genre that has become overpopulated with *Godfather* clones and *Goodfellas* wannabes, this visually striking, densely plotted and lyrically unique film earns a spot at the top.

Mad Dog and Glory (1993)
   Director: John McNaughton
   Starring: Robert De Niro, Uma Thurman, Bill Murray, David Caruso
   Low-key dramedy finds Wayne (De Niro), a timid police photographer, saving the life of Frank (Murray), a local crime boss. As a gesture of gratitude, Frank gives Wayne a present: Glory (Thurman), an attractive young woman who is supposed to spend a week as Wayne's companion. This absorbing character piece allows all three stars to effectively play against type, and the sly script and nuanced performances are further appreciated with repeated viewings.

Cabin Boy (1994)
   Director: Adam Resnick
   Starring: Chris Elliot, Ritch Brinkley, James Gammon, Brian Doyle-Murray
   Spoiled snob Nathaniel (Elliot), a "fancy lad" embarking on a journey to Hawaii, mistakenly boards a run-down fishing ship and causes havoc for the drunken crew, including steering the vessel into the mysterious region known as the Devil's Cauldron. It takes a special sense of humor to appreciate the comedy of *Cabin Boy*, and even then, that sense should probably be chemically enhanced before watching it.

Dumb & Dumber (1994)
   Director: Peter Farrelly
   Starring: Jim Carrey, Jeff Daniels, Lauren Holly, Mike Starr
   Lloyd (Carrey) and Harry (Daniels) are two good-hearted dimwits who embark on a journey to return a briefcase filled with money to the lovely Mary (Holly). Unbeknownst to them, this innocent act of kindness is actually an interruption of a criminal scheme that puts Harry and Lloyd in danger, making them targets of hitmen looking to retrieve the cash. The movie is exactly as advertised: Incredibly dumb and extremely funny.

Ed Wood (1994)
   Director: Tim Burton
   Starring: Johnny Depp, Martin Landau, Sarah Jessica Parker, Patricia Arquette
   Incredibly entertaining biopic of filmmaker Edward D. Wood Jr. (Depp), widely regarded as the worst director ever. Instead of mocking his failures, the movie humorously—and sincerely—celebrates his

love for storytelling, a passion that clearly outweighed his actual abilities. Depp is absolutely perfect, and it's his relationship with Landau as the drug-addicted Bela Lugosi that comprises the heart of this wonderful film. Winner of two Academy Awards for Best Supporting Actor (Landau) and Best Makeup.

James and the Giant Peach (1996)
Director: Henry Selick
Starring: Paul Terry, Richard Dreyfuss, Jane Leeves, Joanna Lumley
Young James (Terry) is an orphan being raised by two evil, slave-driving aunts. His dream of escaping and traveling to New York arrives via a magically enhanced peach, where James encounters and befriends an eclectic group of insects who are in for the adventure of a lifetime. Based on the beloved book by Roald Dahl, the film is a visually dazzling combination of live-action and stop-motion animation, with a few songs thrown in for good measure. Oscar-nominated for Best Original Music.

The Ice Harvest (2005)
Director: Harold Ramis
Starring: John Cusack, Billy Bob Thornton, Oliver Platt, Connie Nielsen
Darkly comic film noir stars Cusack as Charlie, a lawyer who steals $2 million from the mob with the help of his low-life partner, Vic (Thornton). Their escape plan doesn't go quite as smoothly as the theft, complicated by the involvement of a sexy strip club manager (Nielsen), Charlie's drunken friend (Platt), and a hitman (Mike Starr) on the trail of the stolen loot. *The Ice Harvest* has flown under most people's radar, but with spot-on performances, tight direction and an intelligent script, it's a movie worth seeking out.

www.ingramcontent.com/pod-product-compliance
Lightning Source LLC
Chambersburg PA
CBHW050552170426
43201CB00011B/1666